J. William Fulbright and America's Lost Crusade: Fulbright's Opposition to the Vietnam War

Lee Riley Powell

Rose Publishing Company
Little Rock, Arkansas

Powell, Lee Riley
    J. William Fulbright and America's
lost crusade: Fulbright's opposition
to the Vietnam War.

    Bibliography: p. 243
    Includes index.
    1. Fulbright, James William, 1905-   —
Political and social views. 2. Vietnamese
Conflict, 1961-1975. 3. United States—
Foreign relations—1956-   . I. Title.

E744   973.90924   84-61295
ISBN 0-914546-51-1

Cataloging information provided by
the Central Arkansas Library System.

2263266

To my mother and father

Author's Note

The research for this book was begun in 1978, while I was working as an intern in the office of U.S. Senator Kaneaster Hodges of Arkansas. At that time I did research in the Library of Congress and wrote a brief essay on Senator J. William Fulbright's opposition to extreme anti-communism during the postwar era. I would like to thank Senator Hodges and his administrative assistant, Bob Snider, for giving me this opportunity.

While I was in graduate school at the University of Virginia a few years later, I expanded the original essay into a master's thesis on Fulbright's opposition to President Lyndon Baines Johnson's Vietnam policy. I would like to thank Professor Norman A. Graebner of the University of Virginia for his suggestions concerning my thesis, which is Part Two of this book. Two copies of the thesis are in the Alderman Library at the University of Virginia.

The University of Virginia thesis was expanded into *J. William Fulbright and America's Lost Crusade.* I have done extensive research in the J. William Fulbright Papers at the University of Arkansas Library in Fayetteville, Arkansas. Betty Austin, Ellen Shipley, and former Curator Sam Sizer of the Fulbright Papers were always most helpful in assisting my research. Scholars interested in writing about Senator Fulbright's foreign policy positions may wish to consult my original manuscript, including footnotes, bibliography, and other material, which is in the University of Arkansas Library at the Special Collections Room, where the Fulbright Papers are filed.

I have deleted the footnotes, extended bibliography, and some of the text from this book because of tight limitations of space.

The writing I deleted dealt in detail with the 1966 China hearings and Fulbright's role in the anti-Vietnam war movement during late 1966-67. The China hearings were related to the 1966

Vietnam hearings, which are discussed in this volume. My material on the China hearings is in the Special Collections Room at Fayetteville. I also deleted an essay I had written on Fulbright's role in Arkansas politics from 1954 to 1965. I might include all of my essays on this subject in a larger book at some later date, but this volume contains the heart of my writings on Fulbright.

Since this book is *not* a biography of Fulbright, it will not deal with the Senator's civil rights record and other issues which were not directly related to Fulbright's responses to the Cold War and the Vietnam war.

I would like to thank Professors Franklin Wright of Southwestern at Memphis for his helpful commentary on one of my earliest essays on Fulbright. Professors George M. Apperson and James Lanier of Southwestern and David A. Shannon of the University of Virginia also encouraged this project. Professor Willard B. Gatewood, Jr., of the University of Arkansas has my thanks for facilitating my research in the Fulbright Papers. I accept responsibility, of course, for any errors of fact or interpretation.

Aides to Senators Dale Bumpers of Arkansas and Claiborne Pell of Rhode Island helped me to obtain access to some Senate Foreign Relations Committee documents. I would also like to thank Senator John Sparkman of Alabama and U.S. Representative Claude Pepper of Florida for allowing me to interview them.

Bob Snider, who was an aide to U.S. Senator John L. McClellan of Arkansas before he became Senator Hodges' administrative assistant, gave me some suggestions about McClellan's relationship with Fulbright.

Senator Fulbright generously took the time to write three detailed comments on the drafts of the book's chapters as I have sent them to him over the last few years. The Senator and I also had five hour-and-a-half conversations concerning this monograph.

Needless to say, the views expressed in this volume are somewhat different from those of Senator Fulbright concerning some issues.

Lee Riley Powell
Little Rock, March, 1984

Contents

Foreword

This intensive study of the role of a Senator in the events preceding and during the Vietnam war will be useful to present or future Senators who, of necessity, must vote on matters of importance affecting our relations with foreign nations. It is also useful to anyone considering the adequacy of our form of government in the conduct of our foreign relations. Many serious students of government are presently concerned about the obvious disarray in our foreign relations, especially the alienation of our N.A.T.O. allies and the escalation of the arms race with the Soviet Union. They are concerned that the absence of continuity and experience in the higher echelons of our leaders is inherent in our system and is a serious disadvantage in the conduct of our foreign relations.

It is clear from this study that a typical Senator assumes that office with a very limited understanding of foreign relations. Due to our geographical location and our history prior to World War II, we have had very little involvement in foreign affairs. For the first 200 years of our national existence we generally followed George Washington's advice not to become entangled in the affairs of Europe or other foreign nations. We are the only major nation that has never been occupied by a hostile army, a very educational experience. Under this policy of isolation, we prospered materially, but our understanding of our proper role in the world and how to play it successfully has not developed in a manner commensurate with our economic and military power. As some observer has said, we are like a loose cannon, unpredictable, emotional and often arrogant. Above all, perhaps we are self-righteous and hypocritical, and superior in our attitude toward less powerful nations, evidence I believe of our "immaturity as a nation."

This study by Mr. Powell reveals in many instances all of these characteristics. Personally it reveals my own lack of knowledge of

China and Vietnam especially and consequently my vulnerability to misinformation supplied by an administration concerned only with its own purposes and not with candid consultation.

The structure of our government, with its separation of powers between the Executive and Legislative, results in an adversary relationship which inhibits candid consultation and which puts the Congress at a disadvantage with regard to knowledge of foreign affairs. Senators and Congressmen are experts on the conditions in their own constituencies and do not need to rely upon the executive for information, but very few speak a foreign language or have any significant experience in or knowledge about any foreign lands. These circumstances in addition to many others too extensive to deal with in this brief piece such as the proliferation of primaries and the cost of elections, the low esteem of Congress as revealed by the polls, and the effect of television on rational discussion of issues, all indicate that it is time to review and re-evaluate the relevance and the validity of our present constitutional system to present world conditions. It suggests to me that it may be time to consider changing our adversarial division of power to a system combining these powers in the legislative body in which a more cooperative spirit would prevail between those who enact the laws and treaties and those who execute them.

The years of the Vietnam war and my differences with President Johnson were not only tragic for the country and the people suffering personal mutilation and death, but were personally painful and unhappy years for me. It is obvious that in the early period of the war I was quite unaware of the relevant history of the area and the issues involved, that I was unduly influenced by my former close association with the President as Majority Leader and by the power of "group think" as Professor Janis described it. It was only at the end of that experience that I developed sufficient knowledge and skepticism about the executive to have the confidence in my judgment which I should have had at the beginning. However, I think that could be said of most of the other Senators.

The most consistent theme in my conduct, although with some lapses, was my conviction that a war with the Soviet Union would be a catastrophe and therefore I supported a policy of detente rather than confrontation. I still do. I believe the agreements made in 1972 between Nixon and Brezhnev if implemented in good faith as I believe they could and would have been by more experienced leaders would serve the interests of our country and the world.

Mr. Powell has given us the material from which we can learn much about our government if we are willing to recognize that conditions have changed and our Constitution is not a divine instrument for eternity, but is a human document well suited for its time, but now in need of review. The 200th anniversary of its adoption is in 1987, an appropriate time for all thoughtful citizens to consider how we can make this great country live up to its traditions and aspirations, which we have been unable to do in recent years.

J. William Fulbright

Part One:

Fulbright and the Cold War, 1945-1963

Part One:
Fulbright and the Cold War, 1945-1963

Chapter One
The Early Years of the Cold War

Introduction

In his first Senate speech of March, 1945, Senator J. William Fulbright juxtaposed his bewilderment and dismay at the American fear of communism with his hope that the creation of the United Nations would inaugurate a new peaceful world order in the postwar era. Fulbright believed that the most destructive of all the American xenophobias was the hatred of the Soviet Union and communism. Why, he asked, are we so hostile to the Russians when "the Russian experiment in socialism is scarcely more radical, under modern conditions, than the Declaration of Independence was in the days of George III?" In Fulbright's view, emotional super-patriots who constantly played upon popular fears and hatred of communism and Russia only revealed the weakness of their faith in the American system; he concluded that "We must demonstrate the superiority of individual initiative under capitalism by our results, by the provision of a superior way of life, not by the violence of our oratory."

Despite his concerns over the damaging effects of extreme anticommunism, the prevailing spirit of the March, 1945 speech was a resilient optimism. Only two years earlier the House of Representatives had apparently embraced the principle of collective security by passing the Fulbright Resolution, a declaration of support for the creation of and American participation in an international peacekeeping organization; and now the United States seemed willing to adopt the Charter of the United Nations. The Senator appealed to the nation's leadership to avoid repeating the tragic error of 1919-1920, when the rejection of U.S. participation in the League of Nations had "left our people divided and unable to agree upon any policy." In the closing passage of his address, Fulbright reminded the Senate that America now held an opportunity to play a crucial role in establishing a powerful United Nations organization and

15

averting another world war: "By the greatest good fortune, and enormous sacrifice, we have earned a second opportunity to help save the world and ourselves from self-destruction."

Seven months later the explosion of the atomic bomb at Hiroshima, the failure of the United States to embrace the axiom that all nations must accept United Nations supervision of armaments, and the emergent hostility between America and Russia had transformed Fulbright's earlier optimism into a pessimism which essentially lasted the remainder of his career. In his speeches during the autumn of 1945, he deplored the reality that instead of cooperating with the Soviet Union in the United Nations, the United States had "already fallen to quarreling with Russia like two dogs chewing on a bone."

Fulbright predicted that America would not be able to retain exclusive control over the atomic bomb, for "any one of several industrial nations probably can produce bombs in from three to five years." He vigorously advocated the effective international control of nuclear weapons by the United Nations. The young Senator lamented the fears and uncertainties which the terrifying new force of atomic weapons had engendered, comparing contemporary men to primitives living in the darkness of caves and jungles who faced "elemental and infinite forces which we do not understand, forces which threaten to snuff out our lives as one does a candle between the fingers."

In that first year of his Senate career, Fulbright advised his colleagues to play their proper role in the formation of American foreign policy: if the Senate "cannot consent to the measures presented by the Executive it seems to me imperative that it offer our Nation and the world an alternative." By the autumn, it was clear that Fulbright could not consent to the basic foreign policies of the Truman administration, and it was equally clear that the executive did not intend to adopt Fulbright's alternative of basing U.S. policies upon the creation of a U.N. with adequate power to curb the Soviet-American arms race. In late 1945, the Arkansan criticized the Truman administration for claiming to support the U.N. while insisting upon the veto provision for the Security Council, for demanding exclusive control of military bases in the Far East while asserting the right of American participation in eastern European affairs, and jealously guarding atomic secrets "under the guise of a self-appointed sacred trusteeship." According to Fulbright, if the President did not adhere to the concept of an international security community, then he should understand that his anti-Soviet posture would lead to a policy of imperialism in which America would have to incessantly enlarge its military establishment and expand its domination of strategic areas throughout the Atlantic and Pacific.

Fulbright's speeches of 1945 foreshadowed his later critique of postwar American policy. He had established his renowned themes of opposition to rigid anti-communism and conventional nationalism, his plea for an amelioration of Soviet-American relations, and his concern for maintaining the Senate's role of advising, consenting, or offering alternatives to the policies of the executive branch. In 1972 he was to write that the foreign policy of the United States from the final months of World War II until President Richard Nixon's journey to China in February, 1972 was shaped by two fundamental perspectives on international relations: first, the idea of founding an international security community through the United Nations, and then the belief in a relentless global ideological struggle between "freedom" and "communism."

The ephemeral ascendancy of those who advocated the establishment of a powerful United Nations was already weakening by the later stages of World War II, as nationalistic sentiments, anti-communism, disillusionment with the prospects for cooperating with the Soviets in the U.N., and other forces shattered the hopes for a genuine international security community. After Stalin's ruthless consolidation of Soviet domination in eastern Europe and the Chinese communists' triumph over Chiang Kai-shek, a generation of American political leaders emerged who were dedicated to the proposition that the Soviet Union and China could be prevented from executing their alleged designs for world conquest only by the intimidating effect of American military power.

In the late 1960s Fulbright would agree with John Kenneth Galbraith that a third generation of Americans had now recognized "that in fact limited areas of common interest are developing between us and, above all, that the survival of civilization requires at least a tacit understanding among the nuclear powers." This new generation recognized the diversity of the communist bloc, and no longer regarded international communism as an aggressive and monolithic conspiracy to rule the world. The third generation, Fulbright would write in 1967, "advocates a creative competition between the communist countries and the West to see who can build the stronger and more prosperous society at home, who can more effectively help the world's less developed nations, who can build better schools and raise healthier children, who, in Khrushchev's colorful phrase, can provide more and better goulash." These advocates of creative East-West competition appeared to enjoy successes in 1963 with the passage of the Nuclear Test Ban Treaty and a general relaxation of Soviet-American tensions. Yet at precisely the moment, in Fulbright's view, when the third generation "seemed

17

about to take full control of America's affairs," a tragic regression to the earlier dogmas occurred: "The Vietnamese war is a manifestation of second-generation attitudes toward communism. It is basically an ideological war." The Senator would conclude that underlying the crusade in southeast Asia was the discredited dogma that the United States was fighting the centrally directed, global communist monolith, a force so evil that America must search for and destroy it in every corner of the world. In 1965, as in 1945, the hopes for a more realistic and moderate American foreign policy would be dashed.

In the latter years of his career, Fulbright was deeply troubled that the "second generation's" anti-communist ideology had portrayed the Soviet-American relationship as a universal conflict between freedom and the alleged system of international "terror and oppression" directed from Moscow. To the Senator's mind, this attitude led the American public and politicians to respond to the actions, statements, and policies of communist states not on the basis of their varying and specific merits, but in terms of the ideological clash between eastern communism and western democracy. The decisive moment in world history had arrived, the anti-communist crusaders proclaimed, when all nations must choose between diametrically opposed "ways of life," communist oppression or democracy.

As Illinois Senator Everett Dirksen explained in 1967, such a regime as the corrupt and despotic Greek military dictatorship was democratic because it was attempting to "shove back the communist influence." Given such a world view, it was pedantry for Congress to conduct thorough investigations before extending U.S. aid to a particular regime, for the crucial if not the exclusive criterion for that aid was simply whether the regime was sufficiently vehement in its anti-communism. As Fulbright responded to the Illinois Senator's preachments, if America followed the guidelines Dirksen and other Cold Warriors established for choosing the allies of the United States, then the chaotic and authoritarian government of South Vietnam "would also seem to qualify as one of the democracies for whom the United States is resolved to make the world safe."

In his 1972 volume *The Crippled Giant*, Fulbright would regret that the Cold Warriors in Congress had often seemed to prefer the spectacular and the stirring in policy presentations by the executive instead of more pedestrian but more accurate statements. To illustrate this tendency, Fulbright cited the example of the Truman administration's effort to gain Congressional support for its plan to aid Greece and Turkey. At a meeting with Congressional leaders shortly before the famed Truman Doctrine speech in 1947, Secretary of State George Marshall's concise summary of the realities of the Greek civil war left the leaders singularly unimpressed, whereas Under Secretary of State Dean Acheson immediately captivated the imagination and support of the gathering by warning theatrically that once the communist virus had infected Greece it would inexorably spread to Europe through Italy and France, to Africa through Egypt, and to "all the east" through Iran. According to Fulbright, Acheson may have viewed the decision to state the Truman Doctrine in sweeping ideological terms rather than in precise strategic terms as a domestic political tactic to arouse the public's combative spirit and thus solidify Congressional support for the funds involved in U.S. assistance to Greece and Turkey; but whatever Acheson's views were, his successors in the State Department literally interpreted the Doctrine as a manifesto for global anti-communist interventions. "I believe that it must be the policy of the United States," the President pronounced in one of the crucial phrases of the Truman Doctrine, "to support free peoples who are resisting attempted subjugation by armed minorities or by outside pressures."

In the analysis expressed in *The Crippled Giant*, postwar American leaders urgently needed to re-evaluate their policies toward the communist world, yet they felt themselves absolved from having to rigorously analyze the actual statements and actions of the communist states and insurgencies by the Truman Doctrine's chimera of the universal communist conspiracy against freedom. The interpretation of the Senator's 1972 work is not that Truman's inflammatory language caused the anti-communist crusade, but that Truman's heated anti-communist rhetoric was a "symbolic and seminal event" which powerfully influenced popular American thinking on the Cold War in the years after 1947.

Fulbright's 1972 argument held a substantial measure of validity, especially when one considers the popular and erroneous American opinions that the Truman Doctrine's thesis explained the outcome of the two famous civil wars which were decided in the late 1940s. By the spring of 1949, Chiang Kai-shek's forces had collapsed on the Chinese mainland, and in October the communist guerrillas in the north of Greece had been defeated. According to the Truman Doctrine, America must assist any nation that was battling communism, which was always based upon "the will of a minority forcibly imposed upon the majority." On the basis of the anti-communists' logic, American aid had been primarily responsible for the triumph of the anti-communist forces in Greece, while the anti-communist "majority" in China had disintegrated because it

19

had not received sufficient support from the free world. In actuality, the Greek and Chinese conflicts bore no real similarity to each other, and the "lesson" the Cold Warriors had learned from the Chinese civil war was palpably false. As Fulbright concluded in *The Crippled Giant*, "Whatever merit the Truman Doctrine may have had in the circumstances of early postwar Europe, the bond with reality became more and more strained as the Doctrine came to be applied at times and in places increasingly remote from the Greek civil war."

America had supplied the corrupt and inefficient Kuomintang of Chiang Kai-shek with substantial amounts of aid, but the Chinese revolution was determined by indigenous forces in China which were essentially beyond the control of the United States. Yet the pathological sense of guilt and failure at having forfeited an opportunity to deliver China from the depredations of the communists continued to plague American political leaders throughout the 1950s and 1960s, culminating in the obsession with preventing a similar communist penetration into southern Asia. President Lyndon Johnson would grimly announce shortly after his inauguration that he would not be the President who would allow Ho Chi Minh's legions to gain control of Vietnam as Mao Tse-tung had triumphed in China, as if the United States might somehow compensate for the world's most populous nation's "loss" to communism by a rigid and unceasing application of the Truman Dotrine to the small, underdeveloped lands of southeast Asia.

Fulbright's opposition to America's crusade against communism was not the only issue he emphasized in his dissent against postwar U.S. diplomacy, but it was the single most important issue. As he would concede late in his career, he had frequently not opposed American foreign policy in the earliest period of the post-1945 era. It would require many years and many crises before Fulbright would arrive at his warning to America to avoid the "arrogance of power."

Summer, 1940

In the years before 1945, Fulbright had closely studied the central issues of international relations throughout World War II. During the period before the U.S. entry into the war, Fulbright (then the young president of the University of Arkansas) advocated intervention against the Nazis. He supported William Allen White's Committee to Defend America by Aiding the Allies. In 1940, the thirty-five-year-old university president delivered a series of speeches repudiating isolationism and pleading with Americans to recognize that Hitler's relentless career of conquest posed a dire threat to American security. As he argued in a July, 1940 address at the University of Oklahoma,

> Too often today we hear the profound pronouncement by an isolationist senator that this country does not want war. Of course, we do not want war, just as Austria, Czechoslovakia, Poland, Norway, Holland, Belgium, France, and England did not want war. The fact is, the world has war, and the question is what should we do about it?

Fulbright contended that America should fight to defend the "Atlantic highway," and approvingly quoted a 1917 *New Republic* article by Walter Lippmann in which the famous journalist had written:

> On the two shores of the Atlantic Ocean there has grown up a profound web of interest which joins together the western world. Britain, France, Holland, the Scandinavian nations, and Pan-America, are, in the main, one community in their deepest needs and their deepest purposes. They have a common interest in the ocean which unites them.

The young Arkansan regarded the 1917 *New Republic* essay as even more poignant for the 1940 crisis than it had been in 1917, and concluded that "it is far better to fight for and to lose than to meekly acquiesce." Throughout the pre-Pearl Harbor period, Fulbright reiterated his conviction that Nazi Germany was a uniquely dangerous and insatiably aggressive force that must be crushed.

For the first time in his career, Fulbright's foreign policy statements in 1940 attracted a certain amount of national attention. A noteworthy controversy occurred after his July, 1940 Oklahoma address, when the University of Missouri invited the president of the University of Arkansas to give the summer commencement address. Fulbright initially accepted the invitation and sent to Missouri a copy of his speech, which resounded with a bitter attack upon the isolationists: "The weasling, timid, and fearful policy of the isolationist senators is one of the greatest dangers to our true interests." The Missouri officials were expecting the famous isolationist Senator Champ Clark of Missouri to appear at the commencement, and therefore they asked Fulbright to delete the reference to "the weasling, timid, and fearful policy." He refused to alter his words, with the eventual result that he did not deliver the address at Missouri; and Senator Clark was able to attend the ceremonies undisturbed by the ideas of the young internationalist from Arkansas.

A quarter of a century later,the apologists for the Vietnam war would charge that Fulbright was guilty of "appeasement" because of his opposition to the U.S. intervention in southeast Asia. President Lyndon Johnson would compare the threat of Hitler's expansionism and the alleged threat of Ho Chi Minh in the 1960s; as he once succinctly explained to Doris Kearns, "Someone had to call Hitler and someone had to call Ho." Supporters of Johnson's escalation policy in Vietnam would allege that Fulbright was a starry-eyed pacifist who had no conception of the realities of power politics, or that he was an "appeaser" who was following in the tradition of Neville Chamberlain in failing to resist aggression.

These condemnations of Fulbright were distorted. First, Fulbright had not been an "appeaser" in 1940, as his speeches of that year clearly demonstrated; in fact, he had advocated resistance to Hitler earlier than the great majority of Americans had (as a young university president in 1940 he was not, of course, as nationally prominent as he later became). The Arkansan understood that the nation had to resort to its military power to protect itself against the limitless expansionism of a Hitler, and he would have preferred that American intervention against the Nazis had occurred earlier than it did. During the Vietnam war, he was convinced that Ho Chi Minh's small nation of North Vietnam could not possibly represent a threat analogous to Nazi Germany. In both World War II and the Vietnam war, Fulbright argued that U.S. foreign policy should be based upon a realistic analysis of how to defend America's vital interests. In his view, the danger posed by a fascist conqueror leading a powerful, industrialized Germany demanded a military response from the West, but in the post-World War II era Ho Chi Minh's quest to win a civil war in a small third world nation in southeast Asia did not endanger any important American interests and should have required no American intervention. Fulbright's opposition to the Vietnam war would involve a wide variety of complex issues; but there was nothing inconsistent about his support for resistance to Hitler and his later dissent against the U.S. intervention in Vietnam.

In the early Cold War, hard-line anti-communists would frequently contend that Ho Chi Minh was an agent of the Kremlin; according to the Cold Warriors, the Soviets were similar to Hitler in conspiring to dominate the globe. As will be shown in Part Two, Fulbright and other critics of U.S. involvement in southeast Asia would demonstrate that the extreme anti-communists ignored Ho's nationalism and other indigenous forces in Vietnam. The Arkansan and his intellectual allies would later elaborate upon the argument that the fundamental pattern of Soviet foreign policies did not display the Nazis' insane thirst for destruction and endless military conquest. Over a period of a few years, Hitler had conquered or warred upon the majority of the world's most advanced nations in western, central, and eastern Europe, Russia, north Africa, and upon the high seas. While Fulbright disapproved of some of the Soviet foreign actions, especially in eastern Europe during the Stalin era, he later concluded with George F. Kennan and other Soviet experts that the U.S.S.R. and Nazi Germany were basically different as far as their foreign policies were concerned; and Fulbright appropriately responded to them differently during the course of his career.

1945-1946

Fulbright's support for the creation of the United Nations was his crucial interest in the realm of diplomacy during his first and only term in the U.S. House of Representatives after his election to Congress in 1942. In 1943, when he served as a freshman member of the House of Representatives Foreign Affairs Committee, he had sponsored the first Congressional Resolution advocating a postwar international organization. The Fulbright Resolution stated that the House of Representatives "hereby expresses itself as favoring the creation of appropriate international machinery with power adequate to establish and to maintain a just and lasting peace and as favoring participation of the United States therein." Secretary of State Cordell Hull, Undersecretary of State Sumner Welles, and Harry Hopkins supported the Fulbright Resolution.

In June, 1943, President Franklin D. Roosevelt wrote to Hull inquiring about the prospects for "pushing" the Resolution. "It seems to me pretty good," the President maintained, "and if we can get it through the House it might work in the Senate." Roosevelt displayed much less enthusiasm for the Resolution than Hull did, and the President informed Fulbright that he would endorse it provided the Resolution acquired widespread Congressional and popular support. By the fall of 1943, such support had clearly emerged. In July, 1943, a Gallup Poll reported that 78 per cent of the American public favored the Fulbright Resolution. On September 21 the House passed the Resolution by a vote of 360 to 29. Hull believed that the overwhelming margin of the Resolution's passage improved the American position in subsequent negotiations with the British and the Soviets concerning the postwar world, for it suggested that the American people approved their country's participation in a postwar international organization.

Between September, 1943, and January, 1945, Fulbright continued to support the establishment of a powerful United Nations. On November 5, 1943, the Senate followed the House's

23

example and passed the Connally Resolution, which advocated an international authority to prevent aggression. Many internationalists regarded the Senate document as weaker than the Fulbright Resolution, since the Connally Resolution specifically endorsed national sovereignty. Nevertheless, in late 1943 and 1944 Fulbright remained optimistic concerning the strength of internationalist sentiment. He implored Americans to maintain the wartime spirit of cooperation with the Soviet Union into the postwar period. Fulbright did not, however, espouse the extreme pro-Russian perspective exemplified by Joseph Davies, the former Ambassador to Moscow; Davies averred that "to question Stalin's good faith was bad Christianity, bad sportsmanship, bad sense." In Fulbright's view, after the war Russia might become a friend or it might become an enemy of the United States, depending upon how diligently the great powers supported the forthcoming United Nations organization. In a typical speech of late 1943, he asserted that "Either we cooperate with Russia and other nations in a system to preserve peace" after the war, or America might confront the dangers of competing with an industrialized Russia of 250 million people or a China of 450 million in a chaotic world of warring nations.

In the spring of 1944, Fulbright became the chairman of the London conference on postwar educational and cultural reconstruction. The Allied ministers of education from seventeen nations attended the London conference, which many internationalists envisaged as an important stepping stone in the formation of the U. N. The delegates to the conference drafted a tentative plan for a United Nations agency which would reconstruct the war-ravaged educational institutions of the world; however, later in 1944 American officials decided to postpone the establishment of any such educational organization pending the actual creation of the United Nations.

During his visit to England Fulbright enjoyed a luncheon appointment with Prime Minister Winston Churchill. As the Arkansan later recalled his conversation with Churchill, the Prime Minister did not express any criticisms of the Soviet Union and seemed to regard the Soviets as invaluable military allies; he did, however, consider General Charles de Gaulle an abrasive character who pugnaciously insisted upon a prominent French role in Allied wartime planning. Churchill briefly discussed a wide range of topics, including the preparations for the D-Day invasion which occurred two months later. Churchill was also interested to learn that Fulbright planned to run for the United States Senate in 1944. The conversation with Churchill was very brief, but Fulbright's chairmanship of the London conference and his appointment with the Prime Minister reflected the surprising prominence which the Arkansas Congressman had acquired by 1944. Despite the tentative nature of the conference's proposal for an international education agency, his journey to England pleased Fulbright. During his 1944 Senate campaign, he publicized his central role at the London conference.

Fulbright ended his trip to England with a radio broadcast to the English people over the British Broadcasting Company. In the B.B.C. speech he repeated his theme of the need to reform the system of international politics as it had existed before World War II: "Call it what you will—fascism, democratic decadence, general ignorance—the fact remains that something was wrong with that old world" which the war had destroyed, and "some new machinery with adequate powers must be created now, if our fine phrases and noble sentiments are to have substance and meaning for our children." He closed the B.B.C. address by informing the British public that he was "returning home to campaign for a seat in our Senate, and thereby an opportunity to contribute further, perhaps, to our mutual understanding." During his 1944 Senate campaign he reiterated his ideas for postwar international relations, although his position on domestic issues provided his margin of electoral victory in Arkansas. Upon entering the Senate in January, 1945, Fulbright persuaded fifteen freshman Senators to join him in sending a bipartisan letter to President Roosevelt which urged vigorous and prompt action in creating a United Nations organization.

As the debate over the U. N. intensified, Fulbright sought the advice of an old friend and mentor. During 1945 and throughout Fulbright's career, the Oxford scholar R. B. McCallum exerted an important influence upon the Senator's thinking. In the 1920s McCallum had tutored Fulbright in history when the Arkansan held a Rhodes Scholarship. A British Liberal Party supporter, McCallum had championed the League of Nations and in 1945 endorsed the United Nations. In a January letter to McCallum, Fulbright asked the Oxford sage for his ideas on the "present state of the world," and congratulated him for the flattering reviews of McCallum's book *Public Opinion and the Last Peace*, which analyzed the British public's response to the Versailles Treaty. McCallum replied to Fulbright by briefly expressing concern over potential international controversies which might destroy the wartime friendship between the United States and the Soviet Union. Although he advocated continued cooperation between the great powers, he warned that America and Russia might become embroiled in conflicts over the internal disputes of the smaller countries of the world, where the Russians would support the communist factions while the Americans and British supported the non-communist factions. He also suggested that the Russians did not respect the Anglo-American tradition of support for free elections.

McCallum described future Soviet actions on their pledges at the February, 1945 Yalta conference as the "real test" of their intentions. At Yalta Joseph Stalin had accepted Soviet membership in the forthcoming United Nations organization and agreed to promote free elections in Poland. In *Public Opinion and the Last Peace*, McCallum emphasized his hope that the "mutual sympathy and respect bred in this war" would facilitate amicable relations between America, Russia, and Great Britain after the war. The Oxford scholar's book espoused the internationalist viewpoint which he had impressed upon his pupil Fulbright many years before: security against future warfare depended upon "the disposition of the peoples to avoid war" by moderating their conduct and uniting to prevent aggression. In 1945 Fulbright did not devote his primary attention to the controversies over Soviet expansion into eastern Europe: he regarded the creation of an effective U.N. and later the question of international control over atomic weapons as the two central issues of Soviet-American relations.

In his maiden speech in the Senate on March 28, 1945, Fulbright had stressed his themes of opposition to anti-communism, support for the U.N., and concern for the Senate's proper role in foreign policy (the 1945 speeches are discussed in the introduction). He had also decried the efforts of certain newspapers and politicians to arouse hatred of the British, the Russians, and other foreigners. The United States had an interest, he argued, in the preservation of a strong Great Britain: "In this troubled and violent world is it not true that we would feel quite alone in the world if the British Commonwealth of Nations had been subjugated by the tyranny of the Nazis, and its resources directed against us?" Fulbright admonished the Senate that a lasting foundation of peace could not be established solely by the defeat of the Nazis and Japan and the signing of the U.N. Charter. In his view, American leaders should inform the people that "the price of peace is high," for

> The making of peace is a continuing process that must go on from day to day, from year to year, so long as our civilization shall last. Our participation in this process is not just the signing of a charter with a big red seal. It is a daily task, a positive participation in all the details and decisions which together constitute a living and growing policy.

The Senator believed that statesmen should not promise the people utopian benefits from any American policies, for the preservation of peace was an onerous and never-ending burden.

When President Roosevelt died two weeks after Fulbright delivered his speech, the freshman Senator became distressed over the prospects for creating a viable international organization under the inexperienced leadership of Harry Truman. Fulbright met with Truman immediately after Roosevelt's death in an attempt to reassure the new President. Truman sent him a cordial note thanking him for the visit: "It was a pleasure to see you at the Senate today, and I hope I will have that privilege often." Only two weeks later delegates from fifty nations gathered at San Francisco to draft the U.N. Charter. Truman's July 2 address to the Senate temporarily heartened Fulbright, for the President implored the Senators to approve the U.N. Charter, and he recalled that the Congress had participated in the founding of the Charter through the passage of the Fulbright and Connally Resolutions.

During the Senate debate on the United Nations, Fulbright and his friend Senator Claude Pepper of Florida questioned the prevailing belief that the Charter would provide genuine collective security. In late July the Senate overwhelmingly approved the Charter. Fulbright voted for the U.N. Charter, but he criticized its principle of the sovereign equality of all members in the General Assembly. No document, he asserted, could transform the tiny states of Nicaragua and Luxembourg into the equals of the United States and the Soviet Union. The Senator did not expect nations to immediately renounce their nationalism, but he wanted the Charter to begin placing limits on national sovereignty. In the fall of 1945, he contended that the Charter did not curb extreme nationalism, and he focused his criticism on the U.N. Security Council veto. He described the veto as a "hopeless" principle in any governmental organization, because he regarded it as "another way of saying that we shall go along and abide by the rules if it suits us in each particular instance." In Fulbright's view, the fundamental American foreign policy should not have been merely to praise or oppose Russia or any other nation, but to obtain their assistance in the formation of a bona fide peace-keeping organization. Since 1943 Fulbright had argued for a powerful United Nations, but he did not believe the U.N. Charter created an effective organization, for it endorsed the Security Council veto and the principle of national sovereignty. He based his vote for the Charter on the assumption that advocates of genuine collective security might gradually strengthen the United Nations in future years.

During the autumn, Fulbright was sharply critical of the Truman administration in speeches the Senator delivered at the Foreign Policy Association in New York City in October and a nation-wide address over N.B.C. radio in November. He continued to stress that the Soviet Union would develop atomic weapons within a few years, and that a U.N. system of inspection and control of atomic weapons needed to be established. The Senator did not pretend to have a definitive answer to the problem of how to prevent some future aggressor from unleashing an atomic war upon the world, but he argued that one indispensable requirement for an effective U.N. program of inspection and control would consist of all nations' acceptance of an important infringement on their sovereignty by delegating to the U.N. their powers over atomic armaments. No system of effective international law could be established if the principle of absolute national sovereignty continued, for "There is no law in the real sense between sovereign nations."

Fulbright urged the United States to support a system whereby any disputes regarding international control of the atom would be submitted to the compulsory jurisdiction of the U.N., with the judgment against any recalcitrant member (and here again Fulbright stressed that the Security Council veto should be abolished) to be enforced by all other members of the organization. In making these suggestions, the Arkansan was simply fulfilling his duty of offering alternatives to the administration's policies, for he was fully aware that Truman was not following the approach he advocated. The Senator believed that Truman's policies too often displayed a "get tough" attitude towards the Soviet Union, and that the President frequently "improvised on the spur of the moment." Fulbright's criticisms infuriated Truman. At a press conference after the Senator's N.B.C. speech, the President abruptly rejected Fulbright's views, and then declined further comment.

In terms of Fulbright's direct personal relationships with other major critics of Truman's diplomacy, the Senator was much closer to Claude Pepper than to Secretary of Commerce Henry A. Wallace. Twenty years earlier, young Fulbright had enrolled in Pepper's law course at the University of Arkansas and engaged in lengthy philosophical discussions with the brilliant, loquacious Floridian. In 1945 their relationship remained cordial. Pepper had also criticized Truman for failing to cooperate with the Soviets in the U.N. and endorsed international control over atomic energy, although the Florida Senator espoused a more fervent anti-Cold War perspective than did Fulbright. A minor example of this difference occurred in early 1946, when Fulbright chose not to endorse Pepper's proposal that the United States destroy its arsenal of atomic bombs and the machinery for producing them.

By the spring of 1946, Fulbright had begun to adopt a more favorable attitude towards Truman's diplomacy and a more critical view of Soviet foreign policy. In an important speech at New York City in May, 1946, he sharply criticized the Soviets for the first time, concluding with profound reluctance that recent Soviet policies contradicted the desire to bring peace to the world under the aegis of the United Nations. The Senator's positive response to the Acheson-Lilienthal Report (a proposal for international control of atomic weapons) and his increasing abhorrence of Soviet actions in eastern Europe, Manchuria, and elsewhere were the central reasons for the transition in his position. He wondered if Russia would ever submit to "rules of conduct in any field," and asked "is it the purpose of Russia to dominate the world or is she only seeking security?" He did not give a definite answer, and he suggested that Americans should consider the extent to which Stalin may have based his actions upon the legitimate and ancient Russian quest for warm water ports. Yet he deplored as acts of aggression the Soviet annexation of the Baltic states and Polish territory, the Soviets' stripping of factories in Manchuria, the demands for bases in the Dardanelles, and the violation of pledges to establish free governments in eastern Europe.

At the same time, however, Fulbright pointed to the flaws in American diplomacy. In his May, 1946 address, he alleged that U.S. policy before the Acheson-Lilienthal Report was often indecisive or negative, and he cited the excessive haste in terminating lend-lease aid to Russia as an example of the earlier negativism. The Acheson-Lilienthal Report proposed that no nation should manufacture atomic bombs or the materials for them, and that an international authority of atomic scientists should carry on all dangerous atomic energy activities. Fulbright commended the Report and predicted that Soviet acceptance of it might end the vicious cycle of suspicion and hostility between the two great powers; but if the Soviets rejected it, their rejection "will provide a very significant clue as to her future policy, and we should shape our own policy accordingly."

In the summer of 1946, the United States presented an altered version of the Acheson-Lilienthal Report called the Baruch Plan to the United Nations. The Baruch Plan deeply disappointed many of the experts who helped to prepare the Acheson-Lilienthal Report. The Atomic Development Authority, which Bernard Baruch's proposal would have established, provided for an inspection system over which the Soviet Union could not exercise its Security Council veto. The Baruch Plan assumed the United States would hold a monopoly of atomic weapons for an indefinite period. Moreover, by controlling a majority within the Atomic Development Authority, the United States could have controlled the development of industrial uses of atomic energy within the Soviet Union. Fulbright failed to observe that the Baruch Plan significantly weakened the Acheson-Lilienthal Report. The Soviets rejected the Baruch Plan and Fulbright, true to his position in the May, 1946 speech, became increasingly critical of Soviet diplomacy and increasingly sympathetic to the Truman Cold War policies. He supported the President during the 1946 Congressional campaign.

The administration's endorsement of Fulbright's effort to establish the international scholar exchange program contributed to the Arkansan's more favorable assessment of the Truman administration. Assistant Secretary of State William Benton and Democratic Senator Elbert D. Thomas of Utah assisted Fulbright in passing the legislation creating the Fulbright program. On August 1, 1946, Truman signed the Fulbright Act, which permitted the sale of U.S. surplus property abroad to finance the international exchange of scholars. Fulbright eventually considered the exchange program as the greatest achievement of his long career (1942-1975) in politics.

Political pressures may have influenced Fulbright's 1946 transition from a critic to a supporter of Truman's foreign policy. Truman enjoyed considerable popularity in Arkansas, and Fulbright knew that it was politically dangerous for a freshman Senator to continue criticizing a President of his own party. During the 1940s some of the Senator's opponents darkly hinted that he had displayed a sympathy for communism, but these charges were infrequent. However, in Arkansas in the late 1940s domestic issues usually attracted more attention than foreign policy questions. As long as Fulbright vigorously supported the economic development of the state and maintained a conservative stance on civil rights, most of his constituents tended to grant him extensive freedom of action concerning his foreign policy positions. His controversial ideas in foreign policy may have occasionally damaged his political position in Arkansas, but the damage was not fatal to his political career. Concern over the potential political liabilities of criticizing Truman's foreign policy probably played only a secondary role in Fulbright's increasing tendency to support the President. The Senator's genuine belief that the Baruch Plan represented a magnanimous proposal and his antipathy towards Soviet behavior in eastern Europe, Manchuria, Iran, and the Dardanelles constituted the most important reasons for the change in his perspective on the Cold War.

Fulbright's responses to the early Cold War were not unique, for on the question of atomic secrets his views resembled those of Secretary of War Henry L. Stimson. Fulbright and Stimson had known each other during World War II, although they were not close friends and probably arrived independently at their opinions on U.S. diplomacy. In the fall of 1945 Fulbright, Stimson, several other foreign policy analysts, and many scientists had believed that the Soviets would acquire atomic bombs within three to five years, and therefore the United States should have immediately shared atomic information with the Soviets and established definite agreements for international control of the atom. General Leslie R. Groves and Secretary of State James F. Byrnes had contended that the Russians would require approximately ten years to develop atomic weapons, but the Stimson prediction of relatively rapid Soviet acquisition of atomic bombs proved correct; the Soviets exploded an atomic weapon in 1949.

In Stimson's famous September, 1945 memorandum to the President, he had maintained that Soviet-American relations "may be perhaps irretrievably embittered by the way in which we approach the solution of the bomb with Russia. For if we fail to approach them now and merely continue to negotiate with them, having this weapon rather ostentatiously on our hip, their suspicions and their distrust of our purposes and motives will increase." After the delays in presenting the American atomic plan to the U.N., controversies over eastern Europe, and the Soviet rejection of the Baruch Plan, Stimson changed his position. By the fall of 1946, the now retired Stimson advised Secretary of the Navy James V. Forrestal that "the way things had now developed we should not delay in going forward with the manufacture of all the atomic missiles we can make."

Fulbright perhaps did not reverse his position from 1945 to 1946 quite as drastically as Stimson; however, in a typical speech of late 1946 the Senator complained that "Russia has become affected by the fervor of expansion." He averred that if the United States could impress Russia with measures such as the extension of the draft, then a relatively stable relationship with the Soviet Union might continue through a breathing period, and then in the next fifteen to twenty years business connections and the exchange of scholars with the Soviets might gradually remove the suspicions and hostilities from Soviet-American relations.

Despite Fulbright's support for the administration, a curious episode after the 1946 elections led many people to regard the Senator as a bitter enemy of the President. During a fall, 1946 luncheon with his friend Senator Scott Lucas of Illinois, the reporter Ann Hicks, and others, Fulbright repeated a statement he had made publicly in March, 1945. In the 1945 statement, Fulbright had warned that dangerous deadlocks between the President and Congress could jeopardize world peace and domestic prosperity. He advocated a change in the American government to end the adversary relationship between the legislative and executive branches which inevitably arose when one party controlled the Presidency while the other party controlled Congress. Citing the examples of partisan furor in Woodrow Wilson's experiences with the League of Nations after the 1918 elections and Herbert Hoover's difficulties with Congress after the 1930 elections, he asserted that the President should possess the authority to dissolve the government in cases of stalemate between the legislative and executive branches and precipitate a general election. The proposal clearly reflected Fulbright's admiration for British parliamentary government.

In his 1946 conversation with Lucas he predicted that if the Republicans won the elections the Democrats in the White House and the Republicans in Congress would engage in incessant and acrimonious debates, and "each party will place the blame for the inevitable stalemate on the other party." He remarked to Lucas that if the Republicans won, Truman should appoint a Republican Secretary of State and then resign, thus making the Republican the new President (since there was no Vice-President at the time) and preventing another anomalous adversary relationship from arising. Fulbright suggested Michigan's Republican Senator Arthur H. Vandenberg, the symbol of bipartisanship, as the most logical choice for Truman's successor.

After the Republicans captured both Houses of Congress in the 1946 elections, the reporter who had listened to the Fulbright-Lucas conversation published an article on Fulbright's remarks and thus detonated a major furor. Former Secretary of the Interior Harold Ickes, the journalist Walter Lippmann, the *Altanta Constitution*, and the *Chicago Sun* endorsed Fulbright's idea. Truman refused official comment, although his aides dismissed the quixotic proposal as "utterly fantastic." Truman did not appreciate the niceties of Fulbrightian political philosophy, despite the Rhodes Scholar's statement on November 10 that "In urging this proposal there was no intention to reflect in any way upon the character or capacity of President Truman." At an off-the-record dinner a few days later, Truman disparaged Fulbright as an "overeducated Oxford SOB," although many years later he denied having made the statement.

After the fiasco of the 1946 resignation proposal, Fulbright became more cautious in pressing his ideas for eliminating governmental deadlocks; he had learned his lesson, he recalled many years later, about "tilting at windmills." However, throughout the late 1940s and early 1950s, memories of the resignation controversy severely weakened Fulbright's ability to exert an important influence upon the administration's diplomacy or to work constructively with the President, who thereafter harbored a hostility toward the Senator until after he retired from the Presidency.

1946-1954

From late 1946 until early 1951 Fulbright's importance as a foreign policy analyst declined. During this period the Senator devoted most of his time and energy to the development of Arkansas agriculture and other domestic affairs. His disenchantment with the failure of the great powers to create a powerful United Nations may have contributed to his lessened activity in foreign affairs. Much of his concentration on domestic issues resulted simply from his position within the Senate, where his major committee assignment was on the Banking and Currency Committee. He did not obtain a position on the prestigious Foreign Relations Committee until 1949.

From the summer of 1949 to early 1951 he devoted much of his energy to another domestic issue: a Banking and Currency subcommittee's investigation of administration officials' use of favoritism and unethical influence in the Reconstruction Finance Corporation. The R.F.C. investigation reinforced Truman's bitterness toward Fulbright which the 1946 resignation proposal had engendered. Fulbright's R.F.C. inquiry was not related to the Cold War, except in one respect: Walter Lippmann, Ernest K. Lindley, and other political analysts pointed out the contrast between Fulbright's careful, responsible conduct of a Congressional investigation, and the "witch-hunting" of Wisconsin Senator Joseph McCarthy's investigations. Lippmann described Fulbright's conduct of the R.F.C. inquiry as "an example, all the more impressive because its sincerity has been so effortless, of how a good senator can behave."

To the limited extent that the Arkansan involved himself in foreign affairs from late 1946 to early 1951, he continued to support the basic Truman policies. In early 1947 Fulbright commended Truman's appointment of George C. Marshall as Secretary of State after James F. Byrnes resigned in January. A few weeks after the Marshall appointment Fulbright wrote a letter to the President congratulating him for "making extraordinarily good decisions and appointments." The Senator regretted that the press often "put me in a belligerent attitude," for in reality "it is my intention to support you in every way I can."

Fulbright supported Truman's March, 1947 request for $400

33

million in economic and military aid for Turkey and for Greece, where leftist revolutionaries waged guerrilla warfare against the government. In the President's March 12, 1947 speech to Congress he presented his Truman Doctrine, which committed the United States to "support free peoples who are resisting attempted subjugation by armed minorities or by outside pressures." Beyond the specific request for aid to Greece and Turkey, the Doctrine constituted a vague and indeterminate promise to support governments under communist attack. Although Fulbright voted for the specific appeal for aid to Greece and Turkey, he displayed little enthusiasm for the global anti-communist rhetoric of Truman's speech. Throughout his later career Fulbright affirmed that in 1947, given the paralysis of the western European economy, Stalin's expansion into eastern Europe, and the virtual disarmament of the United States in conventional forces, the decision to aid Greece and Turkey represented an intelligent action. But the Arkansan later objected to Truman's inflated rhetoric publicizing the concept of a global ideological conflict between western freedom and Moscow's system of "terror and oppression." Whether the Senator privately held these views at the time was debatable, for he failed to offer any public criticisms of the Truman Doctrine. He did propose an alternative strategy for the management of disputes with Russia. He asserted that the "balance of power" should govern American policy in the Cold War, and that the United States could restore the European balance by promoting the political and economic federation of Europe as a counterweight to Soviet power. One week after the Truman Doctrine speech, Fulbright and Elbert Thomas of Utah introduced a resolution stating that "Congress favors the creation of a United States of Europe within the framework of the United Nations." The administration as well as the Senate did not accept the resolution.

At times during the late 1940s Fulbright indulged in the Cold War rhetoric characteristic of the era. When Henry Wallace charged that aid to Greece amounted to American imperialism, Fulbright complained to an Arkansas newspaper reporter that Wallace's statement "sounded just as though it had been written in the Kremlin." Fulbright's remark was a heated criticism, especially since he had frequently praised Wallace (and most of the other Roosevelt advisers) during the Roosevelt administration. The Senator might have refuted Wallace's view with a temperate, well-reasoned explanation of the need to strengthen the weak Turkish government or to fill the power vacuum in the eastern Mediterranean which the recent British withdrawal from Greece had created. Since Fulbright made his criticism in an impromptu interview with a reporter, he may not have reflected upon the derogatory tone of his remark; nevertheless, the published statement represented a harsh effort to disparage the former Vice-President and Cabinet official. Wallace's views suffered from a pro-Soviet bias, but his ideas deserved respectful criticism.

On another occasion in the late 1940s Fulbright differed with Wallace in a more temperate fashion; in 1948 he delivered an address at Southwestern at Memphis in which he offered a restrained critique of Wallace's third party Presidential candidacy. "Multiple parties," he argued, "in other countries have usually resulted in unstable and ineffective governments." In the Memphis address, Fulbright did not employ any anti-communist rhetoric in opposing the Wallace third party movement.

In 1947 Fulbright demonstrated more enthusiasm for the Marshall Plan than for the Truman Doctrine's global anti-communism. The Senator praised Secretary of State Marshall's June 5 speech at Harvard, in which the Secretary announced the administration's plan for economic aid to Europe. The Marshall Plan differed in purpose and tone from the Truman Doctrine, for it committed the United States to the economic rehabilitation of Europe, and not to a crusade against communism. In July Marshall wrote Fulbright thanking him for his approval of the Harvard speech. The Secretary informed Fulbright that the favorable domestic and foreign responses to the address augured well for the success of the Marshall Plan. Marshall had invited the Soviet Union and its Slavic satellites to join in the economic recovery program. The Soviets eventually rejected the American offer and denounced the program as an American plot to gain control of the European economy. The Soviet repudiation of the Marshall Plan accelerated Fulbright's tendency to attack Soviet diplomacy. In responding to the Soviet rejection, Fulbright charged that the Russians did not desire the rehabilitation of any European country unless "it is communist-controlled and isolated by an iron curtain."

In 1948-1949 Fulbright continued to support Truman's Cold War policies in Europe. The Arkansan endorsed Truman's 1948 Presidential campaign and rejected the third-party movement of Henry Wallace as well as the Dixiecrats under Strom Thurmond. During the 1948 Berlin blockade, Fulbright and Scott Lucas traveled to Berlin, where they conferred with General Lucius D. Clay and approved of Clay's handling of the crisis. In June the U.S.S.R. had attempted to prevent the organization of Germany's three western zones into a West German state by blockading West Berlin. Britain and the United States responded with the Berlin airlift, which supplied the city so effectively that Stalin ended the blockade in 1949 and acquiesced in the subsequent creation of the West German Republic. Stalin countered the Western triumphs in the victory of the anti-guerrilla forces in Greece and the Berlin airlift by establishing the East German Democratic Republic. After the Fulbright-Lucas journey to Berlin, the Arkansas Senator stated "there's little likelihood of war," provided the United States maintained a firm stance against Soviet actions. In 1949 Fulbright voted for the North Atlantic Treaty Organization Pact, through which the United States provided a shield of air and atomic power for western Europe. He demonstrated special enthusiasm for Truman's Point Four program of technical assistance to under-developed countries. As a freshman Senator who devoted much of his time to domestic issues, Fulbright did not play a central role in the N.A.T.O. and Point Four programs.

In 1949 Fulbright defended the administration against the extreme anti-communists who denounced Truman for "losing" China to communism. Upon Marshall's recommendation, Truman had rejected a direct military intervention in the Chinese civil war. He felt he could not immediately desert the Chinese Nationalists because of Chiang Kai-shek's many influential friends within the United States, and therefore he decided to provide the Nationalists with a moderate amount of aid. In the 1940s the United States supplied the corrupt and inefficient Nationalist Chinese with military equipment and around $2 billion in aid, air-lifted entire Nationalist armies at critical junctures during the war, and seized and held vital Chinese seaports for the Nationalists. A few months before the Nationalists collapsed and fled to Formosa, Truman raised the question of terminating military aid to the Kuomintang. Democratic Senator Pat McCarran of Nevada thereupon introduced a bill to loan $1.5 billion to Nationalist China for economic and military purposes. Republican Senator William F. Knowland of California called for an investigation of America's China policy. Fulbright and Tom Connally of Texas defended Truman and the State Department and blocked McCarran's attempt to continue and deepen the American involvement in China. Later in the year Secretary of State Dean G. Acheson, who succeeded Marshall in 1949, and Ambassador at Large Philip C. Jessup supervised the preparation of a State Department White Paper on China. The White Paper accurately portrayed the Chinese revolution as an indigenous uprising beyond American control.

Fulbright won re-election in 1950, the year Joseph McCarthy charged that 205 communists had infiltrated the State Department. A McCarthyite candidate defeated the conservative Senator Millard Tydings of Maryland, who had thoroughly investigated

McCarthy's allegations against the State Department and declared them unfounded. Ohio Senator Robert A. Taft gained re-election after blaming Truman and Acheson for the "loss of China," while the vociferous anti-communist Richard M. Nixon defeated Helen Gahagan Douglas in California. Three of Fulbright's closest friends in the Senate, Claude Pepper, Elbert Thomas, and Democratic Majority Leader Scott Lucas lost their 1950 campaigns for re-election. In all three cases McCarthyite allegations contributed to the electoral results, although George Smathers in Florida and Everett Dirksen in Illinois also used other issues to defeat the incumbents.

Fulbright seemed another likely target for a McCarthyite onslaught. In the 1944 Senate campaign Governor Homer Adkins and other right-wing candidates had denigrated the Rhodes Scholar as a "New Dealer" who had displayed a softness toward communism. They cited as evidence for their charges the facts that Fulbright had served as an Anti-Trust Division lawyer during the New Deal, and as a member of the House of Representatives had voted for an unsuccessful effort to abolish Representative Martin Dies' Special Committee on Un-American Activities. Adkins publicized the Congress of Industrial Organizations' endorsement of Fulbright in an effort to smear him as a tool of socialism. Some observers of Arkansas politics speculated that Fulbright might face a similar right-wing challenge in 1950. Throughout late 1949 and much of 1950 the Senator conducted an exhaustive campaign of speaking engagements in Arkansas. Fulbright had amply demonstrated his non-communist credentials in the late 1940s through his bitter criticisms of Soviet rejections of the Baruch Plan and the Marshall Plan. His vigor in encouraging Arkansas' economic development and conservatism in civil rights deprived potential opponents of any domestic issues to use against him. Moreover, although many of his constituents may not have cared deeply about the specifics of his foreign policy positions, they understood and admired the prestige Fulbright enjoyed as the author of the Fulbright Resolution, the Fulbright Fellowships program, and as a member of the Senate Foreign Relations Committee.

The right-wing threat to end his career did not materialize. Fulbright ran unopposed and in 1951 emerged with a strengthened position in the Senate.

After the 1950 election Fulbright led the Democratic opposition to Republican condemnations of Truman's Asian policy. Republican Senators escalated their attacks on the State Department after the outbreak of the Korean War in 1950. In November, Fulbright wrote Acheson a brief letter assuring the Secretary that

37

the American People would ultimately grow weary of the Republicans' "carping." On December 19 the *New York Times* reported that Fulbright and other Democrats had rallied to a "rare demonstration of solidarity" in opposing Republican suggestions that Truman ask for Acheson's resignation. In a Senate debate on December 18, Senator Knowland provided the Republican rebuttal by claiming that his party had simply fulfilled its duty to lambast Acheson for "having closed the door to communism in Europe while leaving it wide open in Asia." Fulbright decried Republican criticisms as "character assassination" of administration officials. To his mind, the Republican assault on Acheson's patriotism resembled a fascist appeal to human prejudice and emotionalism. The Arkansan affirmed that the Republican attacks might eventually disrupt the confidence of U.S. allies in the American ability to follow a responsible foreign policy.

Fulbright vacillated in his early responses to the Korean War. For months after the North Koreans launched their offensive in June, 1950, Fulbright had remained silent. After thirty-three full Chinese divisions ravaged the over-extended American lines south of the Yalu River, the Senator called for an immediate withdrawal of U.S. troops from Korea. In early 1951, he endorsed Truman's original decision to oppose the "direct and unambiguous aggression" of North Korea, but he asserted that any risk of involvement in a protracted land war with China was unacceptable. When China entered the war, he averred, the dangers of fighting on the Asian continent became militarily "untenable." He followed this assertion with one of the harshest anti-communist statements he ever uttered: "We must not forget that the Kremlin is the primary enemy and China merely a satellite." During the early stages of the Korean War Fulbright and Assistant Secretary of State for Far Eastern Affairs Dean Rusk expressed equally distorted evaluations of the strength of Chinese nationalism, Fulbright describing China as a Russian "satellite," Rusk labeling the Chinese a "colonial Russian government." The context of the Fulbright and Rusk statements differed greatly; Rusk contended that since the Peking regime constituted a Soviet colony the Nationalists on Formosa were the authentic representatives of the Chinese people, while Fulbright's description of China as a Soviet satellite occurred in the context of his appeal for an American withdrawal from the Korean military engagement against China. Nevertheless, Fulbright's allegation that China was a Russian satellite revealed his lack of knowledge of the Far East. He possessed a vast store of knowledge concerning Europe, but in the early 1950s he frequently failed to grasp the complexities of Asian affairs.

During 1951, the radical right's attack on Truman's Asian policy increasingly led Fulbright to focus his attention on the Far East. In the spring he engaged in an acrimonious public debate with General Douglas MacArthur when the General entered the political arena to advocate the escalation of warfare against China. MacArthur delineated his strategy for crushing the Chinese in a speech before Congress on April 19, 1951, shortly after Truman relieved him of command in Korea for publicly defying the President's decision to stalemate the war and seek a truce. The General declared that "military necessity" demanded the bombing of Manchuria, the "unleashing" of Chiang Kai-shek to invade China, the massive reinforcement of American forces in Korea, and the blockade of the Chinese mainland. The powerful U.S. Representative Joseph Martin and other ultraconservatives in Congress jubilantly publicized and endorsed MacArthur's appraisal of the military situation in the Far East. On May 16 a Gallup Poll reported that 66 per cent of the American public favored MacArthur's war strategy, while only 25 per cent favored Truman's limited war strategy.

Although Fulbright had often played the role of the skeptical gadfly of the administration in earlier years, he vigorously defended Truman against the avalanche of verbal abuse the President sustained for the dismissal of MacArthur. A week after the General's address to Congress, Fulbright delivered a speech to the Senate in which he denounced the proposal to expand the Korean War as almost certain to precipitate a third world war. He began his speech by condemning MacArthur's challenge to the venerable American principle of subordination of the military to the civilian authority, stating that only a constitutional amendment could abrogate the President's authority to remove commanders in the field.

Fulbright proceeded to discuss the strategic consequences of MacArthur's plan. In a passage which foreshadowed his analysis of American involvement in Laos and Vietnam in later years, he argued that even if the General's critics granted the doubtful contention that Russia would remain passive while Chiang's armies and American bombers invaded China, the Soviets would relish nothing more than the prospect of watching as the United States dissipated its resources in interminable and debilitating conflicts on the periphery of the Soviet empire.

Fulbright contended that MacArthur's strategy represented an ineffable danger, for he believed the Soviet Union almost certainly would intervene once the bombing began. The Senator regarded any lack of specificity in the 1950 Sino-Soviet treaty as irrelevant, because if the U.S.S.R "should stand idly by and see her Chinese ally knocked to pieces," such inaction would inflict irrevocable damage upon Soviet prestige and security. Finally, although MacArthur commanded the first United Nations army in history, he had not consulted or even mentioned America's allies fighting in Korea. The General proposed that the United States unilaterally reach a decision likely to commit American allies throughout the globe to total warfare. Fulbright raised the possibility that MacArthur's drastic plan (if America accepted it) might drive the western Europeans into making an accommodation or even an alliance with the Soviet Union rather than meekly acquiescing as the United States determined their destinies.

In May, MacArthur testified at joint hearings of the Senate Armed Services Committee and the Foreign Relations Committee. At the hearings Senators Fulbright and Wayne Morse of Oregon exposed the glaring inconsistencies in MacArthur's allegation that a land war in continental China would not follow the proposed bombings. Fulbright questioned MacArthur as to whether the primitive economy of China, which possessed thousands of widely dispersed handicrafts industries but no heavily industrialized areas, did not constitute a formidable defense against aerial devastation of its productive capacity. In the Senator's opinion, the United States could not have crippled the Chinese war effort by destroying the Manchurian munitions factories, because the Chinese manufactured only small arms for themselves and received the bulk of their military equipment from the Soviet Union. MacArthur evaded Fulbright's questions by stating that a blockade of the mainland would produce a famine which might kill fifteen million Chinese and that a failure to adopt his program would signify the degradation of the American "moral tone."

During the MacArthur hearings Fulbright charged that the General's view of the military realities suffered from an erroneous assumption of American omnipotence. The Japanese in World War II had never been able to starve China into submission. Considering the enormous difficulties Japan encountered in attempting to subdue China during the eight years of warfare before Pearl Harbor when the Japanese commanded virtually complete control of the air, the Arkansan dismissed MacArthur's prediction that the United States could subdue the Chinese through naval and air power alone. In Fulbright's view, the air strikes were the inevitable prelude to the commitment of combat forces in China. Fulbright argued that Soviet military power might represent a threat to U.S. security, but communist ideology alone could not harm America. The General disagreed vehemently, identifying the fundamental threat to American interest as "communism wherever it exists," both within the United States and throughout the world. Fulbright contended that MacArthur's appeal for a "total victory" had distorted American perspectives on the Cold War by dividing policy alternatives into the absolute polarities of "appeasement," or an utter obliteration of Asian communism which the General imagined would serve as a panacea for all the failures of recent American diplomacy.

The temporary hysteria which accompanied the General's return to the United States after his dismissal gradually abated. The administration's strong defense of its actions and the Senate hearings helped to puncture the legend of MacArthur as the dethroned and noble warrior. However, to many Americans the General remained a hero, and his program of building future policy around Chiang Kai-shek and U.S. sea and air power exerted a pernicious influence on American foreign policy. Truman did not reverse his Far Eastern policy under pressure of the General's assault; but the combined fears and pressures of the Korean War, MacArthur's Asia-first strategy, and McCarthy's attacks on the State Department influenced the Truman administration to adopt a more rigid stance in favor of Chiang and to accelerate aid to the Nationalists on Formosa.

In October, 1951, Fulbright resisted McCarthy's onslaught against Ambassador at Large Philip Jessup, the former editor-in-chief of the China White Paper. Truman nominated Jessup to fill the post of representative to the U.N. General Assembly. Jessup had previously delivered speeches at the U.N., where his record as an ardent Cold War orator had often led Fulbright to criticize him for abetting the Soviet attempt to transform the Assembly into a forum for exchanging insults. Yet McCarthy and former Minnesota Governor Harold Stassen questioned Jessup's patriotism because of his association with Acheson and his membership in the Institute for Pacific Relations. The Institute included among its members Owen Lattimore, the former adviser to Chiang Kai-shek who now led the organization's vociferous criticism of Chiang. During a Senate Foreign Relations subcommittee's hearings on Jessup's nomination, Fulbright pressed McCarthy to document his claims that Jessup held a "great affinity for communist causes." At one juncture of the hearings, McCarthy virtually conceded that he had not yet made a convincing case against Jessup, but he urged the Senators to wait and weigh the evidence in its totality. Fulbright responded, "A number of zeros doesn't amount to one if you put them all together." McCarthy ranted that "men of little minds" were trying to make communism a political issue, whereupon Fulbright sarcastically replied, "You would not do anything like that, would you?"

Despite McCarthy's failure to substantiate his accusations, only Fulbright and Senator John Sparkman of Alabama among the members of the Foreign Relations subcommittee voted in favor of Jessup. Republican Senator H. Alexander Smith of New Jersey explained his crucial vote against the Ambassador at Large by conceding that he held absolute confidence in the ability, loyalty, and integrity of his old friend Jessup, but that Jessup had embraced a "group attitude toward Asia" which brought disaster in China. After Jessup's defeat, McCarthy exulted, "This is a great day for America and a bad day for communists." At the time of Fulbright's clash with McCarthy at the Jessup hearings, the Arkansan confided to his friend Senator William Benton of Connecticut that he "hadn't imagined that the man could be as bad as he turned out to be."

In 1952, Fulbright contended that McCarthy was vilifying the Democratic Presidential nominee, Governor Adlai E. Stevenson of Illinois. McCarthy directed a series of scurrilous charges against Stevenson: he "exposed" Stevenson's membership in the Institute for Pacific Relations, and charged that the *Daily Worker* had endorsed the Governor, which was not true. McCarthy's charges disgusted the Arkansas Senator. Fulbright and Stevenson had met when they were New Deal government lawyers and remained friends until Stevenson's death.

In October, 1952, the *St. Louis Post-Dispatch* reported that Fulbright had sent Stevenson extensive information concerning the techniques the McCarthyites had used in defaming earlier opponents, such as their use of a falsified composite photograph of Millard Tydings supposedly conversing with the communist leader Earl Browder. The Stevenson organization invited Fulbright to come to Springfield and act as an adviser to the Governor during the final stages of the campaign. Fulbright and George W. Ball, Executive Director of the National Volunteers for Stevenson, publicized the similarity between McCarthy's allegations against Stevenson and the McCarthyite campaign against Tydings in 1950. The Arkansas Senator and Ball helped mobilize the Democratic counter-attack against McCarthy. Truman criticized Republican Presidential nominee Dwight D. Eisenhower's reluctant endorsement of McCarthy as a desertion of the General's former comrade in arms George Marshall, since McCarthy had frequently denounced Marshall's role in Asian policy. The Senatorial electoral results in Wisconsin and Connecticut discouraged many of McCarthy's opponents, however. McCarthy gained re-election, although he won only 54 percent of the vote. McCarthy's most vocal antagonist in the Senate, William Benton of Connecticut, lost his campaign for re-election.

In November, 1952 R. B. McCallum wrote a letter to Fulbright analyzing Eisenhower's election to the Presidency. "As an English Liberal I have always been pro-Democrat," McCallum observed, "but in many ways it was becoming very dangerous to have the Republicans excluded from office for so long." If the Republicans had again lost the Presidency after twenty years in opposition, he believed they would have vented their frustrations and bitterness on Stevenson and thus placed the Democrat in an untenable position. He thought Eisenhower might become a good President. In Fulbright's February, 1953 reply to McCallum, he described Eisenhower as a "good man," although he expressed uncertainty about the President's political astuteness. He regretted that McCarthy and Senator William Jenner of Indiana "are having their way at the moment," and hoped "their day of glory will be short lived." Fulbright thought Eisenhower must provide the leadership in beginning the repudiation of McCarthy.

In an early 1953 letter to William Benton, Fulbright elaborated upon his views concerning the proper strategy to employ in opposing McCarthy. According to the Arkansan, the Republicans would rally around McCarthy and accuse the Democrats of partisanship if a Democrat made the initial move to condemn the Wisconsin Senator. The President or a leading Republican must first "take the curse of partisanship off the matter" before a Democrat could present some type of formal condemnation against McCarthy. He believed that the "political overtones" of McCarthyism were extremely difficult to diagnose, but he assured Benton that he would continue to study the issue of condemning McCarthy. In an early 1953 letter to Fulbright, Benton urged his former colleague to act aggressively in opposing McCarthy. "I was one of eleven Senatorial candidates who ran ahead of Stevenson," he informed Fulbright, "which would not seem to indicate that the McCarthy affair hurt me noticeably—there is no doubt that it hurt, but a good case can be made for the fact that it helped in other directions even more than it hurt." In explaining these "other directions" which helped him, Benton observed that he had received over 1,000 contributions to his 1952 Senate campaign from people all over the country who had applauded his dissent against McCarthyism. He predicted that if Fulbright would lead a movement to publicly repudiate the Wisconsin Senator, he would receive a "tremendous response" from the legal profession and from people throughout the United States. Benton has accurately analyzed his 1952 defeat. His opponent William Purtell may have gained a few thousand votes from McCarthy's endorsement, but his 88,000-vote margin over Benton primarily resulted from Eisenhower's ability to generate support for the entire Republican ticket in Connecticut. As the *New York Times* summarized it, Benton "got caught in the Eisenhower landslide."

During early 1953, Fulbright erred in depending on Eisenhower to commence hostilities versus McCarthy. The president refused to openly challenge the Wisconsin Senator and expected the Senate to discipline its miscreants. Nor did McCarthy's opponents receive any encouragement from Eisenhower's Vice President, Richard Nixon, who had earlier competed with McCarthy in vilifying the Democratic "traitors in the high councils of our own government who make sure that the deck is stacked on the Soviet side of the diplomatic table." By the summer of 1953 Fulbright began to realize that the Eisenhower administration would not assume leadership of the movement to repudiate McCarthy.

At the July, 1953 Senate Appropriations Committee hearings concerning funds for the Fulbright Fellowships, Fulbright launched the counteroffensive which culminated in McCarthy's censure in December, 1954. McCarthy threatened to terminate the educational exchange program through his charges that it awarded scholarships to communists. He requested that the Senate Committee place in the record of the hearings several statements which Fulbright Scholars had allegedly made "praising the communist form of government." Fulbright revealed that he had come prepared to insert into the record thousands of statements concerning Fulbright Scholars which would refute McCarthy's assertions. Fulbright's response startled McCarthy. The Republican Senator gesticulated, raised his voice, and derisively referred to Fulbright as "Halfbright," but he eventually withdrew his demand and never again challenged the exchange program. The State Department official Francis Colligan and the scholar Walter Johnson believed that Fulbright's performance in the July, 1953 hearings represented the first successful resistance to McCarthy within the U.S. government since McCarthy had launched his anti-communist crusade with the 1950 "Communism in the State Department" speech.

In early 1954 McCarthy, as well as many of his enemies outside the Senate, portrayed the imminent decision on appropriations for his Permanent Investigations subcommittee as a test vote of confidence in the Senator. On February 2, the Senate overwhelmingly approved the $214,000 appropriation for the subcommittee. McCarthy's margin of victory was 85 to 1, with Fulbright casting the lone dissenting vote. The Arkansan's dissent shocked some of the influential leaders of the liberal bloc in the Senate, especially Senator Herbert H. Lehman of New York, into more vigorous support for the movement to condemn McCarthy. Even before the ap-

44

propriations vote, Lehman had been one of McCarthy's important critics. On February 4, Lehman paid a visit to Fulbright's office. He said he admired Fulbright's vote, apologized for not having voted with him, and promised that he would not fail to join him in opposing McCarthy in the future.

A few weeks after his vote to terminate the funds for McCarthy's subcommittee, Fulbright rejected a Federal Bureau of Investigation request for information concerning an anonymous, minor State Department official who had known the Arkansan. The F.B.I. was investigating the official as a possible subversive. Fulbright explained his refusal by observing that F.B.I. Director J. Edgar Hoover granted McCarthy access to F.B.I. files, and that McCarthy misused the F.B.I.'s information to defame responsible citizens. The Associated Press reported on March 13 that "the Arkansan is the first Senator to refuse to give information to the F.B.I." The A.P. report stated that Fulbright had "declined any further dealings with the F.B.I." after the initial request. Fulbright affirmed that his report on the State Department official "would have been favorable" if he had given it, but he chose to withhold information from the F.B.I. rather than allow McCarthy to twist the words of his report into an anti-communist "smear" against the official.

Throughout the early months of 1954, Fulbright broadened his dissent to charge that McCarthyism exerted a destructive impact not only on American foreign policy, but upon the entire social and intellectual environment within the United States. He elaborated upon the theme that the extremists of the radical right were acting in league with communists to undermine the foundations of democracy. In his view, McCarthyism fostered the stifling of dissent, the attack on American social institutions and "the swinish blight of anti-intellectualism" which strengthened the international appeal of Soviet propaganda depicting the decadence of American society. Fulbright quoted a passage from the works of V. I. Lenin to buttress his arguments in a February speech to the Senate. In analyzing the post-World War I anti-communist hysteria in western Europe and the United States, Lenin had written: "They [the western capitalists] are hunting down bolshevism with the same zeal as did Kerensky and Company; they are overdoing it and helping us quite as much as did Kerensky."

Fulbright especially lamented the pernicious impact of McCarthyism upon the Eisenhower administration's Asian policy. In his opinion, "The current hysteria and fear generated by recent attacks upon the Foreign Service and the State Department" had prevented State Department officials from objecting to unwise

45

ventures, such as a recent decision to ship arms to Pakistan. Fulbright alleged that many State Department Asian experts understood that the U.S. arms shipment to Pakistan risked the alienation of India. The administration delivered the arms in the hope that the Pakistanis would employ them in defense against Asian communists, but many experts feared that the Pakistanis would eventually use the weapons against India. Yet the experts' "mouths are closed," Fulbright lamented in a Senate speech, "simply because criticism of the proposed alliance and arms program might be interpreted by some—unjustly, I believe—as being soft toward communism." The Pakistan arms shipment was one among several examples Fulbright cited to demonstrate the destructive McCarthyite impact on U.S. Asian policy. After the U.S. arms shipment, the Pakistanis agreed to join the Southeast Asia Treaty Organization, an attempted anti-communist coalition which Secretary of State John Foster Dulles created after the Vietnamese communist Ho Chi Minh's forces defeated the French at Dienbienphu.

Many years later, Fulbright wrote in *The Arrogance of Power* that the initial American involvement in the Vietnamese civil war was conditioned by two extraneous factors: McCarthyism and the Korean War. In the late 1940s Truman had cultivated the belief that only a resolute American will to aid anti-communists was necessary to forestall communist revolutions. A failure to have supported the non-communists in Vietnam would have contradicted his logic and subjected the President to another barrage of vilification from McCarthy and the other extremists. Thus by 1951 the United States was financing 40 per cent of the French military effort in Vietnam. The Truman administration considered Vietnam peripheral to Europe, the epicenter of the struggle against communism in Acheson's view. Acheson regarded American support for French colonialism in southeast Asia as a necessary concession to be granted the French in order to secure France's position as the cynosure of the anti-communist coalition in Europe. After war erupted in Korea the Truman administration had virtually ignored Vietnamese nationalism and anti-colonialism and interpreted the Viet Minh's resistance to the French as being analogous to the blatant aggression of the North Korean communists in 1950.

During the Truman and Eisenhower administrations Fulbright regarded Vietnam as peripheral to America's vital interests, and he usually did not devote significant attention to Vietnamese affairs. However, he briefly focused his attention on Indochina after the French collapse at Dienbienphu in 1954. In the summer of 1954 he questioned American policy in southeast Asia for the first time. At a Foreign Relations Committee hearing with Dulles in June,

Fulbright opposed any direct U.S. intervention to uphold French colonialism in Indochina. Dulles had proposed such an intervention earlier in the year. Fulbright suggested that Ho Chi Minh was a Vietnamese nationalist as well as a communist, and therefore might not act as a Soviet puppet. He was particularly concerned about the lack of flexibility in the administration's southeast Asian policy. At one juncture of the hearings he urged Dulles to scrutinize the background of the Indochinese situation in order to prevent a frozen American attitude:

Senator Fulbright: Is it true that at one time Ho had been allied with Chiang Kai-shek? Was he ever in the employ of Chiang Kai-shek?

Secretary Dulles: Well, he was operating in China; as I say, he worked there primarily with Borodin, and there was a period when Chiang Kai-shek was working himself rather closely with the left-wing elements in China, was himself somewhat of a revolutionary figure, and I think it is probably that period you are referring to.

Senator Fulbright: I do not know that it is particularly important, except that some knowledge of the background of these situations sometimes will help to develop a policy. It at least prevents us from freezing our attitude with regard to some of these people, where there is no possibility of any alternative.

Secretary Dulles: Yes

Senator Fulbright: It might permit us to develop a more flexible policy when we realize that even in Ho Chi Minh's case he from time to time might have been allied with people on the other side of the fence. I vaguely remember that at one time Ho Chi Minh was financed by funds which we supplied through [General Joseph] Stilwell. I have read things about it from time to time, but I believe you will find that he had been on both sides of the fence.

Secretary Dulles: I expect he has taken money from both sides of the fence.

Secretary Fulbright: Yes, but it could be interpreted, and I am not interpreting it that way because I do not know, but it could be interpreted that he tried to lead the independence movement without Communist help. Having failed, he took Communist help. That is a possible interpretation, is it not?

Dulles conceded that Fulbright's conjecture was possible, but he contended that Ho's earlier training and indoctrination in Moscow was much more important than his commitment to the Vietnamese independence movement, which he thought "was always a communist plot." The tentative nature of Fulbright's brief questioning

47

was typical of his statements on Vietnam in the 1950s and early 1960s: he constantly confessed to his scant knowledge of Vietnamese affairs and displayed a lack of confidence in pressing his suggestions concerning southeast Asia.

Fulbright demonstrated more assertiveness when he asked Dulles to explain why the British displayed uncertainty regarding America's Far Eastern policy. Dulles replied, "I do not get terribly worried by those matters . . . I would not want to make an answer which would seem to suggest that we concede that the United Kingdom has a veto power over anything we might want to do." Fulbright opposed a "solitary policy" of acting unilaterally in the Far East regardless of British actions. He believed that the United States should be seriously concerned over British misgivings regarding the rigid American hostility to China. The Senator again decried the impact of McCarthyism upon American diplomacy. He attempted to elicit from Dulles an admission that McCarthy's witch-hunting obstructed the administration's ability to conduct a constructive foreign policy, but Dulles dismissed this suggestion.

One should emphasize that Fulbright's questioning concerning southeast Asia and China at the hearing was one very brief episode in the summer of 1954; at the time Fulbright was preoccupied with his role in the Senate opposition to McCarthy's redbaiting campaign. He did not fully analyze all the details of the 1954 Geneva conference and Dulles' policies in Vietnam until much later in his career.

In a series of public statements during the summer of 1954, Fulbright rebuked the extreme anti-communist attitudes of Senators McCarthy and Knowland for causing America's European allies to "question our capacity to lead and to manage our own affairs." Fulbright argued that "McCarthy's effect in Europe was largely responsible for recent foreign policy differences between the United States and Britain." The issues of Chinese admission to the United Nations was the specific difference Fulbright discussed; the Eisenhower administration was adamantly opposed to Peking's entry, while the British and French were more favorably inclined towards China's admission. Fulbright rejected Knowland's assertion that the United States "should walk out of the United Nations if Red China were admitted." The Arkansan also disagreed with the opinion (similar to Knowland's) of Senator Lyndon B. Johnson of Texas that the majority of the American people would support a U.S. withdrawal from the U.N. if China became a member. In two brief public statements in July, Fulbright pointedly informed Senator Johnson that to support such a withdrawal "would be evidence of political immaturity." As an alternative to

Knowland's belligerent anti-communist attitude, Fulbright endorsed Winston Churchill's plea for "peaceful co-existence" with the communist states. The Arkansan believed that ultimately the only alternative to Churchill's approach was war, and he observed, "We have co-existed in this same world with them ever since there has been a communist group." "I think it is a mistake," Fulbright averred, "for us to give to other nations the impression that we are now making up our minds that at no time in the future will we ever change our relationship with China."

Fulbright's disagreement with Senator Johnson concerning China policy was a brief episode which attracted little attention in 1954. The Arkansan and the Texan usually did not criticize each other and often assisted each other during the 1950s. It was somewhat unusual for Johnson to actively encourage the far-right-wing Republicans as he did in the particular episode regarding China and the U.N. Fulbright's relationship with Johnson would improve in the period after the Texan supported the censure of McCarthy later in 1954. Yet this early disagreement between the two men was interesting. Johnson seemed primarily concerned with demonstrating his zeal in helping to shackle China as a pariah nation. In contrast, Fulbright was concerned with fostering reflections as to whether a frozen anti-Chinese policy would serve any interests of the United States.

Fulbright stopped short of advocating American support for Chinese entry into the U.N. In light of his general reluctance to approve of the bellicose anti-Chinese attitudes which were prevalent in the early 1950s, his refusal to endorse U.S. support for Chinese entry might appear inconsistent; however, the political difficulties of challenging basic Cold War policies in Asia should be considered in order to place Fulbright's position in proper perspective. During 1954, Fulbright had publicly rebuked a series of powerful right-wing political figures. He had criticized Republican Senator John Bricker of Ohio for attempting to pass a constitutional amendment denying the President's power to commit the nation with executive agreements and rejecting the broad interpretation of the President's constitutional authority in foreign affairs. When Bricker first introduced his amendment, it enjoyed extensive support in the Senate. Fulbright and other Senators successfully opposed the Bricker Amendment as an isolationist effort to obstruct the President's "duty of conducting our foreign relations by and with the advice of the Senate." The Arkansas Senator had advanced a series of other controversial foreign policy positions throughout 1954 in addition to his vigorous opposition to the Bricker Amendment. He sharply criticized Vice President Nixon for continuing to blame former Secretary of State Acheson for current problems in Asia. In Fulbright's opinion, Nixon's carping "made it almost impossible to have a bi-partisan or non-partisan policy." During a year in which he had publicly challenged Bricker, Knowland, McCarthy, and Nixon, rejected the F.B.I. request for information on a State Department official, and questioned the Eisenhower administration's Asian policies, it was perhaps understandable that Fulbright did not wish to assume the additional burden of advocating American encouragement of Communist China's entry into the U.N. Fulbright was certainly not immune to the anti-communist pressures of the early Cold War, and even his mild and tentative suggestion that the United States should not permanently "freeze" its negative attitude towards China was a controversial statement in 1954.

Fulbright's support for the movement to censure McCarthy represented his central endeavor in 1954. Fulbright encouraged the senior Senator from Arkansas, John L. McClellan, to change his position regarding McCarthy. McClellan had a reputation as a staunch anti-communist and was the ranking minority member of the Permanent Investigations subcommittee. In earlier years he had usually not opposed McCarthy. By 1954, McClellan increasingly tended to believe that no American institution, including the Senate and the U.S. Army, was safe from McCarthy's attacks. McClellan exerted a crucial influence in assuring that the Army-McCarthy hearings were televised, so that the American people could witness first hand McCarthy's demagogical methods. The Army hearings from April to June marked the turning point in McCarthy's career.

Many leaders of the Republican Party had tolerated and encouraged the McCarthyites when they attributed the defeat of Chiang Kai-shek to treason within the Truman administration and waved spurious lists of communists in a Democratic State Department. Fulbright wrote in 1972 that, in retrospect, the Republican electoral defeat in 1948 was probably a misfortune for the country. In their desperate search for a winning political issue the Republicans seized upon the threat of foreign and domestic communism with a ferocity born of having been denied the Presidency for the fifth successive campaign. Thus McCarthy's slander concerning "twenty years of treason" under Democratic Presidents was an immensely powerful political weapon for the Republicans during the early 1950s. But in the 1954 hearings, McCarthy began to destroy himself by his attacks upon a Republican State Department and the U.S. Army. The Wisconsin Senator probably sealed his political doom by making these charges and mercilessly badgering witnesses before the national television cameras at the Army-McCarthy hearings.

Fulbright rapidly capitalized on the public's revulsion against McCarthy during the hearings. In the summer of 1954, he persuaded the Republican Senator Ralph Flanders of Vermont to introduce a censure resolution against McCarthy, thereby emphasizing its bipartisan nature. Republican Senator John Sherman Cooper of Kentucky also provided important assistance to the censure movement. The most important of the thirty-three counts against McCarthy charged that he had publicly incited government employees to violate the law and send him classified information regarding national security, made unwarranted attacks upon General George Marshall, injured the morale of the Army, and brought disrepute upon the Senate. Flanders and Fulbright recommended a condemnation of McCarthy for his contempt of the "Senate, truth, and people." The Senate Select subcommittee on the censure deleted "truth" and "people" from the document in order to assure its passage. The majority of McCarthy's most ardent opponents, including Fulbright, Flanders, and Wayne Morse, did not gain positions on the Select subcommittee. The conservative Senator Arthur Watkins of Utah headed the subcommittee. The final version of the resolution simply censured McCarthy for his contempt of the Senate.

McCarthy condemned the censure resolution leaders for presenting "scurrilous, false charges" on the Senate floor. He bellowed that "Flanders, Cooper, Lehman, Morse, Monroney, Hennings, and 'Halfbright'" should testify under oath concerning their charges against him. "I assure the American people," McCarthy alleged, "that the senators who have made the charges will either indict themselves for perjury or will prove what consummate liars they are, by showing the difference between their statements on the floor of the Senate and their testimony in the hearing." Shortly after the Wisconsin Senator finished his remarks, Fulbright took the Senate floor to answer McCarthy's diatribes:

> Mr. President, we have already had a very slight example of what we can expect. I think the junior senator from Wisconsin is a great genius. He has the most extraordinary talent for disrupting and causing confusion in any orderly process of any body of men that I have ever seen . . . I am interested in that kind of character as a psychological study. But I think it is doing incalculable harm to the work of the Senate. I know it has already done tremendous harm to the relations of the United States with all the rest of the world, because the people of the other countries think we

51

have lost our minds if we are willing to follow such a leader.

During the censure debate Fulbright received an avalanche of abusive mail from McCarthy's admirers. The tremendous volume and the obscenity of the letters so appalled Fulbright that he inserted a number of them into the *Congressional Record* to publicize the irrationality of "McCarthyism." McCarthy, he asserted, "has so preyed upon the fears and hatred of uninformed and credulous people that he has started a prairie fire, which neither he nor anyone else may be able to control." *Time* magazine observed that all public men occasionally received offensive letters, but conceded that Fulbright "had a point to make last week about the character of what has come to be known as McCarthyism." Fulbright read a few of the less abusive McCarthyite letters to the Senate: "You refused to vote one dollar to the McCarthy committee. A fine dirty red rat are you . . . Who were the birds that voted not to allow Senator McCarthy time off to recover from his illness? I'll tell you: it was red loving Fulbright and the rotten Jew, Herbert Lehman." Another letter denounced Fulbright as a "dirty, low-down, evil-minded traitor," while yet another urged the Arkansan to "do the country a big favor and drop dead." In Fulbright's view, the thousands of letters he had received revealed "a great sickness among our people, and that sickness has been greatly enhanced and increased during the course of the past year." He hoped that the censure of McCarthy would help to repudiate "the reckless incitement of the hatreds and fears of people who are suffering from a lack of information or a lack of understanding."

The anti-McCarthy movement inexorably gained strength in late 1954; Senator Lyndon B. Johnson of Texas belatedly endorsed the censure, thus ensuring widespread Democratic support for the resolution. Nevertheless, 22 Senators voted against the censure, with John F. Kennedy of Massachusetts (Kennedy was in the hospital at the time) and several others abstaining. In the early 1950s Kennedy privately explained his silence on McCarthyism to Arthur Schlesinger, Jr.: "Half my voters in Massachusetts look on McCarthy as a hero." Despite the many frustrations Fulbright encountered during the censure struggle, the 67 to 22 vote against McCarthy in December encouraged the Arkansan. After the Senate action, McCarthy possessed no power to challenge the President or any other citizen. The political leadership of the United States had officially disassociated itself from the Wisconsin demagogue. Flanders later stated, "I could not have accomplished censure" without Fulbright's assistance. Well before the final vote in December, William Benton had congratulated Fulbright on his leadership in the censure movement. He asserted not only that Fulbright's opposition to McCarthy would be vindicated, but that the Arkansan had now established himself "to a far greater degree as one of the great leaders of the Democratic Party."

Conclusion

Fulbright had displayed adroit maneuvering in guiding the censure resolution through the Senate, and he had delivered many eloquent orations in pleading with his colleagues to revive the spirit of free discussion. But the shrewd parliamentary tactics and the eloquence of the censure leaders did not precipitate the fall of Joe McCarthy. In 1954, McCarthy wrought his own destruction because of his political ineptitude and his profound contempt for human dignity. The nation's abhorrence of McCarthy's performance at the Army hearings focused upon his abrasive demeanor, his boorish methods of interrupting and browbeating witnesses, and the pathetic appearance of his victims. To a certain extent, the precipitous decline in McCarthy's prestige and power after 1954 signified a revulsion against his personality rather than a definite repudiation of the blind and counterproductive hostility to communism which he embodied.

The virulent anti-communism of the early 1950s frequently echoed in the positions of some Americans in later years. The Republican nominee for President in 1964, Barry Goldwater, publicly accepted MacArthur's philosophy of war, which held that once hostilities had begun the civilian authorities could place no restraints on the use of force until a total victory had been achieved. Clearly there is an affinity between MacArthur, who declared that his proposal involving the possible starvation of fifteen million Chinese would strengthen the moral fiber of the United States, and the American officer who explained during the Vietnam war that the Vietnamese town of Ben Tre had been destroyed "in order to save it" [from the communists]. At the Vietnam hearings of 1966, Dean Rusk justified the bombings of North Vietnam with a rationale similar to MacArthur's arguments for the proposed air raids against China in 1951. And the anti-communist crusaders' 1951 vision of America as the omnipotent anti-communist gendarme, unilaterally exorcising all the communist devils from Asia, was to find its most concrete and powerful expression in Lyndon Johnson's 1966 Asian Doctrine, which Fulbright described as an effort to "make the United States the policeman and provider for all non-communist Asia."

The extreme anti-communism of the McCarthy era inflicted

almost irreparable damage upon many Americans' ability to think rationally and objectively about Asian communist insurgent movements throughout the 1950s and early 1960s. McCarthy's denial of the legitimacy of the Chinese revolution crippled the American capacity to recognize the genuine patriotism and vigor of Asia's incipient nationalism. McCarthyism disseminated the belief in an international communist conspiracy against democracy, while it inculcated in many politicians fear of the "soft on communism" charge. In 1963, President John F. Kennedy privately remarked that he planned to order a military withdrawal from Vietnam, but "I can't do it until 1965—after I'm re-elected. In 1965, I'll be damned everywhere as a Communist appeaser. But I don't care. If I tried to pull out completely now, we would have another Joe McCarthy red scare on our hands, but I can do it after I'm re-elected." Shortly after he became President, Lyndon Johnson declared, "I am not going to be the President who saw southeast Asia go the way China went." In addition to his belief in the inherently aggressive nature of communism, Johnson maintained that a failure to check the expansion of communism in Vietnam would precipitate a debate over "who lost Vietnam" which would have exceeded in vituperation the controversy over the Chinese revolution.

McCarthy, Nixon, McCarran, and other redbaiters were primarily responsible for inflaming the extreme anti-communist sentiments of the early Cold War; but the Truman administration bore part of the responsibility, for the Truman Doctrine encouraged many Americans to envisage international relations as an arena of universal conflict between western democracy and Moscow's totalitarianism. The years roughly from 1946 to 1950 represented the period of Fulbright's career during which he adhered to a basic anti-communist position. But even in that era he was not an extremist. As early as 1949 and 1950 he had vigorously defended the administration against the McCarthyite charges that Truman had "lost" China to communism. In the early years of the Cold War and throughout his career he believed that the Truman Doctrine's application to Asia was vastly more destructive than its application to Europe. A quarter of a century after the Truman Doctrine speech, Fulbright argued in his book *The Crippled Giant* that the specific decision to aid Greece and Turkey was logical; it was the universalism of the Doctrine which he opposed: "The Truman Doctrine, which made limited sense for a limited time in a particular place, has led us in its universalized form to disaster in Southeast Asia and demoralization at home." John Foster Dulles and Dean Rusk would interpret the Doctrine as the charter for the incessant military interventions and global ideological warfare of the next two decades.

Fulbright had shared many of the Cold War assumptions in the late 1940s and the early 1950s, as he demonstrated with such statements as his denunciations of Soviet eastern European policies and the Soviet rejections of the Baruch Plan and Marshall Plan. Yet he had opposed the redbaiting of the McCarthyites and received a series of accolades from Benton, Lehman, Flanders, and others for his role in the anti-McCarthy movement. By 1954 he was beginning to advance beyond criticisms of McCarthy's methods to reject the Cold War myth that all third world communists acted as puppets of Moscow. There was obviously a divergence between some of Fulbright's anti-communist statements during the early Cold War and his dissenting views in later years, and some analysts might consider this disparity as inconsistency on Fulbright's part; but the Senator's increasing tendency to question American foreign policy might more accurately be considered evidence of flexibility. During the early 1950s he witnessed the destructive effects of extreme anti-communism, and was flexible enough to begin changing his position. He was becoming increasingly skeptical of American efforts to fashion anti-communist allies out of politically unstable, underdeveloped Asian nations which did not possess the skilled manpower and industrialized base which had enabled the western European nations to successfully utilize America's Marshall Plan aid. Fulbright emerged from the McCarthy era with a determination to repudiate the extremism which had ravaged the nation's intellectual environment as well as its foreign policy.

The Senator was certainly not alone in his nascent role as a dissenter; a minority of politicians and foreign policy analysts including Herbert Lehman, Wayne Morse, and John Kenneth Galbraith resisted the anti-communist hysteria of the 1950s. The record of Fulbright's opposition to McCarthyism confirmed William Benton's prediction that dissent against extremism would ultimately strengthen a Senator's prestige. His experience in challenging McCarthy reinforced the Arkansan's conviction that in foreign policy, a politician should not merely react according to his perception of his constituents' whims, but that he held a responsibility to influence and educate public opinion. In the late 1950s and 1960s, he displayed a burgeoning inclination to return to his 1945 critiques of anti-communism in the United States, and eventually led a powerful challenge to the Cold Warrior mythology which dominated America's postwar diplomacy.

Chapter Two

Critique of the Dulles Policies and the Bay of Pigs Invasion

A basic corollary of the anti-communist ideology was the belief that Congress' role in foreign policy must be to help create a national consensus in support of the President in order to present an image of unity to international communism. Through a series of what were represented by the postwar administrations as national emergencies arising from allegedly imminent threats of communist aggression, the Congress became habituated to acquiescing to the Presidential will, usually after only the most perfunctory debates. Fulbright stated in 1972 that in the period from Truman's waging of the Korean conflict without a Congressional declaration of war to the invasion of Cambodia in 1970, the executive virtually usurped the war and treaty powers of Congress and reduced the "advise and consent" function of the Senate to the privilege of attending ceremonial briefings regarding decisions which had already been made.

The notion that Congress should not challenge the President's judgment in an emergency and the tendency of American political leaders to confuse nationalism and communism in the third world seem to have been the determining characteristics of American policy in the Middle East crisis of the mid-1950s, leading to the Eisenhower Doctrine of 1957. President Eisenhower presented this Doctrine (as it came to be known) to Congress in January, 1957, claiming that Russia had "long sought to dominate the Middle East." If Congress accepted Eisenhower's (or Dulles') plan, it would be authorizing the President to extend economic and military aid to any Middle Eastern country requesting help "against overt armed aggression from any nation controlled by international communism." Fulbright opposed the Eisenhower Doctrine, arguing that it was an attempt to eliminate debate through an emotional appeal to patriotism and stampede Congress into giving the President an unrestricted grant of power over the Armed Forces and American economic resources. Senate Majority Leader Lyndon Johnson disagreed with Fulbright, concluding that Congressional disunity would create an impression of weakness around the world and might inspire further communist adventurism. Johnson controlled enough votes to frustrate Fulbright's opposition and save Secretary of State Dulles' policy.

Beginning in January of 1957 Fulbright directed an inquiry by a Senate subcommittee into American diplomacy in the Middle East. The study was cancelled in July 1957 when Fulbright decided that the limitations upon research imposed by the State Department's secrecy requirements had rendered it almost impossible to arrive at a definitive assessment of all the intricate details of the recent Middle Eastern policies. Fulbright delivered a speech to the Senate in August in which he summarized the incomplete results of the subcommittee's seven-month investigation.

He began his address by discussing the $54.6 million grant to Egypt which had been proposed in December, 1955 to help finance the initial stages of construction of the Aswan Dam. In his view, the United States had offered this contribution to the project because it was realized that a Nile River development program was vital to the future of the Egyptian economy, and that economic instability would lead to social and political unrest in Egypt and thus endanger the unstable peace in the Middle East. When the administration withdrew its offer in July, 1956, it indefinitely postponed "the day when the Egyptian people might seek to build a democratic government upon a solid economic base." The administration's contention that Egypt's ability to devote adequate economic resources to the project had deteriorated between December of 1955 and July of 1956 was not true, Fulbright concluded; for there was no radical worsening in Egypt's economic condition in 1956, since the primary drain on Egypt's resources—the mortgaging of part of her cotton crop in exchange for communist arms—had occurred prior to the time of the U.S. offer.

Fulbright did not elaborate upon the specifics of the meeting between Egyptian Ambassador Ahmed Hussein and Dulles at which the American aid proposal was withdrawn. The Secretary of State had already been disturbed by Egyptian leader Gamal Abdel Nasser's diplomatic recognition of mainland China in the spring of 1956. Hussein pleaded with Dulles at their meeting not to retract the American assistance plan for the Aswan project, because he said the Egyptians had "the Russian offer to finance the dam right here in my pocket." From Dulles' Manichean world view, Hussein's plea was apparently seen as an invitation to the capitalist forces of light to engage in a bidding contest with the communist forces of darkness, and the American offer was peremptorily withdrawn. Fulbright deduced from the Aswan papers that Dulles had considered President Nasser to be a Soviet puppet, despite the judgment of able State Department career officials that Nasser was fully aware of the dangers of aligning too closely with the Soviet Union. In Fulbright's view, Dulles had confused communism with Egyptian neutralism and nationalism, which could have been used to promote political freedom and halt the expansion of communist influence in the Middle East.

In his August, 1957 speech Fulbright described the ruinous concatenation of events set in motion by Dulles' decision not to grant the funds for the Aswan project. The withdrawal had been the direct cause of Nasser's nationalization of the Suez Canal, which had led to the Israeli-British-French attack on Egypt, severe oil shortages and economic dislocations in Europe and the United States. It also seriously damaged relations within NATO when America cooperated with the U.S.S.R. in forcing the British and French to accept a cease-fire in November, 1956 and to evacuate the Canal area. Moreover, the Senator argued that if the Western powers had not been divided over the Suez crisis, they might have been able to use diplomatic pressure to at least mitigate the severity of the Soviet repression of the Hungarian revolutionaries after their abortive revolt against the Russians in October, 1956. As far as the costs of the administration's blunder were concerned, Fulbright noted that the expenditures authorized by the ultimate American response to the chaotic Middle Eastern situation, the Eisenhower Doctrine, had already reached a figure ($174 million by the summer of 1957) over three times greater than the original contribution for the construction of the dam would have been.

Fulbright ended his report to the Senate on the subcommittee's findings by criticizing the administration's failure to appreciate the tremendous emotional significance the entire Arab world attached to American assistance for the Aswan project as a symbol of America's "willingness to help them help themselves." Dulles' rash withdrawal had immeasurably strengthened the Soviet propaganda statements charging that the United States was interested in assisting the economic development of other nations only insofar as its aid could place the recipient nation under U.S. political bondage. In so doing, Fulbright concluded, Dulles had greatly facilitated the consolidation of Soviet influence in the Middle East.

Fulbright prepared a thorough indictment of the Eisenhower administration's foreign policy in the summer of 1958. He challenged Dulles' doctrine of mutual deterrence in a Senate speech in

June. This doctrine held that since the United States would never start World War III, peace could be assured if the American capacity to carry out a massive nuclear retaliation against communist aggression were maintained. Fulbright considered this doctrine "irrational because of the very degree of rationality it requires" in assuming that the supreme political authorities of the two superpowers, the hundreds of direct custodians of the nuclear weapons systems in both nations, and the allies of the superpowers could always be expected to act upon the basis of reason and attempt to prevent "the war of the millennium." Rather than continue an arms race that no one could win, he suggested that the United States should re-evaluate its preoccupations concerning military assistance programs and its vast network of overseas military bases. Perhaps some of the 1,400 American overseas bases (many within short range of the Soviet Union) could be traded for armaments control agreements. The Soviet anxiety over these bases was not unreasonable; Fulbright confessed that "I might find myself plagued by an obsession against Soviet bases if their ballistic-launching facilities were in the Caribbean or Mexico."

Fulbright emphasized the injurious consequences of America's foreign military assistance program in a speech before the Senate in August of 1958. The speech was given shortly after Eisenhower had, in effect, honored the principle of his Doctrine by sending the Marines to Lebanon to counter an alleged threat of communist subversion. Fulbright did not attack Eisenhower's decision at the time, but he felt that the current troubles in the Middle East were symptomatic of a fundamental flaw in American diplomacy. "We have," he said, "on a grandiose scale provided peoples of the underdeveloped nations with the weapons of destructive warfare, and have been miserly in providing them weapons to wage war on their own poverty, economic ills and internal weaknesses." Governments which parroted an anti-communist line were lavishly rewarded, primarily with military aid, while governments which persisted in following a neutral course were aided reluctantly or not at all.

Fulbright proceeded to demolish Dulles' argument that armaments proliferation did not endanger international peace and security since all weapons destined for other countries were accompanied by specific stipulations against their aggressive use. American military equipment furnished to the Chinese Nationalists to fight Mao's communists had eventually been used to kill Americans in Korea. And recently the pro-Western regime in Iraq had been overthrown by the Iraqi army, which had received its weapons from the West. Dulles' "specific stipulations" were clearly meaningless.

In one of the most frequently quoted passages in all of Fulbright's works, the Senator advanced the central point of his August, 1958 speech: "If there is a single factor which more than any other explains the predicament in which we now find ourselves, it is our readiness to use the spectre of Soviet communism as a cloak for the failure of our own leadership." Vice President Nixon had been spat upon and stoned during his Latin American tour, but this was rationalized by saying that only a handful of communists had been responsible. If violence erupted or a pro-Western government fell in any corner of the globe, the comforting American formula for the evasion of reality was immediately applied—it was simply more of the Soviet Union's insidious machinations.

Fulbright urged the Senate to renounce the belief that the Soviet Union was the sole source of America's troubles. "In the fear of the deviltry of communism," he argued, America had "cast itself indiscriminately in the role of the defender of the status quo throughout the world." This fearful attachment to the status quo ultimately derived from the popular misconception that the Chinese Nationalists had been defeated because the United States had not supplied them with sufficient military aid. Fulbright concluded that the opposite was true, that America had become too deeply involved with a corrupt and reactionary government which never could have inspired the loyalty of the Chinese people. "Those tragic events in China seem to have set a rigid pattern which has been followed almost unbrokenly ever since." Unless American policy were drastically revised to concentrate foreign aid in the economic rather than the military sphere and to avoid identifying America with the status quo in a revolutionary epoch, Fulbright predicted that the errors in American diplomacy of the 1950s would become the disasters of future years.

The Eisenhower administration's most costly mistake was probably its inept performance during the U-2 crisis. Fulbright conducted a Foreign Relations Committee investigation in the summer of 1960 into the flight of the U-2 surveillance plane which was shot down over Russia on May 1, 1960. As had been the case after the Suez crisis, Fulbright encountered difficulties in gaining access to all the facts regarding the flight, but presented the Committee's report along with his personal views on the controversy in a Senate speech of June, 1960. The administration claimed that the May 1 flight had been seeking information which would never again have been available. Since the Senate was not told, "even under conditions of the utmost secrecy." what that information was, Fulbright described the administration's justification as a "cover story" for its incompetent handling of the episode. Several Republican Senators accused Fulbright of giving aid and comfort to the enemy after his

June speech, although at least one subsequent monograph (*The U-2 Affair*, by David Wise and Thomas Ross) vindicated his position.

Fulbright believed that Eisenhower's reaction to the U-2 flight's failure was essentially a reversion to the rigid anti-communism of the late Dulles (who had died in 1959). The traditional impersonal diplomatic forms were abruptly cast aside in dealing with the Soviets in the aftermath of the U-2 incident. It was unfortunate that Eisenhower had taken personal responsibility for a covert intelligence operation, for one of the reasons for the CIA's existence was to serve as a "whipping boy" in such incidents. Fulbright criticized the alibi for the flight (NASA's statement that the U-2 had been a weather plane that strayed off course) as having made the United States appear foolish when the Russians produced the U-2's surveillance equipment and the pilot, Francis Gary Powers, who admitted that he was on an espionage mission. Lastly, the administration had inexcusably assumed the self-righteous attitude that the Soviet Union should be blamed for the U-2 flights, because if the Soviets had not been so secretive and threatened to "bury us" with nuclear missiles, America would not have been forced to spy on them.

The disastrous timing of the U-2 debacle inflicted almost irreparable damage upon Soviet-American relations for the remainder of the period Khrushchev was in power (until 1964). Fulbright was deeply disturbed that in the spring of 1960, the apparent relaxation of Soviet-American tensions of 1959 had already vanished; at the September, 1959 Camp David meeting, Eisenhower and Khrushchev had jointly declared a willingness to negotiate existing disputes. Khrushchev briefly visited the Senate Foreign Relations Committee shortly before the Camp David conference and was cordially received by Fulbright, who became chairman of the Committee in 1959. On that occasion Khrushchev had vehemently denied that his "We will bury you" slogan was a threat of nuclear devastation, saying that he had been referring to economic competition. At a Foreign Relations Committee coffee in Khrushchev's honor, the Russian leader grandly autographed the place cards of all the Senators, including an absent junior Committee member, John F. Kennedy. Fulbright mailed Senator Kennedy his autographed card, jovially remarking, "Dear Jack: Maybe this will enable you to get out of jail when the revolution comes." (The Foreign Relations Committee in 1959 was far less active than it would become several years later, and possibly the least active member in the Committee's affairs was Kennedy, who was vigorously campaigning for the Presidency and rarely attended Committee meetings. The Arkansan would have preferred that Kennedy's attendance had been better, and the Fulbright-Kennedy relationship at that time was not close.) The pleasant atmosphere of Khrushchev's 1959 visit had not been followed by any major improvements in Soviet-American relations, and Russian and American officials had maintained conflicting positions on Berlin and most other issues on the eve of the scheduled conference at Paris in May, 1960. The U-2 incident had occurred two weeks before the Paris summit meeting, at a time when Khrushchev was trying to convince the ultra-conservatives in the Kremlin that all Americans were not arrogant imperialists and that Eisenhower was a reasonable man. Charles E. Bohlen, an adviser to Eisenhower at the Paris summit, viewed the "plane incident" as largely responsible for Khrushchev's hostility at Paris. Fulbright carried this critique even further, stating that the administration's ineptitude had "forced Khrushchev to wreck the Paris conference."

The Bay of Pigs

Undaunted by the failure of its aerial espionage over Russia, the CIA began plotting during the final months of the Eisenhower administration to overthrow Fidel Castro's regime in Cuba. When Fulbright learned of the CIA's plan in March, 1961, he prepared a memorandum arguing against an invasion of Cuba. Fulbright contended that the idea represented by Castroism, the program of radical social reform with anti-Yanqui overtones, could not be destroyed by overthrowing Fidel Castro. If the CIA ousted Castro behind a facade of American-trained and equipped Cuban exiles, the United States would be denounced as an imperialist power throughout Latin America. A successful invasion would burden America with the costs of rehabilitating a war-ravaged nation in an advanced state of political and economic disorder. If the exiles unexpectedly encountered formidable resistance, the United States could not conceal its role in the enterprise by refraining from direct military involvement, for the fact that the CIA had been training the exiles in Guatemala had been such a poorly kept secret that the press had almost daily carried detailed accounts of the leaders, equipment, and possible strategy that would be used in the invasion. An American intervention would nullify "the work of thirty years in trying to live down earlier interventions," the Senator warned.

Fulbright concluded that for the administration to provide even clandestine support for the CIA's plot would be "of a piece with the hypocrisy and cynicism for which the United States is constantly denouncing the Soviet Union in the United Nations." Moreover, it would be an entirely unnecessary action, since Castro's regime was not a grave threat to the military security or the vital national interests of America unless the Soviets attempted to install nuclear weapons in Cuba. Removal of Castro would not exclude communist agitation from the Western Hemisphere as long as the Soviets retained their embassies in Mexico, Montevideo, and elsewhere, and more importantly as long as the social and economic causes of Latin American political unrest remained. Fulbright averred that it should always be remembered that Castro was "a thorn in the flesh, but not a dagger in the heart."

President Kennedy received the Cuban memorandum in late March, 1961, and on April 4, Fulbright attended the last major policy review before the Bay of Pigs invasion. Secretary of State Dean Rusk, Secretary of Defense Robert McNamara, three members of the Joint Chiefs of Staff, CIA director Allen Dulles, and most of the other high-level advisers of the administration were present at the April 4 strategy session. The historian William A. Williams (whose views differed from those of Fulbright on many issues) has written that Fulbright displayed "magnificent personal and political courage" at that meeting. The Arkansan elaborated upon the basic points of his memorandum on April 4; that if the invasion succeeded, a Cuba which was an American puppet, an American Hungary, would be a liability to the United States both financially and in the forum of world opinion. The CIA's proposal would violate the principle of nonintervention enshrined in the OAS charter, "the keystone of all Latin American policies toward the U.S." Fulbright was also not convinced that the conquest of Cuba would be such a simple undertaking from the military standpoint, rejecting Dulles' claim that the Cuban people were able and willing to assist any invasion from the outside. No one else openly opposed Dulles' plan at the April 4 meeting.

Dulles contended that if America did not execute the Cuban invasion plan, the administration would create an impression of being "soft on communism," and the anti-communist movement in Latin America would wither. According to Dulles, the Cuban exiles would have adequate air support, and even if they were unable to immediately capture Havana they could easily escape into the Escambray Mountains and continue fighting as guerrillas. The fiasco at the Bay of Pigs two weeks later proved all of Dulles' arguments to have been totally inaccurate. Castro quickly gained control of the air, and the CIA had deliberately refrained from informing the exiles that dispersing into the mountains was an alternative strategy. It would have been exceedingly unlikely that the exiles could have initiated guerrilla warfare, for they had been trained as conventional Army units using World War II infantry tactics. Attorney General Robert Kennedy and other administration figures analyzed the Bay of Pigs shortly after the debacle occurred. Kennedy contended that the Joint Chiefs of Staff had been negligent in their study of the situation, and that the chance of the exiles becoming guerrillas "was practically nil." The Chiefs, Kennedy wrote in a June 1, 1961 memorandum, "didn't make any study whether this country was proper guerrilla country. It was proper guerrilla country, but it was guerrilla country between 1890 and 1900. Now, with helicopters, it is no longer guerrilla country and there was no way these men fighting in here in this swampy area could possibly supply themselves." The Attorney General emphasized the importance of the CIA's distorted advice to the President that anti-Castro uprisings in support of the exiles' landings would erupt. But there was no internal revolt against Castro at the time of the Bay of Pigs.

The false allegations presented by the CIA at the final strategy review before the Bay of Pigs partially explain the near unanimity with which administration officials supported the plan. The Kennedys, for obvious reasons, tended to place the major share of the blame for the Bay of Pigs upon the CIA and the military; but the egregious advice of Dulles and his allies was not the only reason for the administration's decision. The President also had to consider the political dangers that would have been involved if he had disbanded his predecessor's Cuban liberation phalanx in the face of the "experts'" advice that the project would be a triumph; Robert Kennedy claimed that "If he hadn't gone ahead with it, everybody would have said it showed he had no courage because . . . it was Eisenhower's plan, Eisenhower's people all said it would succeed, and you turned it down." To some extent the explanation for the President's decision may lie in the precedent set by the events in Guatemala in 1954, when the CIA engineered the overthrow of a leftist government with the approbation of President Eisenhower. The Guatemalan coup was accomplished so easily that it became the model for the Bay of Pigs. But perhaps the fact that John F. Kennedy and the intelligent group of men gathered in the State Department that April evening in 1961 could have expected a tiny band of 1,500 men to wage a powerful assault on a nation of seven million inhabitants can best be explained by Fulbright's belief that an ideological obsession concerning communism beclouded the judgment of American political leaders in the postwar period. The administration's reasoning seems to have been subtly conditioned by a basic precept of the Truman Doctrine. It was not essential to scrutinize the facts of the internal situation in Cuba, for communist governments were by the Doctrine's definition imposed upon the oppressed majority by the ruthless communist minority. Thus, because of the opinions of a few over-emotional and highly imaginative Cuban dissidents, the administration envisaged a massive sympathy uprising sweeping the emigres to power in Cuba, when the evidence had clearly indicated that Castro was strengthening and consolidating his dictatorial control over the island in 1960-1961.

On April 19 Kennedy resisted Vice-President Lyndon Johnson's pressure to "will the means to victory" by ordering air strikes by American planes against Cuba. Apparently this was the only time during the crisis that Kennedy followed the advice of Fulbright's Cuban memorandum. Castro had moved fifty anti-aircraft guns to the area shortly after the invasion began. Even if the proposed American air strikes had been tactically successful in spite of Castro's anti-aircraft arsenal, the CIA Cubans would still have been stranded on the beachhead, surrounded by a vengeful enemy army two hundred times its size. Kennedy's wise decision in avoiding direct U.S. military participation obviously does not alter the reality that the Bay of Pigs invasion was a disaster. At a meeting with Congressional leaders on April 19, Kennedy turned to Fulbright and said grimly, "Well, you're the only one who can say I told you so."

Fulbright later stated that the Bay of Pigs seriously aggravated many of the ills which beset American foreign policy throughout the early 1960s. One of the reasons Khrushchev attempted to intimidate Kennedy at the Vienna conference of 1961 and later gambled on the installation of Soviet missiles in Cuba in 1962 was, in Fulbright's opinion, that he misjudged Kennedy as inexperienced and perhaps weak after the Bay of Pigs. Conversely, Kennedy became determined to prove that he could be as "tough" as any leader; in Fulbright's words (in 1978), that "he was a man, not a little boy." Shortly after the Bay of Pigs, Kennedy bolstered American forces in Berlin and Saigon and dispatched Lyndon Johnson to South Vietnam. When Johnson returned he reported that the decisive moment had arrived when the United States would either have to uphold the cause of freedom in southeast Asia or "pull back to San Francisco and a Fortress America concept." A failure to "move forward promptly with a major effort to help these countries defend themselves" would demonstrate to the entire world that America did not honor her treaty commitments, according to the Vice-President.

Fulbright had been at once the only dissenter and the only member of Congress consulted at the final strategy review before the Bay of Pigs (Chester Bowles, Arthur Schlesinger, and a few others opposed the CIA plan, but they were either absent or

66

remained silent at the April 4 strategy session). Yet the atrophy of Congress' role in foreign policy which was to have such pernicious consequences for American policy in Vietnam accelerated rather than abated in the years after 1961. One year and six months after the Bay of Pigs Fulbright was not included in any meaningful fashion in the administration's deliberations during the Cuban missile crisis. Kennedy and his advisers had already decided to blockade Cuba when they briefed the Congressional leadership on October 22, 1962, immediately before Kennedy informed the nation of his decision on television. Fulbright and Senator Richard Russell of Georgia argued that an invasion of Cuba which would pit American soldiers against Cuban soldiers and allow the Russians to stand aside would be less likely to provoke a nuclear war than a blockade which might involve a forcible confrontation with Russian ships. The most obvious problem with Fulbright's contention was that air strikes probably would have killed some of the 22,000 Russian soldiers in Cuba. The Arkansan later re-considered his recommendation; in 1966 he wrote that if the administration had advised him at the time of all the facts that were later made public he might have recommended a different course of action. In later years the Senator emphasized that the administration did not give the Congressional leaders any time to consider alternatives or reflect about the crisis, since the President's nationally televised address was to be delivered only two hours after Kennedy briefed Fulbright and his colleagues; more importantly, the executive branch did not provide the Congressional leaders with all the relevant data concerning the emergency. From beginning to end of the entire crisis Fulbright was excluded from the small group of advisers who determined the nation's course during October, 1962.

After Khrushchev withdrew the missiles from Cuba, Fulbright praised the President for having "proved to the Soviet Union that a policy of aggression and adventure involved unacceptable risks." Khrushchev, who was faced with a clear American military superiority in 1962, agreed to remove the missiles in return for a U.S. guarantee not to invade Cuba; and in a private agreement unknown to Fulbright and almost everyone else until many years later, Robert Kennedy had verbally assured the Soviet ambassador that the obsolete American Jupiter missiles would be removed from Turkey in four or five months, provided that the Soviets did not make any public mention of the private understanding regarding the Turkish missiles. The Turkish arrangement was secret because the Kennedys felt that American "hawks" would have lambasted the administration if it had appeared to be granting concessions under duress. Moreover, Khrushchev could point to the U.S. "no-

67

invasion of Cuba" guarantee as well as the Turkish arrangement in his efforts to justify Cuban missile withdrawal to the "hard-liners" in the Kremlin. The Jupiter missiles were removed from Turkey in the spring of 1963. Although the Kremlin "hawks" were angered by Khrushchev's performance during the crisis, they did not prevent the relaxation in Soviet-American tensions which occurred in 1963. Fulbright enthusiastically supported the ephemeral post-missile crisis detente; in particular, he led the fight for the ratification of the Nuclear Test Ban Treaty, which was designed to slow down the arms race by eliminating atmospheric testing.

Arthur Schlesinger alleged in *The Imperial Presidency* that if Fulbright had participated directly in the administration's decision-making process during the Cuban crisis of 1962, he would probably have agreed with the strategy Kennedy decided upon; considering Fulbright's later approval of Kennedy's performance and his re-evaluations of the advice he gave on October 22, Schlesinger's argument is plausible. Yet as Schlesinger aptly observed, the very brilliance of Kennedy's handling of the emergency "appeared to vindicate the idea that the President must take unto himself the final judgments of war and peace," and thus one of the tragic legacies of the missile crisis was "the imperial conception of the Presidency that brought the republic so low in Vietnam." The Arkansas Senator's exclusion from the inner councils of the administration in October, 1962, did not damage U.S. diplomacy in the specific case of the Cuban missile crisis, but there would be other crises in the Caribbean and in Asia when the executive branch desperately needed the genuine participation of Fulbright and other Congressional leaders in making crucial decisions. But later Presidents would attempt to maintain their exclusive grasp of the nation's destiny in the international arena just as John F. Kennedy had in that legendary autumn of 1962.

Years after the President's assassination in November, 1963, Fulbright came to believe that Kennedy had not fully recognized that Khrushchev was immersed in an internal power struggle with the Soviet military in the early 1960s. The Senator did not assert that he had the definitive explanation for Khrushchev's Cuban blunder, and indeed the Soviet leader's motivations have been a subject of scholarly debate. But a number of Soviet specialists would agree that a theory Fulbright described in 1972 as "plausible" held a substantial measure of validity. According to this perspective, Khrushchev placed the missiles in Cuba as a desperate gamble to counter the domestic pressures emanating from the coalition of generals and ultra-conservatives who opposed his program of decreased military spending and his rejection of the Stalinist form of authoritarianism. Kennedy contributed to the deterioration of Khrushchev's position by expanding both American conventional forces and the American nuclear missile arsenal, even though the United States enjoyed an enormous strategic superiority by 1962. As Fulbright phrased it in *The Crippled Giant*, the placement of missiles in Cuba was largely an effort to "narrow the Soviet missile gap in relation to the United States, without forcing Khrushchev to concentrate all available resources on a ruinous arms race."

In retrospect, the Senator argued that especially during the early Kennedy Presidency the United States had not understood that "Khrushchev was a world statesman with whom business could be done"—and that Khrushchev's Cuban adventure was not simple, flagrant aggression, but was influenced by the American military build-up of 1961-1962 as well as by internal pressures. By 1972, Fulbright regretted the aftermath of the Cuban crisis within the U.S.S.R.; the Kremlin "hawks" resented the October, 1962 episode as a resounding diplomatic defeat for the Soviet Union, and thus the long-term effect of the missile crisis complemented Eisenhower's errant policy during the U-2 affair in hastening the downfall of Khrushchev, who for all his excesses was still the Soviet leader who "repudiated the Marxist dogma of the inevitability of war between communist and capitalist states." The Senator always believed that the prospects for negotiating armaments control agreements and a political settlement in southeast Asia received a setback when Khrushchev fell from power in 1964. Khrushchev's successors escalated the arms race and brought the Soviet Union to a rough strategic parity with the United States by 1972, ended Khrushchev's de-Stalinization policies, and greatly increased Soviet aid to the Vietnamese communists in response to the American escalation in southeast Asia.

In reflecting upon the Kennedy administration a decade later, Fulbright would lament the President's basic misunderstanding of Khrushchev in 1961. To his mind, Kennedy had misinterpreted Khrushchev's endorsement of the communist doctrine of "wars of national liberation" as a formal declaration of a Russian intention to sponsor subversion, guerrilla warfare, and revolution in southeast Asia and throughout the globe. Khrushchev's outrageous rhetoric was largely a response to the Chinese communists' accusations that the U.S.S.R. was betraying the cause of communist revolution by some of the recent relatively conciliatory Soviet policies towards the United States. If Kennedy's judgment in 1961 had not been distorted by a residual belief in the myth of the global communist monolith, he might have been able to correctly analyze the effects of the internal divisions in the communist world. He initially interpreted Khrushchev's verbal support for "wars of national libe-ration" as being essentially analogous to the communist threat in Europe in the late 1940s. By 1963, Kennedy was beginning to re-evaluate many of the dogmas of the Cold War, although whether he was considering any changes in Vietnam policy in the months before his death remains unclear. But in 1961-1962, the Kennedy administration concluded that the containment policy of the Truman administration had frustrated Stalin's alleged expan-sionist designs; now a similar containment policy in the 1960s must demonstrate to the Chinese as well as to the Russians that "indirect aggression" through subversion and guerrilla warfare was not a rel-atively safe and inexpensive method of expanding communist power.

In dissecting the errors of those years, Fulbright did not claim that he had been immune to many of the intellectual fallacies which were the conventional wisdom in the early 1960s. When he remem-bered the inflated anti-communist rhetoric of Kennedy's speeches in 1961, the Senator would reflect, "I do not recall these words for purposes of reproach; they represented an assessment of Com-munist intentions which most of us shared at that time." At several junctures of that era, notably his dissent from the Bay of Pigs adven-ture, Fulbright had demonstrated an unusually lucid ability to per-ceive and warn against the emotional and ideological biases which afflicted U.S. foreign policy. Yet as an analysis of his foreign policy positions in 1961-1963 will show, he did not always oppose and at times embraced the assumptions of America's Cold War diplomacy.

Chapter Three
Fulbright's Foreign Policy Positions 1961-1963

Fulbright did not extend his critique of the anti-communist prejudice in American diplomacy to the Kennedy and Johnson administrations' policies in Vietnam until 1966. During the early 1960s the attention of Congress was primarily focused upon Cuba and Europe, and Indochina appeared to be an area of peripheral concern. More importantly, from 1961 to 1965, Fulbright basically accepted his contemporaries' ingenuous view of the inordinate power the Presidency had acquired by the 1960s. He was convinced that the individuals who were President during those years would use that power with wisdom and restraint. Fulbright, Kennedy, and Johnson generally supported efforts to emasculate the political influence of the extreme right in the United States. The fact that Kennedy's and Johnson's policies seemed moderate when juxtaposed with the radical rightists' demand for a "total victory" over world communism tended to obscure for Fulbright the militancy of the administration's strategy in Vietnam.

Lyndon Johnson's influence upon Fulbright was one of the reasons that some of the Senator's statements on Vietnam and the Cold War in the early 1960s exhibited a somewhat hostile attitude towards the communist powers. On March 5, 1960, Fulbright delivered a Senate speech in which he denounced the Eisenhower administration for neglecting federal aid to education, defense research, and missiles in its obsession with balancing the budget. Fulbright stated that it was then being argued whether the Soviet missile superiority was "three to one or maybe only two to one." This statement was a remarkable departure from Fulbright's long-standing opposition to any issue which might accelerate the arms race. Fulbright apparently based this speech to some extent on information given to him by Johnson (who had obtained the information through leaks from the Air Force) which indicated that

Eisenhower's budget-cutting economies had created a "missile gap" between the Soviet Union and the United States. The "missile gap" was, of course, later discovered to have been nonexistent, though after (in David Halberstam's words) "many God-fearing, Russian-fearing citizens had cast their votes to end the gap and live a more secure life, only to find that they had been safe all along."

There has been much speculation concerning the close Fulbright-Johnson relationship in the late 1950s and early 1960s. Fulbright admired Johnson's political skills and his ability to manage the Senate as Majority Leader. Probably Fulbright concluded that Johnson at least partially approved of his general critique of U.S. foreign policy, since Johnson referred to Fulbright as "my Secretary of State" in the late 1950s and early 1960s. Actually there is little evidence that Johnson agreed with Fulbright's foreign policy positions in the 1950s. The Majority Leader had supported Dulles while Fulbright was excoriating the Eisenhower administration. During his first fifteen years in the Senate, Fulbright had frequently been in an adversary relationship with the executive branch, and he understandably relished the prospect of playing a more creative role in politics, possibly as Johnson's Secretary of State. But he never displayed any great eagerness for the Secretary of State post; he was perfectly content to remain in the Senate as a supporter and counselor to Kennedy and Johnson.

Perhaps Johnson's choice of Fulbright as "my Secretary of State" was similar to John F. Kennedy's selection of Chester Bowles as his foreign policy adviser for the 1960 Presidential campaign. In order to receive the nomination of the Democratic Party, the major political difficulty of a centrist candidate such as Kennedy or Johnson was to conciliate the Stevenson wing of the Party. This could be achieved by associating the name of a political figure who was closely identified with Stevenson, such as Fulbright or Bowles, with the centrist candidate's campaign. When Kennedy and Johnson became President, in turn, each considered his major political problem to be the necessity of preventing a right-wing backlash against his administration's policies. Johnson was preoccupied with the fear that he might be vilified for "losing" Vietnam as Truman had "lost" China. Thus Dean Rusk, the friend and admirer of John Foster Dulles, the chosen candidate of Robert Lovett, (and hence an unlikely target for any charges of being "soft on communism") and the author of the description of Mao Tse-tung's regime as a "colonial Russian government" in 1950, became the most congenial choice for Secretary of State by the two Presidents who in 1960 had grandly displayed the names of Chester Bowles and J. William Fulbright.

The Arkansas Senator did not object to Rusk's appointment in

1960, and he was able to influence the selection of several secondary level advisers. Fulbright played a crucial role in persuading Kennedy to appoint as Under Secretary of State George Ball, who would later gain fame as one of the few administration officials who advised Kennedy and Johnson not to escalate the American military involvement in Vietnam.

Kennedy had almost appointed Fulbright Secretary of State in December, 1960. But several problems arose. The Arkansan's position during the Suez crisis had offended many Jewish leaders, who complained that Fulbright was pro-Arab. Henry Luce, founder of the *Time-Life* empire and undaunted champion of Chiang Kai-shek, warned the administration that Fulbright would be unacceptable as Secretary of State because the Senator was not an advocate of unceasing hostility to Mao's China. Luce was one of the partisans for the selection of Dean Rusk, and he let it be known that Rusk was blessed with impeccable credentials as a knight-errant against Asian communism. There were several other considerations in the selection process; but in a February, 1961 memorandum, Robert Kennedy explained the most important reason for John Kennedy's decision: "Jack always wanted William Fulbright" for Secretary of State, but the Kennedys were concerned that the Senator's appointment would offend many Africans and American blacks because of his conservative civil rights record. In reflecting upon the consequences of Rusk's elevation to the State Department, it might be recalled that Arthur Schlesinger was always convinced that the President would have cancelled the Bay of Pigs adventure if only one Cabinet official had opposed it in early 1961; Rusk and the others did not do so. The divergence between Fulbright's views and Rusk's hard-line anti-communist stance concerning the Far East was already significant by 1960; and the divergence would become a chasm in later years. Of course, the Senator had no strong ambition to be Secretary of State, and opinions as to what he might have accomplished in the Cabinet are only speculation. It will never be known whether Fulbright might have changed the American diplomatic history of the 1960s if he had served as Kennedy's Secretary of State instead of Dean Rusk.

Fulbright delivered two speeches in April and May of 1961 in which he virtually subscribed to the notion that the Cold War and nuclear technology had rendered the traditional constitutional balance between the legislative and executive branches of government almost obsolete. He was at least partially influenced by his personal respect for Kennedy. The Senator did not criticize the young President in the aftermath of the Bay of Pigs, arguing that Kennedy would learn from his errors and mature as a world leader.

In an address at the University of Virginia, he contended that "we now have the kind of President" who can impart to the people "that zest of action so greatly needed if we are to win the contest of will which engages us today." "My question," he continued, "is whether we have any choice but to modify and perhaps overhaul the eighteenth century procedures that govern the formulation and conduct of American foreign policy. I wonder whether the time has not arrived, or indeed already passed, when we must give the executive a measure of power in the conduct of our foreign affairs that we have hitherto jealously withheld." It is especially revealing that Fulbright complimented Johnson for his support of the Eisenhower administration's foreign policy. Although Johnson may have erred on particular issues, Fulbright noted, the Texan had correctly followed the "proper long-term procedure" of the Senate, which should be to support the administration's basic policy while offering judgments on how best to execute that policy. This view is almost diametrically opposed to Fulbright's statement in 1966 that the Senate should attempt to exert influence "not on the day-to-day conduct of foreign policy but on its direction and philosophy as these are shaped by major decisions."

The discrepancy between Fulbright's praise for Johnson in 1961 and his criticism of the Majority Leader in 1957 goes beyond the fact that Johnson had been, in one writer's words, "Capitol Hill's chief flag-waver for Dulles," whose policies Fulbright had execrated. Johnson had been a champion of the Eisenhower Doctrine in 1957, and to eulogize his record as Majority Leader is to espouse a theory of Congress' role in foreign affairs which tends to foster the Congressional resolutions through which Congress bestowed unrestricted grants of power upon the executive in order to counter alleged threats of communist aggression. Fulbright reconsidered his position only after he helped to guide the most infamous of these resolutions through Congress: when the Johnson administration portrayed the incidents in the Gulf of Tonkin in 1964 as incontrovertible evidence of North Vietnam's deliberate and systematic campaign of aggression, Fulbright reacted almost exactly as had Johnson in 1957, immediately endorsing the administration's effort to acquire unrestricted authority to oppose the communist "conspirators."

In the summer of 1961, Fulbright cooperated with Kennedy and McNamara in alerting the nation to the dangers of the "strategy for survival conferences" which attempted to propagate the belief that internal communist infiltration represented the principal, if not exclusive peril to America's freedom and security. Right-wing orators and military personnel dominated these conferences, which

74

were based upon a 1958 National Security Council directive authorizing the U.S. government to enlist the military's assistance in arousing the public to the menace of the Cold War. Fulbright suggested that the administration should cease reprimanding military personnel who engaged in propaganda activities on an individual basis, and issue a general directive re-affirming the principle of the military's subordination to the civilian authority. McNamara issued such a directive shortly afterwards, and the National War College indicated at least nominal acquiescence in the reform by applauding a speech given by Fulbright at the College in August. Fulbright concluded in a memorandum to McNamara in August that the radicalism of the "strategy for survival conferences" could be expected to have considerable mass appeal during the "long twilight struggle" (Kennedy's phrase) with international communism. In Fulbright's view, the primary task of leadership in the republic "is to restrain the desire of the people to hit the communists with everything we've got, particularly if there are more Cubas and Laoses. Pride in victory and frustration in restraint during the Korean War led to MacArthur's revolt and McCarthyism."

Fulbright and Vietnam, 1961-1963

When Fulbright analyzed the problem of communist expansion in southeast Asia in a Senate speech of the summer of 1961, he was preoccupied with his confrontation with the radical right and the larger question of the impact of the Cold War upon international politics. There is more material in this speech on the American-Soviet competition for political influence in the third world, the after-effects of the Bay of Pigs misadventure, and the communist threat in Laos than there is on the Vietnam controversy, which did not appear to be of overwhelming significance at that time. Fulbright began his discussion of Vietnam in a somewhat theoretical fashion, interpreting the collapse of the French empire in Indochina as a demonstration of the validity of Mao Tse-tung's principle that if guerrillas have the support of the civilian population in subverting a reactionary social and economic structure, they will "multiply and flourish like fish in warm water." According to Fulbright, France wasted seven billion dollars, eight years, and the lives of 100,000 French and Vietnamese soldiers in its abortive effort to defeat the Vietminh. "But France bore the heavy burden of its colonial record and its unconcern with political and social reform. Inevitably, France lost."

Fulbright proceeded to criticize American policy in Laos. America had recently failed in a quixotic venture to transform Laos into an armed anti-communist bastion. Fulbright stated that there was neither pro-communist nor anti-communist motivation in Laos, an incredibly primitive country even by regional standards. This passage is consistent with Fulbright's tendency throughout his career to emphasize the irrelevance of ideology to poor, peasant populations. The people of Laos were interested in their village, family, and religious life and were totally apathetic about the question of whether the ruling faction in their distant capital labeled themselves socialist commissars, royalty, or a military junta. The illusion that the United States could inspire the Laotians to become staunch democrats and anti-communist zealots resulted in a cost of $300 million and an immeasurable blow to American prestige.

Fulbright considered American policy in South Vietnam to be heavily prejudiced in favor of military assistance. In his view, economic and social progress would ultimately determine the outcome of South Vietnam's "struggle for independence," yet there had been no evaluation of Vietnam's long-range economic weaknesses, nor any coherent attempt to measure aid programs against specific economic targets. Paramilitary operations within Vietnam could not assure South Vietnam's independence, and neither could a protracted and inconclusive military conflict in Laos. President Ngo Dinh Diem's regime was "of necessity authoritarian" but Fulbright felt that Diem had been excessively severe. The South Vietnamese government should begin the process of social and political reform which would eventually thwart communist infiltration tactics by desisting from its present policy of suppressing all internal opposition to its rule, including anti-communist elements.

Fulbright's fundamental argument in the June, 1961 speech was reminiscent of what he had said in 1958 concerning the popular misconception that the Chinese Nationalists had been overthrown because the United States had not vigorously supported them. He believed many Americans were drawing the wrong conclusion from the "lesson of Cuba" (the Bay of Pigs) that inadequate methods had been employed to achieve a worthy objective, that America must "beat the communists at their own game" of subversion, saturation propaganda, and terror. In Fulbright's view such a strategy would not only violate America's traditional moral values, but would "draw the United States into costly commitments of its resources to peripheral struggles in which the principal communist powers are not directly involved." Senator Barry Goldwater denounced Fulbright's address as advocating a dangerous doctrine of "nonintervention." In the same speech (also in the summer of 1961) Goldwater expressed astonishment that the Kennedy administration had not declared its purpose to be a total victory over the tyrannical forces of international communism.

The June, 1961 address by Fulbright seems prescient if only the above passages are cited. Fulbright did not, however, apply the logic of what Goldwater had called a doctrine of "nonintervention" to Vietnam. American policy in Vietnam had been a classic example of the tendency in American diplomacy which Fulbright had abhorred since the 1950s, for the primary objective had not been to assist in the creation of viable political institutions or a sound economy in South Vietnam but to prevent communist expansion beyond the 17th parallel. Approximately 90 percent of American aid throughout the Diem era was concentrated upon developing the South Vietnamese army and military bureaucracy. Fulbright had attacked this bias in the aid program but had nevertheless described both American policy in Vietnam and the performance of the Diem regime as "qualified successes." Diem had been "courageous, diligent" and "strong in a situation where strength has been essential."

It was strangely out of character for Fulbright to defend any dictator, and particularly one as brutal and inept as Ngo Dinh Diem. Apparently Fulbright accepted the view which was popular in Washington in the early 1960s that Diem was a capable Asian strong man whose authoritarian methods would be necessary during an interim period until the communist guerrillas could be defeated. Such an opinion was based upon a lack of knowledge of Vietnamese affairs. Frances Fitzgerald has written that the "Saigon government bore no resemblance to a strong, Asian-style government" but rather "resembled nothing so much as an attenuated French colonial regime." Diem had ignored every article of the constitution he had so ostentatiously promulgated, incarcerated thousands of critics of his government in concentration camps, and by distributing the bulk of U.S. relief aid to Catholic villages, he perpetuated the French policy of rewarding Catholics at the expense of the majority of the population. The Vietnamese courts continued to follow the French colonial code, there were no substantive changes in the French administrative system, and over a third of the Diemist administrators had formerly collaborated with the French. Diem claimed to be a proud Vietnamese nationalist, but the fact that his regime was tainted by vestiges of colonialism was an almost unsurmountable disadvantage in its struggle with the Vietnamese communists led by Ho Chi Minh, the leader of the resistance against the French and Japanese and perhaps the only authentic Vietnamese national hero.

The most surprising error in Fulbright's June, 1961 speech was the fundamental distinction he drew between the communist dangers in Laos and Vietnam. Laos emerges in this address as a country where a "peripheral struggle" must be avoided at all costs; Vietnam does not. It would be absurd, he argued, to commit thousands of American troops to interminable warfare in the jungles of primitive Laos, where the simple, peace-loving peasants had no understanding of what the terms "communism" and "capitalism" signify. The United States must search for a political settlement in Laos, even if it meant the participation of communists in a coalition government. But in Vietnam, Fulbright confidently declared that "the people are anti-communist." Therefore, America should redouble its efforts to develop the economic infra-structure of South Vietnam, while continuing its support for the South Vietnamese army.

The image of the South Vietnamese people as resolute anti-communists was as erroneous as the conception of Diem as a strong and competent dictator. It is probable that there were as many anti-Diemists as there were anti-communists at that time. Diem was conducting an increasingly violent campaign of terrorism against both communist and non-communist opponents to his rule, thereby alienating all factions within the country except possibly the Catholics and those who could derive some private advantage by currying favor with his venal administration. By 1961 the communist guerrillas had extended their influence to over 80 percent of the rural population in South Vietnam. The American officials in Saigon supported Diem in his refusal to adopt a system of electoral democracy, for all intelligence estimates indicated that the communists would have won a majority of the votes in normal elections. (It should be added that since Vietnam possessed no real democratic tradition, the significance of elections was unclear.)

Fulbright's distorted view of the prospects for a non-communist state in South Vietnam can be partially explained by the problem that the executive branch was the major source of information concerning Vietnam during the first six years of Diem's dictatorship. American journalists generally did not travel to Vietnam until 1961. By 1966 Fulbright had detected a pattern in which a professional reporter from a newspaper such as the *New York Times* or the *Washington Post* would write an article saying that the communists were inexorably gaining strength, that the South Vietnamese government had failed to inspire the loyalty of the people, and that the difference between American anti-communism and French colonialism was not recognized by the South Vietnamese. The Kennedy and Johnson administrations would then dismiss the journalists' accounts as irresponsible. Two or three years later Fulbright would discover that the reporters had been correct, at which time the administration would respond with a new set of optimistic evaluations contending that only a few thousand more troops or more extensive air raids for a few more years would assure the final victory of America's stalwart ally.

The fact that a Senator is often absorbed by the interests and opinions of his constituents must be considered in order to place Fulbright's statements concerning southeast Asia in the early 1960s in their proper perspective. This was especially true of Fulbright in late 1961 and 1962. Senators John Tower, Barry Goldwater, and Strom Thurmond came to Arkansas to campaign against Fulbright, and there was widespread speculation that Governor Orval Faubus might be able to defeat Fulbright in the 1962 primary election. In late 1961 Fulbright traveled throughout Arkansas speaking to small groups of Arkansans, and by early 1962 had demonstrated enough political support to eliminate the possibility of a Faubus candidacy for the Senate. The Senator eventually received about seventy percent of the total vote in the 1962 general election, defeating a politically obscure dentist named Kenneth Jones.

It was unfortunate that Fulbright was at least partially preoccupied with Arkansas politics in late 1961 and 1962, for in October of 1961 the President's Special Military Representative, Maxwell Taylor, and Walt Rostow (then the chairman of the Policy Planning Council) were reporting to President Kennedy after their mission to southeast Asia that combat troops and advisory units would be necessary to check the expansion of communism in South Vietnam. Rostow was particularly enthusiastic about the potential military impact of American air power in Vietnam. Kennedy resisted the pressure to authorize a massive, systematic bombing campaign or the direct commitment of combat troops, but endorsed the proposal to increase the number of advisers to the South Vietnamese army. Within fifteen months after the Taylor-Rostow mission, Kennedy expanded the contingent of advisers from 500 to 10,000, allowed these advisers to engage in combat, promised continuing assistance to Diem, ordered U.S.A.F. units to attack Vietcong strongholds in South Vietnam, and attempted to pacify the countryside by approving a Strategic Hamlet program which uprooted and alienated the South Vietnamese peasantry. Thus, during much of the period when Kennedy was making the fateful decisions escalating the American commitment in Vietnam, Fulbright was traversing the delta and hill country of Arkansas, cultivating the support of the local power structure, defending his controversial August, 1961 memorandum to McNamara (mentioned above) by referring to the American tradition of strict subordination of the military to the civilian authorities, and discussing the significance of U.S. economic aid in developing foreign markets for Arkansas cotton, rice, soybeans, and chickens.

In 1963, Fulbright continued to devote the majority of his time and energy to issues other than Vietnam; but a brief exception occurred in October, 1963, when the Senate Foreign Relations Committee listened to a briefing by Secretary of Defense McNamara and General Maxwell Taylor, who had recently returned from Vietnam. After the briefing Fulbright told reporters that McNamara and Taylor had reported "impressive progress" in the military situation and that the Vietnamese countryside would be pacified by 1965 unless "political unrest" complicated matters. As Fulbright was speaking of "impressive progress," events were unfolding which epitomized the futility of the American involvement in Vietnam.

By October, 1963 Kennedy had posted 16,000 American soldiers as advisers to the South Vietnamese army, increased military aid to South Vietnam, and authorized a CIA-sponsored program of clandestine sabotage operations in Laos and North Vietnam. Having accepted defeat at the Bay of Pigs and agreed to a compromise neutralization formula for Laos, the President was not prepared to accept a communist triumph in South Vietnam. However, the administration became increasingly impatient with Diem's failure to institute reforms and effectively fight the guerrillas. After the Diem government perpetrated the massacre of thirty Buddhist monks at a Saigon pagoda in August, the administration rapidly lost confidence in Diem. With the knowledge if not the approval of Washington, the Vietnamese generals plotted a conspiracy against Diem and assassinated him on November 1, 1963. Kennedy had known of the coup but not of the assassination attempt and was shocked by the South Vietnamese leader's murder. The inept dictator the United States had supported for eight years had finally been eliminated, and yet the overthrow of Diem apparently exacerbated the problem of political instability in South Vietnam. It was not until 1965 that Nguyen Cao Ky and Nguyen Van Thieu, with massive American support, terminated the succession of South Vietnamese coups and countercoups which followed Diem's fall.

In the early 1960s Fulbright accepted the nominal American objective of securing the independence of South Vietnam. As he later came to realize, American policy was working against the independence of Vietnam. The continuation of the war weakened the ability of North Vietnam to pursue the traditional policy of all the small states of the Far East, which was to remain independent of China. American aid for South Vietnam created a total dependency on the United States. An American economist who visited Vietnam in 1961 concluded that the aid program represented a gigantic relief project rather than an economic development program, and consequently withdrawal of the aid would produce both political and economic collapse. When the former Pentagon official Daniel Ellsberg testified before the Senate Foreign Relations Committee in 1970, he described the political systems of Diem and Thieu as "Diemism." Ellsberg defined Diemism as a government based upon the military, Catholics, bureaucrats, landlords, and businessmen; the Diemists rigidly excluded the Buddhists and other religious sects, students, trade unions, and the smaller political factions from participating in the exercise of power. The basic characteristics of Diemism were the use of police state methods to suppress freedom of speech or other political activities, a total unwillingness to negotiate with the communists, and an extreme dependence on the United States.

Later in the 1960s, the Arkansas Senator would investigate the U.S. Vietnam policy in exhaustive detail; but in the summer and fall of 1963 Fulbright regarded the American dilemma in southeast Asia as peripheral to the fundamental issue of Soviet-American relations. Fulbright approved of President Kennedy's nascent efforts to reduce Cold War animosities in 1963, and he was especially pleased with Kennedy's eloquent speech at American University in June. Both the United States and the Soviet Union had a "mutually deep interest," the President had declared at American University, "in a just and genuine peace and in halting the arms race . . . If we cannot end now all our differences, at least we can help make the world safe for diversity." After the Nuclear Test Ban Treaty was signed in Moscow, Kennedy had not attempted to exaggerate its significance. He conceded the Treaty would not resolve all conflicts with the U.S.S.R. or reduce nuclear stockpiles, but it would eliminate atmospheric testing and represent an "important first step toward peace." He quoted a Chinese proverb in summarizing the importance of the treaty: "A journey of a thousand miles must begin with a single step." On September 14 the Senate ratified the Treaty with Fulbright's vigorous support. Kennedy praised the Senate's action as "a welcome culmination of this effort to lead the world once again to the path of peace."

A few days after Kennedy's assassination on November 22, Fulbright eulogized the fallen leader's willingness to listen to dissenting opinions: "He was the most approachable President. I never had the slightest hesitancy in saying anything I thought to him. I never thought he might take offense at any idea I might have contrary to his own." In late 1963, Fulbright believed that Lyndon Johnson would also listen sympathetically to his ideas concerning foreign policy. On the evening of November 22, President Johnson arrived at the Executive Office Building in Washington, where he conferred for more than two hours with intimates and political leaders. The first person he consulted was his old friend J. William Fulbright. In the early days of his Presidency, Johnson frequently invited the Senator to lengthy personal conferences, and Fulbright regarded himself as an influential foreign policy counselor to the new administration. The Senator attempted to encourage Johnson in the weeks after the assassination, publicly stating that his former Senate colleague would probably become a great President. In a January, 1964 letter to Will Clayton, Fulbright was somewhat less effusive: "The Texas President is doing a fine job under difficult circumstances . . . He will come out all right, I think." The cordial relationship between Fulbright and the new President was symbolized by a famous photograph of the two men aboard Air Force One in December, 1963. The President autographed the picture with the words, "To J. William Fulbright, than whom there is no better. Lyndon B. Johnson."

"I thought," Fulbright would later reminisce concerning the America of January, 1964, "we were on the verge of entering our golden age." The Senator was especially enthusiastic that Johnson would divert America's energies away from the Cold War and concentrate upon solving the nation's domestic problems. Despite the frustration and the tragedy of the previous years, the early Johnson Presidency was a season of euphoria for many progressive political analysts, who expected Johnson to lead the nation in domestic affairs while relying heavily upon the advice of Fulbright, Lippmann, Mansfield, Ball, and other moderates in foreign policy. For many enlightened Americans of that day, 1964 promised to be the dawn of an era of greatness for the Senate, the Presidency, and the nation.

Part Two:
Fulbright and Vietnam

Part Two:
Fulbright and Vietnam

Chapter Four
1964

In 1964 Senator J. William Fulbright was one of the principal Congressional apologists for President Lyndon Johnson's foreign policy in southeast Asia. Fulbright delivered two important analyses of the Vietnam war during the first year of Johnson's Presidency: in a major Senate address on March 25, 1964, he endorsed the President's policy of supporting the non-communist regime in Saigon, and in August he praised the administration's Gulf of Tonkin Resolution. Yet Fulbright did not devote great attention to Vietnam in 1964, for he was primarily concerned with opposing the Presidential candidacy of Arizona Senator Barry Goldwater. Fulbright later asserted that until the early 1960s he had considered the American military and economic aid to South Vietnam as "a very small operation. I wasn't at all concerned. I was entirely preoccupied with Europe. I don't recall we ever had a hearing on Vietnam." The Arkansas Senator tended to rely on the administration for information concerning southeast Asia, largely because he was not particularly knowledgeable about Vietnam in 1964. Thus, in March he accepted the administration's contention that the United States should not seek an immediate negotiated settlement in Vietnam, and five months later he did not challenge the President's allegations of flagrant North Vietnamese aggression in the Gulf of Tonkin.

Fulbright briefly analyzed American policy towards Vietnam in a passage of his March 25, 1964 Senate speech entitled "Old Myths and New Realities." The only "realistic options" in Vietnam, he declared, were "the expansion of the conflict" or a "renewed effort to bolster the capacity of the South Vietnamese to prosecute the war successfully on its present scale." In Fulbright's view, "Whatever specific policy decisions are made, it should be clear to all concerned that the United States will continue to meet its obligations and fulfill its commitments with respect to Vietnam."

85

Fulbright opposed an immediate negotiated settlement, arguing that it was exceedingly difficult for a party to a negotiation to achieve by diplomacy "what it has conspicuously failed to win by warfare." He expressed the idea which later became the Johnson administration's private justification for expanding the American military involvement in southeast Asia: the United States would intervene in order to substantially alter the military "equation of advantages" in favor of the anti-communist forces, and thus establish the existence of an independent, non-communist South Vietnam as a precondition for any diplomatic conference. The Senator did not speculate about the future duration of the American military presence in South Vietnam. He did not indicate whether he recommended expanding the conflict, although he approved of the first air strike against North Vietnam a few months later.

Fulbright did not elaborate upon what would be required in a "renewed effort to bolster" the South Vietnamese military capacity, nor did he define America's obligations and commitments to South Vietnam. His ambiguity was typical of the perennial difficulties which Johnson's supporters experienced in presenting specific, cogent justifications for the American intervention in Vietnam. When Fulbright expanded the March 25 Senate speech into his book entitled *Old Myths and New Realities* later in 1964, the only "evidence" he offered to demonstrate the alleged threat to American security in Vietnam was a vague and inaccurate charge of Chinese and North Vietnamese aggression. In 1964 he believed that the Congress must rely upon the thousands of experts in the State Department and the Central Intelligence Agency for expertise in the realm of diplomacy, largely because the half-dozen staff members of the Senate Foreign Relations Committee could not comprehensively analyze all the myriad controversies of America's foreign relations. Fulbright's dependence on the administration for information was unnecessary, as he eventually realized; during the late 1960s he employed a larger number of Congressional investigators, sought the ideas of journalists and scholars, conducted frequent Foreign Relations Committee investigations, and diligently attempted to acquire independent sources of information concerning American foreign policy in Vietnam and elsewhere. But it was only after the massive military interventions in Vietnam and the Dominican Republic that Fulbright would become wary of depending on the executive's evaluations in foreign affairs; in 1964 he accepted the administration's judgment on the southeast Asia crisis.

The lack of detail in Fulbright's passage on Vietnam in "Old Myths and New Realities" may be partially explained by the fact that the speech was a general review of American diplomacy, and the Vietnam policy was only one of many controversial issues which Fulbright discussed on March 25. His analysis of the Vietnam war constituted less than one-tenth of the material in the address. The brevity of the section on Vietnam was characteristic of his inattention to southeast Asia in the early 1960s.

"Old Myths and New Realities" was one of Fulbright's most famous critiques of the Cold War mentality. He urged the United States to renounce "the master myth of the Cold War that the communist bloc is a monolith composed of governments all equally resolute and implacable in their determination to destroy the free world." According to Fulbright, some communist states, such as Yugoslavia and Poland, posed no threat to the West, while China posed an immediate threat. Nikita Khrushchev's diplomacy was much more prudent than the aggressive Stalinist foreign policy of the early postwar period. Communist imperialism and not communism as a doctrine represented a danger to the West, Fulbright asserted. He concluded that as long as any nation was content to practice its doctrines within its own frontiers, regardless of how repugnant its ideology appeared to be to Americans, the United States should have no quarrel with that nation.

The most controversial passage of "Old Myths and New Realities" dealt with Cuba. Fulbright stated that American policies designed to overthrow Fidel Castro had been failures. Neither military invasion nor an American trade ban had succeeded in the past, and such aggressive policies would not succeed in the future. The United States should accept the reality that the Castro regime was a "distasteful nuisance but not an intolerable danger" and stop flattering "a noisy but minor demagogue by treating him as if he were a Napoleonic menace."

Many liberal politicians and journalists praised Fulbright's March 25 address before the Senate. Walter Lippmann eulogized the Senator in an article written for *Newsweek* in early April: "He says what he believes is true rather than what is supposed at the moment to be popular. He is not listened to on the floor of Congress until he has been heard around the world. He has become the leading witness to the present truth, but it is not a fatal mistake to be right too soon." The Johnson administration, however, reacted negatively to the speech. Secretary of State Dean Rusk carefully disassociated the administration from Fulbright's foreign policy positions. In two successive press conferences after March 25, President Johnson denied any agreement or connection with the ideas expressed in "Old Myths and New Realities."

The President's hostile response to Fulbright's address was a significant indication of Johnson's intolerance of even mild dissent.

87

Fulbright's views concerning American diplomacy in the Far East were not sharply different from those of the administration; the March speech may have been influenced by Dean Rusk's conception of the relationship between North Vietnam and China. Senator Fulbright wrote in 1972 that Rusk adhered to a modified version of the communist conspiracy thesis. In the late 1940s and 1950s, many foreign policy analysts had imagined international communism to be a global conspiracy, with the head of the "octopus" in Moscow and its tentacles reaching out to the farthest corners of the earth. Fulbright contended that after the Sino-Soviet break became obvious in the 1960s, Rusk professed to be scornful of the conspiracy thesis. Yet Rusk defended the Vietnam war with references to a "world cut in two by Asian communism," the only difference between the earlier and later perspectives being, in Fulbright's opinion, that Rusk had discovered a second "octopus" in Peking. When Fulbright was writing in 1972, Rusk's specter of "Asian communism" seemed farcical. But in 1964 Fulbright may not have clearly understood that North Vietnam was not a Chinese puppet. He spoke of preventing South Vietnam from being dominated by "Peking and Hanoi" as if North Vietnam and China were practically indistinguishable.

Fulbright probably thought his treatment of China in "Old Myths and New Realities" was moderate, since he clearly hoped for an eventual amelioration of Sino-American relations at some unspecified date in the future. A reduction of tensions in the Far East, he hypothesized, might "make it possible to strengthen world peace by drawing mainland China into existing East-West agreements in such fields as disarmament, trade, and educational exchange." He commended the recent French recognition of China, which might "serve a constructive long-term purpose, by unfreezing a situation in which many countries, none more than the United States, are committed to inflexible policies by long established commitments and the pressures of domestic public opinion." The French initiative, he speculated, might facilitate a reevaluation of American foreign policy towards China.

Despite the Senator's favorable response to the French recognition of China, there were no specific differences between Fulbright and the administration with respect to America's China policy. He contended that the United States should not recognize China or acquiesce in Chinese admission to the United Nations, for "there is nothing to be gained by it so long as the Peiping regime maintains its attitude of implacable hostility toward the United States." China represented an "immediate threat" to the West, according to Fulbright, yet he did not explain what the threat was. Fulbright's rhetoric concerning China in 1964 was sometimes conciliatory and never as abrasive as the administration officials' statements; but the fact that his views were influenced by the belligerent anti-Chinese position of the executive branch was revealed in August, 1964, when he described the Gulf of Tonkin Resolution as a device to "deter aggression on the part of the North Vietnamese and Chinese."

In 1966 Fulbright would characterize the Gulf of Tonkin Resolution as a blank check signed by the Congress in an atmosphere of urgency which seemed to preclude debate. On August 5, 1964, Johnson summoned Fulbright and other Congressional leaders to an emergency meeting at the White House and advised them that North Vietnamese naval vessels had flagrantly violated the principle of freedom of the seas by attacking American destroyers in the Gulf of Tonkin. Without questioning Johnson's version of the Tonkin incidents, Fulbright cooperated closely with the administration in guiding the resolution through the Congress. The Senate Foreign Relations Committee and the Armed Services Committee held a joint executive session hearing which lasted an hour and a half on August 6. Fulbright was the floor manager for the resolution, which proclaimed that the United States was "prepared, as the President determines, to take all necessary steps, including the use of armed force, to assist any member or protocol state of the Southeast Asia Collective Defense Treaty requesting assistance in defense of its freedom." The resolution was adopted on August 7 by a vote of 416 to 0 in the House of Representatives and 88 to 2 in the Senate, with Senator Wayne Morse of Oregon and Senator Ernest Gruening of Alaska casting the only dissenting votes.

During the August 6 joint hearing Rusk, Secretary of Defense Robert McNamara, and Chairman of the Joint Chiefs of Staff Earle G. Wheeler defended the resolution and an August 5 air strike against North Vietnam. Rusk emphasized the President's desire to continue closely consulting with Congress. The Secretary of State did not employ John Foster Dulles' domino theory to justify the resolution or the bombings. This theory had been explained by President Eisenhower in 1954, when he averred that if the noncommunists in Vietnam were overthrown, communist expansion into Burma, Thailand, the Malay peninsula, Indonesia, Australia, New Zealand, Japan, Formosa, and the Phillipines would inevitably follow. The Johnson administration's rhetoric may have differed from that of Eisenhower and Dulles, but the policy of supporting the non-communist regime in Saigon persisted. Rusk described the domino theory as unnecessary, for "it is enough to recognize the true nature of the communist doctrine of world revolution and the militant support that Hanoi and Peiping are giving that doctrine in southeast Asia." According to Rusk, the two attacks on American destroyers in the Gulf of Tonkin were not isolated events but were part of North Vietnam's systematic and deliberate campaign of aggression in southeast Asia.

The August 5 air raid was a retaliation against North Vietnam for the two alleged attacks of August 2 and August 4, which had inflicted no damage upon the American destroyers. The bombings destroyed several shore facilities, approximately two-thirds of the North Vietnamese navy (which consisted of patrol boats), and the largest petroleum storage depot in North Vietnam. Senator Russell Long of Louisiana asked McNamara at the August 6 hearing if the American planes had achieved a "surprise attack" against the North Vietnamese naval bases which was similar to the Japanese surprise attack upon Pearl Harbor; McNamara replied, "Yes, that's exactly true." Almost all the Senators congratulated the administration on the promptness and moderation of the decision to bomb North Vietnam. J. William Fulbright commended Rusk, McNamara, Wheeler, and President Johnson for the "restraint with which overwhelming power in the area was used, a new attitude on the part of a great power."

Wayne Morse was the only Senator who opposed the administration's Vietnam policy at the August 6 hearing. Morse criticized not only the resolution but the premise of North Vietnamese aggression upon which the administration's policy was based. He denied that the executive branch had produced a "scintilla" of evidence to prove that regular North Vietnamese army and navy units were engaged in aggressive acts against South Vietnam. The Oregon Senator specifically questioned the validity of the administration's version of the Tonkin incidents, asserting that the American destroyers had committed a provocative act by cruising so close to the North Vietnamese shore. (When the transcript of the secret hearing was finally published in 1966, the State Department deleted the exact distance, although McNamara later admitted that the administration had authorized the American vessels to cruise within four miles of the North Vietnamese coastline.)

McNamara and Rusk answered Morse with the rather lame rejoinders that the American-equipped South Vietnamese sea patrol had searched 130,000 junks in 1963 and discovered 140 Vietcong, and that North Vietnam was infiltrating parties of 100 to 200 guerrillas into South Vietnam through Laos. The administration officials' statements were ambiguous and were not relevant to Morse's questions, for they did not specify the frequency with which the alleged infiltrations occurred and they failed to demonstrate that North Vietnamese regular units were fighting in South

Vietnam.

During the brief Senate debate over the resolution Senator George McGovern of South Dakota asked Fulbright about the South Vietnamese operations in the Gulf of Tonkin on July 30, 1964. Fulbright answered McGovern by saying the administration had assured him that the destroyer patrol "was entirely unconnected or unassociated with any coastal forays the South Vietnamese may have conducted." At the August 6 secret hearing, Secretary McNamara had claimed that "our Navy played absolutely no part in, was not associated with, was not aware of any South Vietnamese actions, if there were any." Four years later in testimony before the Foreign Relations Committee, McNamara contradicted his earlier assertion when he admitted the American warships had been co-operating with South Vietnamese naval raids against North Vietnam in July and August, 1964.

During the August, 1964 debate in the Senate, Senator Gaylord Nelson of Wisconsin attempted to clarify the meaning of the resolution. When Nelson asked Fulbright if the resolution was "aimed at the problem of further aggression against our ships," Fulbright replied affirmatively. Nelson offered an amendment to the resolution declaring it to be the policy of the United States to avoid a direct military involvement in the southeast Asian conflict, and Fulbright indicated that the amendment was "an accurate reflection of what I believe is the President's policy, judging from his own statements." Throughout 1964, Johnson assured the Arkansas Senator that he intended to avoid a massive, direct military intervention in the Vietnam war. Fulbright, as floor leader, did not accept Nelson's amendment because it would have required further consideration by the House of Representatives and thus delayed the Gulf of Tonkin Resolution's passage. The Foreign Relations Committee chairman was under pressure from the Johnson administration to pass the resolution immediately in order to emphasize America's unity in opposing potential aggressors.

At one juncture of the debate Fulbright conceded that "the language of the Resolution would not prevent" the Commander in Chief from landing large American armies in Vietnam or China. But he also maintained that "I have no doubt that the President will consult with Congress in case a major change in present policy becomes necessary." Fulbright believed he was summarizing the general sentiment of the Senate (which was also expressed by McGovern, Frank Church of Idaho, John Sherman Cooper of Kentucky, and others) when he concluded: "I personally feel it would be very unwise under any circumstances to put a large land army on the Asian continent."

Fulbright supported the Gulf of Tonkin Resolution because he did not suspect the President's version of the alleged incidents was untrue, and because he did not wish to cause any political difficulties for Johnson during a campaign in which the alternative candidate was Barry Goldwater, a man whose election Fulbright envisaged as a disaster for the United States. At one point during the campaign Goldwater replied to a question about what policy he would follow in Vietnam by saying, "I would turn to my Joint Chiefs of Staff and say 'fellows, we made the decision to win, now it's your problem.'" He had spoken of defoliating the jungle trails in Vietnam with "low-yield atomic bombs." In contrast, Johnson skillfully played the role of the man of peace, declaring: "We are not about the send American boys 9,000 or 10,000 miles away from home to do what Asian boys ought to be doing themselves." Fulbright was convinced that Johnson would use the resolution with wisdom and restraint.

During the Senate's deliberations over the resolution Fulbright assured his colleagues that Johnson did not intend to expand the war. Many Senators thought of the resolution as a typical Johnsonian political ploy. An anonymous source later quoted Fulbright as having remarked in the Democratic cloakroom at the time that, "This resolution doesn't mean a thing. Lyndon wants this to show he can be decisive and firm with the communists too."

The Johnson administration eventually would refer to the Gulf of Tonkin Resolution and the Southeast Asia Treaty Organization Treaty as constituting the "functional equivalent" of a declaration of war. The language of the resolution included no restrictions upon the authority of the President to "take all necessary measures to repel any armed attack against the forces of the United States and to prevent further aggression."

In 1964 Fulbright was far more disturbed by the threat of Goldwater's presidential candidacy than he was by events in southeast Asia. He believed that Goldwater essentially advocated a policy of "co-annihilation." When the administration requested Fulbright's support during the Tonkin Gulf crisis in August, he was influenced by a partisan desire to help repudiate the extremist Republican and ensure the triumph of the "moderate" candidate, Lyndon Johnson. He interpreted the administration's request for passage of the resolution as not only an appropriate response to the alleged attacks on American ships, but also as a device to deprive Goldwater of the "soft on communism" charge against Johnson. The resolution and the retaliatory air raids against North Vietnam could demonstrate Johnson's determination to oppose communist aggression.

From the standpoint of domestic politics, the administration's handling of the Tonkin affair was brilliantly successful. A Louis Harris poll showed the President's positive rating skyrocketing from 42 per cent before the crisis to 72 per cent after his response to the alleged incidents in the Gulf. Fulbright's support for the Gulf of Tonkin Resolution had helped Johnson to eliminate the Vietnam controversy as an issue in the campaign, a fact which contributed to Johnson's overwhelming victory in November.

During the summer of 1964 the Senator from Arkansas believed that Johnson's account of the events in the Gulf was honest and accurate. It was not until 1966 that he would fully realize his error of substituting his personal trust in the President for a proper institutional balance between the legislative and executive branches, a balance which might have been achieved by holding extended hearings on Vietnam in August, 1964, as Senator Morse advocated. Fulbright later wrote in *The Arrogance of Power* that if the Senate had thoroughly debated the resolution, or if a careful investigation of the alleged attacks on American ships had been conducted, then "we might have put limits and qualifications on our endorsement of future uses of force in Southeast Asia, if not in the resolution itself then in the legislative history preceding its adoption." But in 1964 he believed that if the administration ever contemplated a massive expansion of the war his old friend Lyndon Johnson would consult him and weigh his advice thoughtfully. He still relished his role as senior Senate foreign policy partner to the President. It was not until 1966 that he held the hearings Morse had called for in 1964. And only then would he become convinced that in the allegation of unprovoked aggression on the high seas in August, 1964, the administration had deliberately deceived the American public and the Congress.

Johnson's actions during the Tonkin Gulf controversy produced a temporary political triumph, as the Harris poll indicated. But the long-term consequences of the administration's mendacious performance during the affair weakened the President politically, for Congress and the public began to question Johnson's veracity after the facts of the Tonkin episode became public knowledge in the late 1960s. In the middle and later 1960s, Fulbright's realization that the administration had deceived him during the Tonkin crisis helped to galvanize the Senator into an adamant opposition against the Vietnam war. Fulbright began to investigate the Tonkin incidents in 1966, after his exhaustive analysis of the 1965 American intervention in the Dominican Republic demonstrated that the administration had justified its Dominican policy through false allegations of communist aggression. He would then begin to suspect the administration's accusations of communist aggression in the Gulf of Tonkin had been similarly distorted. His investigations eventually revealed the executive's duplicity during the Tonkin controversy and facilitated the emergence of a "credibility gap" in Washington—a widespread belief that the Johnson administration perennially failed to present candid explanations for its policies.

In 1966 Fulbright investigated the August, 1964 incidents in the Gulf of Tonkin. Cyrus Vance, one of McNamara's chief assistants in the Defense Department, had explained shortly after the first North Vietnamese attack that "We assumed it was brought about by mistake," or by confusion created by the activity of South Vietnamese vessels in the Gulf. Fulbright accepted this view of the first incident.

His doubts about the administration's account of the second attack began when Rear Admiral Arnold True advised Fulbright that the American destroyers probably could not have detected whether the North Vietnamese patrol boats were in attack formation at their reported distance on the night of the second incident. A study by the Foreign Relations Committee staff in 1967 showed that the American destroyers were on an intelligence-gathering mission on August 4, not on a "routine patrol" as the administration claimed.

The executive branch never adduced evidence to prove that the North Vietnamese gun boats committed hostile acts; in fact, the effects of stormy weather on the radar and sonar of the destroyer called the *Maddox*, as well as over-enthusiastic sonarmen, may have accounted for the reports of torpedo attacks. Fulbright received "top secret" briefings from the Pentagon in 1966 and 1967, at which the only "evidence" produced to substantiate the administration's version of the events in the Gulf was one machine gun shell said to have been fired from a North Vietnamese gun boat. He became convinced that the second alleged attack had never occurred, and that the administration had falsely represented the Tonkin incidents as acts of blatant aggression in order to generate public support for military action in Vietnam. In the later 1960s, the Tonkin Gulf controversy became the focal point of Fulbright's increasingly vitriolic critique of the Johnson administration's disingenuousness. Fulbright would also criticize the Gulf of Tonkin Resolution as a Presidential usurpation of Congress' constitutional authority to initiate war (the constitutional arguments are discussed in Chapter 7).

One should emphasize that Fulbright's public opposition to the American involvement in the Vietnam war began roughly eighteen months after the August, 1964 incidents in the Gulf of Tonkin. The obvious question arises: Why was Fulbright so dilatory in challenging the Vietnam policy? The administration's attempt to mislead the Senator concerning the alleged attacks on American destroyers is only a partial explanation, for Fulbright clearly erred in failing to hold extensive hearings to examine the President's account of the incidents as well as the basic policies in Vietnam. Fulbright's fear of the Goldwater threat, his conviction that China was an aggressive power, and his view of Johnson as a moderate were probably crucial in leading him to support American policy in Vietnam during 1964. His lack of knowledge about southeast Asia and his belief that the Foreign Relations Committee staff could not compete with the executive branch in the realm of intelligence-gathering also contributed to his tendency of relying upon the administration's judgment regarding American diplomacy in the Far East.

Fulbright's notion that President Johnson was restrained and prudent in foreign policy was not unusual in 1964; many politicians and foreign affairs analysts believed in Johnson's "moderation" at the time. Walter Lippmann concluded in an August 6, 1964 column in the *Washington Post* that the President intended to exercise American power "with measure, with humanity, and with restraint." The vast majority of the Congress regarded Johnson's actions during the Gulf of Tonkin crisis as prudent. "At that time," Fulbright later admitted in discussing the Gulf of Tonkin Resolution's passage, "I was not in a suspicious frame of mind. I was afraid of Goldwater." Thorough Foreign Relations Committee hearings on Vietnam might have embarrassed Johnson in the midst of the Presidential campaign, with the Democratic National Convention scheduled to begin on August 24.

Despite Fulbright's anxiety over the Goldwater candidacy, the Arkansas Senator held a genuine conviction that the Chinese were in a belligerent and resentful mood in 1964 and 1965. In the spring of 1965, months after Goldwater had been decisively repudiated at the polls in 1964, Fulbright continued to refer to the Chinese as imperialistic in his private communications with the President. Thus, Fulbright's fear that public criticism of Johnson's Asian policy would strengthen Goldwater and precipitate a recrudescence of extreme anti-communist sentiment in the United States was not the sole motive for his support of America's Far Eastern policy. He vaguely perceived the danger of alleged Chinese aggression as the threat of a conventional imperialism, and he never endorsed Rusk's notion that the Chinese were plotting a uniquely nefarious conspiracy to banish freedom from the earth. Nevertheless, Fulbright's belief that the Chinese were resentful and hostile toward the West facilitated the administration's efforts to convince him that there was a coordinated North Vietnamese-Chinese campaign of aggres-

95

sion in southeast Asia. The Senator would clarify his thinking about the Far East in 1965-1966, after the military escalation in Vietnam became the central controversy in American foreign policy.

In addition to the reasons cited above for Fulbright's support of the Johnson administration's Vietnam policy, the Senator had maintained throughout the early 1960s that the Presidency must be the dominant institution in the formulation of American diplomacy. According to Fulbright, members of Congress had to devote the majority of their time to the study of domestic affairs, and hence their "advise and consent" function must be secondary to the President's role in foreign policy. In the early 1960s, Fulbright would recall several episodes of American diplomatic history in which the Senate obstructed the President's endeavors in foreign affairs, notably the defeat of the Versailles Treaty and American membership in the League of Nations, and the Senate's opposition to full American participation in a World Court. He frequently cited the demagogical investigations of former Wisconsin Senator Joseph McCarthy as the classic example of the potentially pernicious consequences inherent in "senatorial excursions into foreign policy." Whatever the merit or lack of merit in Fulbright's historical interpretations, it is clear his plea for a strong, activist President was the standard position of the intellectuals in the Democratic Party during 1964. His favorable perception of the individual who held the Presidential Office in 1964 obviously influenced his theoretical justifications for an increasingly powerful Presidency.

Fulbright would later advocate a much more assertive role for the Senate in foreign policy. "The Senate," he wrote in *The Arrogance of Power*, "has the responsibility to review the conduct of foreign policy by the President and his advisers, to render advice whether it is solicited or not, and to grant or withhold consent to major acts of foreign policy." The fiasco of American policy in southeast Asia was the catalyst which led Fulbright to re-assess his perspective on the proper institutional balance between the executive and the legislative branches of government. In his 1972 work, *The Crippled Giant*, he confessed: "I myself was among those who took an ingenuous view of Presidential power until the disaster of Vietnam compelled me to re-evaluate my position."

Fulbright was basically an enthusiastic supporter of President Johnson in 1964, but several of his ideas in "Old Myths and New Realities" and in the Senate's Gulf of Tonkin debate foreshadowed his future dissent. In "Old Myths and New Realities" he had criticized the administration's belligerent anti-communist stance in its Cuban policy. His attack upon the myth that all communist states were relentlessly expansionist was not congenial with Johnson's

Weltanschauung.

The March 25, 1964 Senate speech had not questioned American policy in Vietnam, but Fulbright's decision to publicly analyze the southeast Asian crisis was disturbing to the President, who did not desire a thorough public discussion of Vietnam during the election year. Johnson's basic strategy was to delay the crucial decisions in Vietnam until after the election. Thus, he merely expanded American assistance and increased the number of American advisers in South Vietnam, for he feared a direct, large-scale intervention would jeopardize his cherished domestic program and his prospects for being elected. Johnson was pleased, of course, that Fulbright did not follow "Old Myths and New Realities" with an effort to generate a public dialogue on Asian policy in August, 1964.

In 1964 Fulbright was harboring private doubts about the American involvement in Vietnam. He sent a newspaper photograph of South Vietnamese soldiers torturing a suspected communist guerrilla to Secretary of Defense Robert McNamara in May, writing, "I have been gravely concerned over the situation in Vietnam even without reports of tortures and indiscriminate bombing. We should cut our losses and withdraw." This letter did not have a significant impact on the thinking of the executive branch, and it was largely forgotten after the turmoil over the Gulf of Tonkin crisis and the Presidential campaign. The President privately assured Fulbright that he would not "send in the Marines a la Goldwater," for his administration's Vietnam policy consisted only of "providing training and logistical support of South Vietnamese forces." During the latter half of 1964 and early 1965, Fulbright came to believe that the danger of being confronted with a stark choice between immediate withdrawal and massive escalation in Vietnam was not imminent. He believed that the President was sincerely interested in a political settlement of the war.

In later years, Fulbright would regard his decision not to hold comprehensive hearings on the Gulf of Tonkin Resolution in 1964 as the fundamental error in his responses to America's Vietnam policy from 1964 to 1966. When the Foreign Relations Committee belatedly conducted its 1966 investigation of the Vietnam war, there were approximately 200,000 American soldiers in South Vietnam. At that late date, the administration would successfully exert pressure on the Congress to continue the appropriations for the war by presenting the issue not as a choice of approving or disapproving of the Vietnam war, but of either supporting or abandoning "our boys out there on the firing line." When the Congress allowed the alternatives to be defined in these terms, there could be little doubt of its support for the war in the late 1960s.

Despite his failure to foster a thorough public debate concerning Vietnam in August, 1964, several of Fulbright's statements during the Senate deliberations over the Gulf of Tonkin Resolution adumbrated his later role as an adversary of U.S. policy in Asia. He clearly did not envisage the resolution as a mandate for an expanded war, since he constantly referred to Johnson's declarations that he sought to avoid a massive military intervention in Vietnam. (It should be acknowledged that the President was uncertain about the degree of military power which would be required to defeat the Vietnamese communists, although he always underestimated their will to fight for a unified Vietnam under Ho Chi Minh). Fulbright also asserted that the President should closely consult with Congress regarding its Vietnam policy in the future.

Most importantly, Fulbright had unequivocally rejected the strategy of deploying American armies on the continent of Asia, for air and sea power were the foundations of America's strength. His response to the administration's decisions during the Tonkin controversy was similar to that of his old friend Walter Lippmann. Lippmann endorsed the President's actions in the belief Johnson was signaling that American involvement in the Vietnam war would be limited to naval and air support for South Vietnam. "The lasting significance of the episode," Lippmann predicted in August, 1964, "is the demonstration that the United States can remain in Southeast Asia without being on the ground." Fulbright concluded in the Senate's August 6, 1964 debate that he would "deplore" the landing of a large American army on the Asian mainland, for "Everyone I have heard has said that the last thing we want to do is become involved in a land war in Asia."

During the fall of 1964, Fulbright was predominantly concerned with his appeal to the nation to reject Goldwater's vague proposals for gaining a "total victory" in the Cold War. He frequently delivered speeches criticizing Goldwater's militant anti-Soviet attitude. As the historian Lloyd Ambrosius has observed, Goldwater failed to propose a peaceful, positive program for winning a "total victory" in the Cold War. Throughout the early 1960s, Goldwater's suggestions for a victorious Cold Warrior policy were almost entirely negative: the United States should withdraw diplomatic recognition from the Soviet Union, avoid negotiations with communist states, eschew disarmament, abolish the cultural exchange program with the Soviet Union, and terminate all trade with communist nations. The Arizona Senator's only positive, non-military proposal was his plea that the administration should announce to the world America's determination to achieve a total victory over communism. But such an announcement would have been a statement of purpose rather than a program for achieving the goal. Yet Goldwater still promised a "total victory" without nuclear war.

In responding to Goldwater's foreign policy positions during the early 1960s, Fulbright stressed the absence of specific methods in Goldwater's recommendations:

It would be beneficial and instructive, I think, if those who call for total victory would spell out for us precisely how it might be achieved . . . Is it to be won by nuclear war—a war which at the very least would cost the lives of tens of millions of people on both sides, devastate most or all of our great cities, and mutilate or utterly destroy a civilization which has been built over thousands of years?

In contrast to Goldwater's opposition to negotiations with the communist world, Fulbright enthusiastically supported such agreements as the Nuclear Test Ban Treaty. The Foreign Relations Committee chairman endorsed increased trade and the expansion of the cultural exchange program with the Soviet Union as policies which could reduce the tensions of the Cold War and introduce "a degree of normalcy into our relations with the Soviet Union and other communist countries." On September 8, 1964, Fulbright delivered a Senate speech repudiating the Arizona Senator's belief in American omnipotence:

The Senator's assumption that the Russians can be counted on to accept humiliation rather than war is a dangerous delusion. It is based on the fantastic premise that the American people will prefer the destruction of their cities and perhaps a hundred million deaths to an adjustment of interests with the communists, but that at the same time, the Russians will surrender to an ultimatum rather than accept the risk of nuclear war . . . The simple point which Goldwater Republicans seem unable to grasp is that no nation can be expected to acquiesce peacefully in its own 'total defeat.'

Fulbright was convinced that the President agreed with him on the need to ameliorate Soviet-American relations, as well as on the necessity of avoiding a military entanglement in the jungles of Indochina. In Fulbright's opinion, only the Goldwater movement and a minority of right-wing Democrats advocated escalation of the American commitment to South Vietnam. The chairman of the Senate Foreign Relations Committee would not have believed that President Lyndon Johnson would begin to implement many of Goldwater's proposals for the Vietnam war within a year after the Gulf of Tonkin crisis.

99

Chapter Five

The Decline of Fulbright's Confidence in Johnson's Leadership

In the final weeks of 1964 Senator Fulbright was optimistic about the prospects for ameliorating America's relations with the communist nations of the world. The Senator's old antagonist and the principal spokesman for the radical right in the United States, Barry Goldwater, had been repudiated at the polls in November. The Republican won only 52 electoral votes, as opposed to 486 electoral votes for the Democratic ticket. Fulbright had repeatedly denounced Goldwater for proposing a radical policy which envisaged the total destruction of communism and the imposition of American ideas of democracy upon the entire world. In contrast, President Johnson proposed a "conservative policy" of preventing communist expansion while negotiating limited agreements with communist nations that would reduce the danger of nuclear war. Fulbright conducted an unusually strenuous campaign of speaking engagements during the Presidential race, and competent observers of Arkansas politics attributed Johnson's victory in Arkansas primarily to Fulbright's vigorous efforts on the President's behalf. The Senator was exuberant after the electoral triumph of the politician he had praised so profusely in his speech at the 1964 Democratic Convention:

> The same understanding of human nature which enabled him to lead the Senate so effectively during a difficult period in our history will enable him to find a way to resolve differences which exist among nations. I commend Lyndon Johnson to this convention and to all our people as a man of understanding with the wisdom to use the great power of our nation in the cause of peace.

Fulbright continued to support the President despite his private concern (which he had expressed in his May letter to McNamara) over the administration's Vietnam policy. During 1964

101

Fulbright discussed the Vietnamese dilemma with Walter Lippmann, who reinforced the Senator's doubts concerning the American military involvement in southeast Asia. But Fulbright's doubts were mitigated by his conviction that Johnson would give a fair private hearing to dissenting views concerning Vietnam. Fulbright's friendship with Johnson strengthened his belief that the President would carefully listen to his ideas. A telegram the Senator and Mrs. Fulbright sent to the Johnsons immediately after the election revealed the cordial personal relationship between the two men and their families: "What a team you are!! Heartfelt congratulations to both of you from both of us, and all best wishes for happy and fulfilling years ahead." Many years later, Fulbright would admit that he had been dilatory in challenging the military escalation policy "primarily because I misjudged the intentions of President Johnson and because I was not informed about Vietnam and China," but he added, "my friendship with the President also contributed to my reluctance to take issue with him publicly." The warm Fulbright-Johnson relationship in 1964 was perhaps an unfortunate example of the tendency David Halberstam has decried, whereby "key congressmen like William Fulbright, rather than playing their true constitutional roles, were often handled as friends of the White House family." The Senator thought the President was sincerely interested in achieving a political settlement in Vietnam, and that by refraining from public criticism of Johnson's policies he could retain the ability to exert a powerful influence on the administration privately.

As Fulbright later admitted, the belief that he was privately persuading the President of the futility in expanding the military commitment to South Vietnam was an "illusion." In *The Arrogance of Power* Fulbright would excoriate the policy of the executive branch to notify Congress of decisions which had already been made rather than genuinely consulting it. This policy continued in 1964-1965, though he was not fully cognizant of it at the time. A memorandum in the Pentagon papers, written by Assistant Secretary of State for East Asian and Pacific Affairs William Bundy in November, 1964, exemplified the administration's attitude towards Congress as one among many external "audiences" to be manipulated in the desired direction (the news media, the American public, and international opinion were the other principal audiences). Bundy wrote that Fulbright and other "key leaders" of Congress should be consulted, but "perhaps only by notification if we do a reprisal against another Bien Hoa." The Assistant Secretary argued that guerrilla assaults, such as the recent Bien Hoa attack, might be repeated at any time and would "give us a good springboard for any decision for stronger action." The memorandum listed Fulbright as one of fifteen Congressional leaders who were to be notified of "stronger action" in Vietnam, but it did not assign any particular importance to the chairman of the Senate Foreign Relations Committee.

Fulbright was not aware of the cavalier attitude represented by the Bundy memorandum in late 1964. During November of 1964 he had rarely held more confidence in an administration. Shortly after the election he departed for Yugoslavia to confer with Marshal Josip Broz Tito and preside over the signing of an agreement inaugurating Yugoslavia's participation in the Fulbright fellowship program. This assignment was especially rewarding for Fulbright, not only because he regarded the student exchange program as the greatest achievement of his career and was always pleased by its expansion, but also because Yugoslavia was the first communist nation to join the program. In Fulbright's view, the new exchange agreement was a classic example of the Johnson administration's "conservative" policy of gradually reducing tensions with the communist world and eroding the ideological prejudices against communism which had plagued American diplomacy since the 1940s. He was highly impressed with Tito after his conversation with the Yugoslav leader. Fulbright's favorable perception of Yugoslavia subtly and significantly influenced his thinking on the dilemma in southeast Asia. If Yugoslavia was a communist state which was not aligned with the Soviet bloc and pursued policies often friendly and seldom harmful to U.S. interests, then he began to speculate that a communist but independent and nationalistic Vietnam would serve American interests in southeast Asia far better than a corrupt, unstable regime dependent on American manpower and financial aid. He persistently emphasized his ideas concerning the value of a "Titoist buffer state" for Vietnam in conversations with Johnson during the months after his visit to Yugoslavia.

The Senator delivered a speech at Southern Methodist University a few weeks after he returned to the United States in which he advocated the "building of bridges to the communist world." Fulbright observed that there was a general tendency among communist countries toward more liberal domestic policies and less aggressive foreign policies. Yugoslavia had demonstrated the most outstanding communist progress by adopting a neutralist diplomacy and permitting substantial liberty for its people. The United States should encourage the independence of Tito's government by engaging in cordial political relations and signing educational exchange agreements with the Yugoslavs, and by according them most-favored nation treatment in trade. Similarly, Fulbright argued that Brezhnev and Kosygin were basicaly pursuing a prudent strategy abroad and had not resurrected the Stalinist apparatus of police terror at home. This increasing moderation of Soviet policy in the preceding decade should be rewarded by arranging limited accommodations with the Soviet Union which lessened East-West hostility and thus reduced the danger of war. Hence, the United States should continue to negotiate constructive agreements with the U.S.S.R. such as the test ban treaty, the prohibition against placing nuclear weapons in orbit around the earth, and the sale of surplus American wheat to the Russians.

The fundamental assumption of the Southern Methodist address seemed to be that change was virtually an inalterable law of human existence which did not cease to exist when nations became communist. Although Fulbright was disturbed by China's "ideological fanaticism," he believed that Peking might eventually follow the progressive evolutionary pattern of the Soviet Union and assume a more moderate attitude toward the West. He approvingly quoted a recent article by George Kennan which stated that Americans should not interpret the current Chinese antipathy towards the United States as absolute and permanent. Kennan wrote:

> Neither these men in Peiping nor the regime over which they preside are immune to the laws of change that govern all human society, if only because no single generation, anywhere, ever sees things exactly the same as the generation that went 10 years before it.

Fulbright concluded that China's admission to the United Nations was inevitable.

The passage quoting Kennan was the only point in the speech in which Fulbright indirectly questioned the view of China as an unchanging and malevolent aggressor. Despite the fact that he thought China's admission into the U.N. was inevitable, he said the United States would have to oppose its entry if that occurred in the near future; the Chinese should not be extended diplomatic recognition or allowed into the U.N. because of their "aggression and subversion." Fulbright referred to Chinese aggression frequently in the address, but he failed to cite any specific instances of this alleged Chinese imperialism. The lack of evidence to support his contentions concerning China was in sharp contrast to the passages where he enumerated specific examples of American cooperation with Yugoslavia and the Soviet Union to buttress his arguments for improving relations with those nations. Apparently Fulbright considered Chinese imperialism in the Far East as so flagrant and obvious that it was unnecessary to adduce evidence to prove Peking's aggression. He was unable to cite any evidence to demonstrate China's alleged imperialism simply because China was not an expansionist power, as he eventually realized.

Fulbright entirely avoided any discussion of the controversy over Vietnam. The Senator as well as several historians later felt that his inaccurate perspective towards China weakened the logic of his critique of the American involvement in Vietnam. Since he accepted the prevailing contemporary view of China as a relentlessly expansionist power, President Johnson could believe in late 1964 and early 1965 that Fulbright agreed with Rusk, McNamara, and the other major advisers on the basic necessity of containing China, and differed only in thinking the existence of a non-commmunist South Vietnam was peripheral to American interests. The President would decide that Fulbright was wrong, that "the experts knew the facts" about South Vietnam's crucial relevance to American security.

The December, 1964 speech at S.M.U., entitled "Bridges East and West," was the subject of a brief set of remarks delivered on the Senate floor by Senator Frank Church of Idaho on January 6,1965. Senator Church placed "Bridges East and West" in the *Congressional Record* declaring, "I have never read a more impressive statement outlining the goals, methods, and policies our Government should have in mind in our dealings with the Communist world." Church was particularly complimentary of Fulbright's analysis of the communist nations as representing a panoply of change and limited progress rather than a monolithic and belligerent bloc. The Idaho Senator also praised Fulbright for his belief in the futility of total military victory as a panacea for all American difficulties in the international arena. Church did not comment upon the section of the address dealing with China.

A week after Church's tribute to "Bridges East and West" Fulbright identified himself with a mild dissent against Johnson's Vietnam policy by placing in the *Congressional Record* a *Ramparts* magazine interview with Church which Fulbright described as "an excellent statement with regard to what our policy should be in southeast Asia." Church strongly opposed escalation and advocated the neutralization of southeast Asia, although he did not endorse an immediate American withdrawal. He speculated that the United Nations might be able to help maintain the territorial integrity of the states in the region. According to Church, the conflict in South Vietnam was a civil war, basically an indigenous revolution against the existing government which only the people of South Vietnam could suppress. America could not "win their war for them," especially in a country where the majority of the populace associated all Western nations with imperialism. The South Vietnamese did not recognize the distinction between white soldiers in French uniforms fighting to preserve a French colony and white soldiers in American uniforms fighting to arrest communist expansion. In Church's opinion, the people of Vietnam were not confronted with a choice between the tyranny of the North and the freedom of the South, because South Vietnam was a military despotism just as North Vietnam was. Finally, he asserted that if the military situation in the South drastically deteriorated,the United States should find the maturity to accept the unpleasant reality of a communist Vietnam and eventually withdraw.

Fulbright's insertion of the *Ramparts* interview with Church into the *Congressional Record*, along with several editorials approving of Church's position, was a significant departure from his complete avoidance of the Vietnam issue in the December address at Southern Methodist University. If he was determined by early 1965 to refrain from direct public criticism of the Johnson administration, he was equally determined to publicly offer alternatives to Johnson's policies. Fulbright's alternative suggestions would lead him to assume the precarious position in early 1965 of professing support for President Johnson while endorsing proposals which contradicted the administration's view of the war in Vietnam. His approbation of Church's perspective on the war in the *Ramparts* article may have been the first of these contradictions, since Johnson and Rusk obviously did not agree with such ideas as Church's assertion that the Vietnamese conflict was a civil war.

It should be acknowledged, however, that Fulbright's endorsement of Church's *Ramparts* article was only a mild and oblique questioning of America's course in Vietnam, for Church avoided mentioning Johnson or the presidential advisers and made several comments favorable to the administration's position. Dean Rusk certainly would not have argued with Church's claim that the United States must continue its massive military and economic assistance to Saigon, and that the interdiction of the Ho Chi Minh trail in Laos would substantially alleviate the Vietcong's pressure on the South Vietnames army. Fulbright did not elaborate upon his opinions concerning Laos or aid levels to Saigon, his only remark on Church's article being the general observation that it was excellent. Fulbright's attitude was indirectly expressed by the editorials he placed in the *Record*, which extolled Church's neutralization proposal and his warnings about the folly of escalating the direct American military involvement in Vietnam.

During January Fulbright began to clarify his thinking about American foreign policy in Vietnam. On January 14 he revealed considerable uncertainty in his letter to an acquaintance stating,

"Like everyone else I am more than a little disturbed by the situation in southeast Asia, and more than a little perplexed as to what our proper course should be." Again, in correspondence a few days later with Frank Stanton, president of the Columbia Broadcasting System, he was unsure: "I have just read the report [a transcript of a C.B.S. documentary on Vietnam]. A classic dilemma if I ever saw one. I confess I have not been able to arrive at a conclusion." By late January Fulbright was becoming more decisive, stating in a letter to a Little Rock constituent, "I agree with your son's idea that we are trying to do the right thing, but the difficulties seem to be beyond our capacity to handle." The letter ended with words which adumbrated his future dissent: "I have been perfectly willing to go along with the efforts of the past, but I am not willing to enlarge this into a full-scale war."

Fulbright's increasing determination in late January to oppose expansion of American military operations in Indochina was expressed publicly as well as in private correspondence. At the end of January a *Time* newsman asked Fulbright a hypothetical question concerning what he would do if given the choice of escalation or withdrawal from Vietnam through negotiations. Fulbright replied that he would withdraw. He firmly rejected arguments in favor of escalation through bombing, contending in the *Time* interview that "You can't selectively do a little bombing." In his opinion, once the bombings began it would be impossible to predict how massive the involvement might become, because "you can't see down the road far enough." The Senator persisted in his belief, however, that the time of the ultimate decision on America's proper strategy in southeast Asia was not imminent.

Late January and early February actually constituted one of the crucial junctures in the administration's deliberations on Vietnam, although in public the President and his aides consistently and disingenuously denied that any major changes were being contemplated. On January 27 Secretary McNamara and Special Assistant for National Security Affairs McGeorge Bundy delivered a memorandum to President Johnson which declared that the fundamental decision could not be delayed any longer and an expanded use of force in Vietnam was necessary. Bundy and McNamara suggested that Bundy should travel to Saigon in early February for an investigation "on the ground." The skeptics within the bureaucracy associated with Under Secretary of State George Ball, who knew of Bundy's inclination to use force, were pessimistic about the prospects for his mission's impact upon American policy. Fulbright was not thoroughly informed of the top-level discussions in the administration, although Johnson attempted to reassure him by arranging for Dean Rusk to have frequent breakfasts with the Senator. The Secretary would report to the President that Fulbright's views remained unchanged by these meetings, whereupon Johnson would prescribe more Rusk-Fulbright breakfasts, which would have similar results. Fulbright was still able to meet with Johnson personally, but their conversations were often dominated by Johnson's monologues on his valiant efforts to resist extremist pressures for escalation.

The euphoria Fulbright had experienced after the electoral triumph in November had not dissipated by January, despite his concerns over Vietnam and his limited consultations with the President. His enthusiasm for Johnson's domestic legislation was one of the important reasons for his continuing favorable assessment of the President. Fulbright argued forcefully in a January 16 speech at Miami that the United States should renounce its self-appointed role as global anti-communist gendarme and instead direct its talents and economic resources toward solving domestic problems. The money which had been devoted to the military demands of the Cold War in the previous two decades could have been used to build myriad schools, housing facilities, and hospitals and to combat poverty at home. Fulbright strongly implied that the Johnson administration would at last reverse the American obsession with opposing communism and channel the nation's energies into domestic affairs. The Senator described Johnson's proposal for federal aid to education, which was presented to Congress a few days before Fulbright's January 16 address, as "a work of high political creativity," and he was confident that "the American people and their leaders are prepared to launch new and creative programs in various areas of our domestic life."

The theme of Fulbright's January 16 speech was almost identical with the central idea of Walter Lippmann's February 2 column in the *Washington Post*. It was not surprising that the opinions of Fulbright and Lippmann were similar, for Fulbright had been a confidant of Lippmann for many years and the two men were communicating frequently in early 1965. The Lippmann article was even more optimistic than the Fulbright address about the prospects for diverting American energies from the Cold War to domestic affairs under the Johnson administration. Analyzing in retrospect the administration's performance in January, Lippmann wrote that for the first time in the quarter of a century since World War II began, the fundamental attention of the President of the United States was focused not upon the dangers abroad but upon the nation's problems at home. The columnist affirmed that "the state of the world today permits and justifies the preoccupation with

American domestic affairs." He eulogized Johnson's domestic proposals, writing, "we have rarely,if ever, seen at the beginning of a new administration such a coherent program, such insight and resourcefulness."

It would be facile to condemn Fulbright's January 16 speech and Lippmann's February 2 column as exercises in wishful thinking; but it should be considered that in earlier articles Lippmann had warned against foreign entanglements which could destroy Johnson's reforms, and Fulbright's *Time* interview had delineated his dissent against bombing. Moreover, the administration's plans for escalation in Vietnam were enveloped in secrecy, while the Johnson agenda for domestic reform was attracting an enormous amount of generally favorable publicity in Washington. It seemed unlikely that a Great Society and a war in southeast Asia could be launched simultaneously. And it had only been a few months earlier that Johnson had dramatically portrayed himself as the "man of peace" in the 1964 campaign, proclaiming his absolute refusal to send American boys 10,000 miles away from home to fight a war Asian boys must fight for themselves. Both the renowned *Washington Post* columnist and the chairman of the Senate Foreign Relations Committee had been assured in conversations at the White House that the Vietnamese conflict would not be expanded. Thus, at the end of January Walter Lippmann and J. William Fulbright imagined broad vistas of time looming ahead, time for the Great Society of Lyndon Johnson to arise and flourish, and time for the gradual termination of America's anti-communist crusade.

The increasing campaign of aerial devastation in February dealt a severe blow to the hopes of those who had counseled restraint in Vietnam. The administration emphatically denied that the February bombings of North Vietnam represented a major policy change, justifying the air raids as retaliatory measures for the February 6 Vietcong attacks on the American army barracks at Pleiku in which nine Americans were killed. In reality the initiation of regular bombing attacks advanced well beyond the limited reprisal strikes during the Tonkin Gulf crisis of August, 1964. As the historian George C. Herring has observed,the Pleiku incident provided the auspicious occasion, not the cause, for implementing the program of air strikes which many administration officials had been advocating for more than two months. Pleiku was not unprecedented; there had been a Vietcong assault on the Bien Hoa air base in November which had resulted in four American deaths; again in December the Vietcong exploded a bomb at Saigon's Brink hotel, killing two Americans. Yet no retaliatory actions had been taken in late 1964, primarily because of fears of provoking a Vietcong offensive against the rapidly weakening South Vietnamese regime. By the end of January there was an overwhelming consensus within the bureaucracy that the Saigon government was so feeble only bombing would revive it. William Bundy's November memorandum on Congressional opinion had maintained that "Bien Hoa" might be repeated at any time and would "give us a good springboard for any decision for stronger action." McGeorge Bundy expressed this attitude more succinctly in February when he averred, "Pleikus are like streetcars" (i.e., one comes along every ten minutes.)

McGeorge Bundy returned from Saigon in February recommending a policy of steadily intensifying air attacks. Fulbright was not invited to the crucial National Security Council meetings on Vietnam escalation in early 1965. Senator Mike Mansfield of Montana was asked to attend the N.S.C. conference immediately after the Pleiku attack, however, and Mansfield's views were quite similar to those of Fulbright. Years later Fulbright would remember Mansfield as the one Senator with whom he was cooperating most closely in his efforts to prevent a disastrous enlargement of the southeast Asian conflict. At the N.S.C. meeting after Pleiku Mansfield stated his concern that the retaliatory policy might lead to Chinese intervention, or that it would eventually cause China and Russia to draw closer together and perhaps heal the growing Sino-Soviet split. He offered the general suggestion that the United States should begin negotiations on the Vietnamese controversy. President Johnson responded that we had disregarded provocation in the past but now communist aggression had become too outrageous, and he was certainly not going to be the President to preside over another Munich.

Mansfield had been the only critic of the retaliatory policy at the N.S.C. meeting, and Fulbright and Mansfield were the only opponents of bombing when the Congressional leaders were summoned to the White House to be informed of the President's decision. Secretary of Defense McNamara and other principal administration officials demonstrated to the Congressional leadership why the sole reasonable course of action was to expand the air war. During these February meetings Johnson would first ask for the opinions of the leaders whose support could be expected, such as Everett Dirksen and John McCormack.

Johnson would ask Fulbright and Mansfield for their views last, after a strong majority seemed to be coalescing in support of the President's position. Fulbright repeated the arguments he and Mansfield had been presenting to Johnson in early 1965, that escalation of the bombing would entrap the United States in a quagmire everyone wanted to avoid. The dissent of the Foreign Relations Committee chairman at that time was largely based upon an instinctive reaction against the excessive use of violence in foreign policy, for he had few facts and figures with which to counter the plethora of intelligence reports and statistics resonating through the phrases of Robert McNamara in the White House conferences of February.

Fulbright did not profess to have a comprehensive knowledge about Vietnam in early 1965. He had always been primarily knowledgeable about European and to a lesser extent Latin American affairs. Throughout the year of 1965 he frequently engaged in lengthy conversations with journalists who had been to Vietnam, and he began to read extensively in the writings of Jean Lacouture, Han Suyin, Philippe Devillers, Bernard Fall, and other experts on China and southeast Asia. Later in the year the Foreign Relations Committee attempted to develop additional independent sources of information on the war by employing two former members of the Foreign Service to travel to Vietnam and send back reports to the committee. By December many competent observers of the Senate felt there were few Senators who had so rigorously studied the history, culture, and politics of southeast Asia as had Fulbright in the course of the year. But it would require considerable time for the Senator to educate himself thoroughly about a region of the world he had considered peripheral to American interests. In early 1965 his opposition to expanding the war was founded on his suspicion of zealous anti-communism and his reluctance to use force, precepts which were derived from his 22 years' experience in Congress of analyzing American foreign policy.

On February 12, 1965 Fulbright once again attempted to offer an alternative to the retaliatory policy by endorsing United Nations Secretary General U Thant's proposal for negotiations. The Senator asserted that "I think it is always wiser to talk than to fight when you can get the parties together." On February 12 U Thant proposed that both sides enter into discussions aimed at preparing the ground for "formal negotiations for a settlement." The Secretary General's plea was essentially a reiteration of his July, 1964 proposal to re-convene the 1954 Geneva Conference on southeast Asia. U Thant did not try to summon the Security Council because of "its past history and the fact that some of the principal parties are not represented in the U.N.," presumably referring (according to a *Washington Post* report) to the facts that North Vietnam and China were not members of the U.N. and the Security Council meetings after the Tonkin crisis had not led to a diplomatic conference. In applauding U Thant's plan of re-convening the 1954 Geneva Conference Fulbright observed that it was quite proper for the Secretary General of the U.N. to urge that negotiations be initiated immediately. The administration's response was diametrically opposed to Fulbright's suggestion. Both the State Department and the White House refused to comment on U Thant's specific proposal, although they definitively rejected the idea that negotiations were in order at that moment.

During the weeks following Fulbright's approval of the February 12 U Thant recommendations, important columnists began referring to him as one of the Senate's prominent critics of military escalation in southeast Asia. On February 21 Drew Pearson stated that Johnson's Vietnam policy was receiving panegyrics from former critics of the President such as Richard Nixon, Barry Goldwater, and Everett Dirksen, while Democratic leaders "Mike Mansfield of Montana, Frank Church of Idaho, and even Bill Fulbright of Arkansas are either openly critical or privately unhappy." Pearson did not elaborate upon his opinions concerning the substance of Fulbright's criticism.

A column by John Chamberlain in the *Washington Post* was explicit in its treatment of Fulbright's critique of American involvement in Vietnam. In an admiring article on Senator Thomas Dodd of Connecticut entitled "The Churchillian Voice of Tom Dodd," Chamberlain maintained that in the early days of the Cold War the Truman Doctrine had committed the United States to protect small nations threatened by communist aggression. Tom Dodd was courageously upholding the Truman Doctrine tradition by defending the Doctrine's application to South Vietnam, the columnist opined, but Chamberlain lamented that "Morse of Oregon, Greuning of Alaska, Fulbright of Arkansas have all sidled away from the Truman Doctrine tradition." There was a distinct implication in John Chamberlain's column that if Tom Dodd was the heir of Winston Churchill and valiant resistance to aggression, then Morse, Gruening, and Fulbright were the legatees of Neville Chamberlain and appeasement.

Pro-administration journalists and several Republican Senators, especially Everett Dirksen, were criticizing Fulbright in early 1965 for hampering Johnson's foreign policy by advocating cooperation with the communist world. The Foreign Relations Committee chairman eschewed direct criticism of Johnson, despite the fact that his endorsement of U Thant's proposal and his public skepticism in January on the efficacy of bombing had contradicted the administration's views of the war. He still clung to the illusion that he might privately dissuade the President from expansion of the conflict, and he regarded his public professions of loyalty to the administration as strengthening his private influence at the White House.

In conversations with the President during March and April he again stressed the value of a Titoist buffer state for Vietnam. A March 3 Fulbright letter to Johnson revealed that the Senator's favorable perception of Yugoslavia continued to influence his thinking about American relations with the communist world. In the March 3 letter he related his belief that Tito was an unusually attractive and intelligent leader, and that Tito had requested in the November, 1964 discussion with Fulbright that the Senator convey to Johnson his wishes for a "further strengthening of friendly relations between our countries." Tito had also mentioned a desire for Johnson to visit Yugoslavia in 1965. The Senator persistently argued in private conversations with the President that a unified, communist Vietnam would be similar to the Yugoslavia of Tito in its nationalism and independence, that like Yugoslavia it might eventually engage in amicable relations with the United States, and that a unified, communist Vietnamese state would not represent a mere extension of Communist China.

In early March Fulbright made only the most oblique references in public to his belief that the strength of nationalism, and not communist ideology, was central to the struggle in Vietnam. He vaguely stated in an address at Johns Hopkins University that "I think we ought to ask ourselves hypothetically whether a Communist regime that leans away from China is worse or better from the viewpoint of our political and strategic interests than a non-Communist state, such as Indonesia or Cambodia, that leans toward China." He did not elucidate the significance of this statement for American policy in southeast Asia. The speech avoided discussion of Vietnam, in keeping with the Senator's strategy of refraining from public criticism of the President. Fulbright's Johns Hopkins address did not attract significant attention.

Fulbright clarified his public position on March 14, 1965 when he appeared on N.B.C.'s *Meet the Press*. On the N.B.C. program Fulbright doubted that southeast Asia was vital to American security "from a long-term point of view," but he conceded that U.S. interests were involved in Vietnam at that moment simply because of the American military presence in that country. He was pessimistic about the prospects for improving the military situation through the large-scale introduction of American ground forces. The Senator was asked for his opinion concerning the recent proposal of Everett Dirksen for a "no concession-no deal policy on further agreements and trade with the Communists until they halt aggression in Vietnam and elsewhere." Fulbright dismissed the Dirksen suggestion, saying, "This so-called hard line, I think, leads no-where." He regretted that the Vietnamese conflict was an obstacle to the amelioration of Soviet-American relations, but he maintained that the United States should continue to negotiate constructive agreements with the U.S.S.R. such as the 1963 Test Ban Treaty. Fulbright reiterated the theme of his January 16 Miami address, calling for a policy of cooperation with the communist world and a re-orientation of American priorities toward solving domestic problems.

In recalling the thesis of the Miami speech, repudiating Dirksen's belligerent ideas, and questioning the wisdom of sending U.S. ground forces to southeast Asia, Fulbright was remaining consistent with his earlier positions on Vietnam. But the general tenor of his remarks contradicted his previous opposition to bombing and his February support for immediate re-convening of the Geneva Conference. He expressed theoretical approval of negotiations, but through the circuitous logic that the air strikes would impress upon the North Vietnamese the "seriousness of the situation" and eventually lead to negotiations. The air raids were appropriate, in Fulbright's opinion, because "the objective of these strikes is to bring about a negotiation." Fulbright accepted the administration's claim that the bombing campaign was a tactic designed to avoid the introduction of American ground troops. He thus reversed the perspective of his public as well as private views in January and February, when he had envisaged bombing as the precursor of a debilitating and inexorably expanding American military involvement in Vietnam.

On the March 14 edition of *Meet the Press* Lawrence Spivak observed that there were contradictory reports concerning Fulbright's analysis of President Johnson's course in Vietnam. Some reports held that Fulbright supported Johnson's Vietnam policy, was being consulted constantly by the President, and wielded immense power within the administration's foreign policy councils. Other reports, notably a recent *New York Times* story, contended Fulbright did not support the February retaliatory policy, did not exert significant influence in the administration's deliberations on Vietnam and was not being adequately consulted by the President. The *New York Times* report was obviously closer to reality, for Rusk's frequent breakfasts with Fulbright and Johnson's monologues to the Senator on his moderation and his need for Fulbright's help can hardly be considered adequate consultation. But Fulbright answered Spivak's request for a clarification of which reports were accurate by affirming his support for Johnson's policy in Vietnam and stating that he had been adequately consulted. He did not

114

speculate on the extent of his influence. The Foreign Relations Committee chairman asserted that it would be improper for the Committee to conduct public hearings on the war "while conditions are so critical in Vietnam." The program ended on a melancholy note, with Fulbright concluding that he would be deeply disillusioned by a massive deployment of American ground forces in southeast Asia, but "when we are in this critical a matter we have to support our President, you know that, in our system."

The notion that Congress must dutifully support the President in time of crisis constituted the most glaring flaw, during early 1965, in Fulbright's campaign to prevent a disastrous American intervention in Vietnam. As long as Fulbright was competing with Robert McNamara, Dean Rusk, Maxwell Taylor, and McGeorge Bundy for the private attention of the President his protests were ineffective; he had been arguing at least as early as his May, 1964 letter to McNamara that the existence of a non-communist regime in South Vietnam was not crucial to American security, and his reasoning never had any significant impact on the administration. The Vietnam hearings of 1966 would demonstrate that Fulbright was most influential when he was revitalizing the public dialogue on American foreign policy which had become quiescent during the years of Cold War diplomacy in the 1950s and early 1960s. But in 1964 and 1965 Fulbright rejected Wayne Morse's plea for hearings on Vietnam. The President professed to be fearful that a public debate would ignite a recrudescence of extreme anti-communist sentiment in the country, and in hopes of strengthening his influence with Johnson the Arkansas Senator did not attempt to foster such a dialogue in early 1965. Thus, Fulbright averred on *Meet the Press* that a public debate on the war led by the Senate Foreign Relations Committee would hamper the President's execution of foreign policy during the southeast Asian crisis.

Fulbright had initiated tentative efforts to develop an open discussion of the Vietnam policy in January and February, 1965. He had publicly denied that bombing was a solution to the conflict and endorsed U Thant's proposal for a diplomatic conference on southeast Asia. His criticism of bombing occurred before the air attacks were escalated, and his endorsement of U Thant's recommendation was announced before the administration's rejection of negotiations was clear. By March he was forced to either follow the logic of his previous statements and openly criticize the President's decisions for escalation, or confine his dissent to private conversations. His comments in the *Meet the Press* appearance revealed his choice of the latter strategy.

It proved to be virtually impossible for the Senator to adhere

115

consistently to this strategy. He would deliver indirect critiques of the administration's foreign policy even when he was attempting to publicize his loyalty to the President. On the Spivak program he had expressed disenchantment with the massive introduction of ground forces into southeast Asia during the same month when Johnson was ordering Marine battalions to South Vietnam.

For a President as intolerant of dissent as was Lyndon Johnson, no public criticism could be allowed. By the summer of 1965 Fulbright concluded that if the President's anti-communist consensus was so stifling that only secret dissent could be tolerated, then the restoration of the proper constitutional balance between the executive and Congress was imperative. That balance might be restored by a public challenge to Johnson's foreign policy. Fulbright's challenge would occur when he became convinced that Johnson had justified the 1965 American intervention in the Dominican Republic through distorted claims of communist infiltration into that diminutive nation. The administration's distortions of the communist threat in the Caribbean reinforced Fulbright's suspicion that the dangers of Asian communist aggression had been similarly exaggerated, that China was not Nazi Germany reincarnate. Thus, by the end of 1965 he was prepared to conduct the comprehensive public investigation of America's Asian policy which the President had feared and skillfully delayed.

An analysis of Fulbright's responses to Johnson's foreign policy initiatives in late 1964 and early 1965 is largely the story of the waning of the Senator's optimism regarding the President. Fulbright was confident in late 1964 that many communist states, especially Yugoslavia and the Soviet Union, were displaying a more cooperative attitude towards the United States. In his praise of George Kennan's November, 1964 article on China there was even the hope that the Chinese might become less hostile towards the West, despite the Senator's inaccurate perception of China as imperialistic at that time. Fulbright believed that Johnson would capitalize on this nascent reduction in Cold War animosities by channeling American energies into domestic affairs, consequently redoubling the nation's vitality. The war in Vietnam had all but destroyed Fulbright's optimism by the spring of 1965. He began to fear that the President would not only fail to "build bridges" to the communist world, but would lead America on a violent crusade into the depths of the ominous Vietnamese labyrinth.

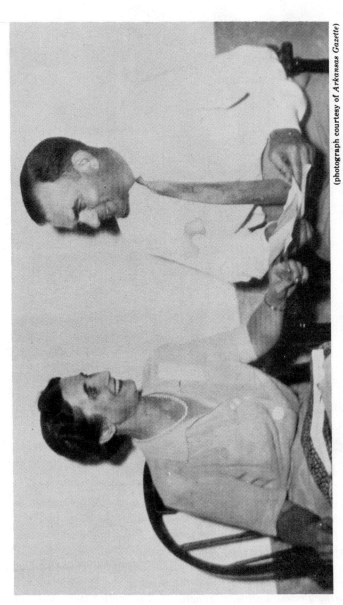

The youthful J. William Fulbright and his wife Betty are smiling in Little Rock a few hours after the returns in the 1944 United States Senate Democratic primary in Arkansas revealed that Fulbright was leading the ticket and would be in a runoff with Governor Homer Adkins. Shortly afterwards he defeated Adkins in the runoff by nearly 32,000 votes.

August 1, 1946: President Harry S. Truman signs the bill which became known as the Fulbright Act, while Fulbright and Assistant Secretary of State William Benton look on. Fulbright and Truman had several widely-publicized disagreements, and the Arkansan would later criticize the universal implications of the Truman Doctrine; but Fulbright actually supported most of the President's policies during the Truman administration. In the early 1950s, William Benton would serve in the Senate, where he and Fulbright became two of the most prominent opponents of Senator Joseph McCarthy's anti-communist investigations.

Fulbright in 1959, the year he became chairman of the Senate Foreign Relations Committee.

Early 1959: The moment of Fulbright's accession to the chairman-
ship of the Senate Foreign Relations Committee. Rhode Island Sen-
ator Theodore Green was resigning, and bequeathed his gavel to Ful-
bright while Senator John F. Kennedy of Massachusetts and Major-
ity Leader Lyndon B. Johnson of Texas observed. Green was 91 years
old at the time, he occasionally fell asleep during committee meetings,
had trouble absorbing the witnesses' testimony and could not make
decisions. His vision and hearing were failing. The Majority Leader
had previously been reluctant to persuade Green to resign, partly
because Green was first in seniority on the committee and Johnson
regarded the seniority system as sancrosanct; and also because the
Texan owed Green a political debt: six years before, Green had deliv-
ered the speech nominating Johnson as Majority Leader. By 1959,
Green's declining mental and physical powers had become such a
serious problem that Johnson and other Senate leaders held private
meetings and decided that the 91-year-old chairman must be re-
placed. Fulbright became the new chairman because he was next in
line in seniority. Even if Green had not resigned in 1959, Fulbright
later would have become the chairman, under the seniority system.

Vice President Lyndon Johnson and his friend, Senator Fulbright, in 1962.

President John F. Kennedy, Secretary of State Dean Rusk, and Fulbright in West Palm Beach, Florida, March, 1963, shortly before the President embarked on a trip to Latin America.

Fulbright, Secretary of Defense Robert McNamara, Georgia Senator Richard Russell, chairman of the Senate Armed Services Committee, and Rusk at a joint meeting of the Armed Services and Foreign Relations Committees in 1963.

Fulbright with Attorney General Robert F. Kennedy, who later joined him as a member of the U.S. Senate. The Arkansan had closer relationships with John F. and Edward M. Kennedy than with Robert Kennedy, although by the late 1960s Fulbright and the former Attorney General would become the Senate's two most influential opponents of the Vietnam war.

The Foreign Relations Committee chairman in 1962.

Fulbright and Johnson outside the White House in late November, 1963, after the assassination of President Kennedy.

Fulbright and President Lyndon Baines Johnson during the period of their friendship, before their estrangement over the American intervention in Vietnam.

The chairman, John Sparkman of Alabama, and Wayne Morse of Oregon at a hearing of the Senate Foreign Relations Committee in the 1960s.

(photograph courtesy of *Arkansas Gazette*)

The faces of Fulbright and Rusk reflect the strain of their conflict over U.S. foreign policy during the later years of the Johnson Presidency.

(photograph courtesy of *Arkansas Gazette*)

Senator Frank Church of Idaho with Fulbright; Church was a vigorous critic of Johnson's Vietnam policy and a prominent member of the Foreign Relations Committee during Fulbright's chairmanship.

David Pryor, then a U.S. Representative from Arkansas and later a Governor and U.S. Senator; Fulbright; and Stuart Symington of Missouri, a member of the Foreign Relations Committee, in 1968.

(photograph courtesy of *Arkansas Gazette*)

Fulbright greets Senator Mike Mansfield of Montana at the Little Rock airport. The two Senators held similar views on the southeast Asian conflict, although they occasionally differed on the most effective strategy to employ in opposing the war.

The Foreign Relations Committee chairman and Secretary of State Henry Kissinger at a Little Rock press conference, February, 1974.

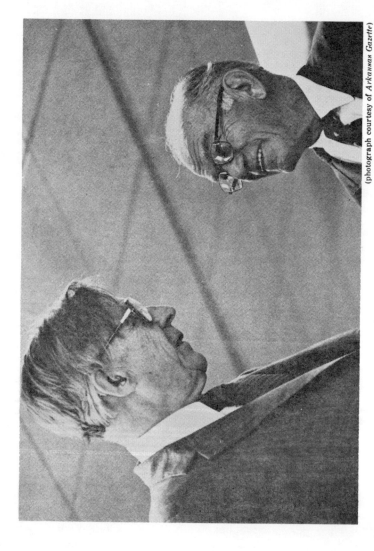

Fulbright and John Kenneth Galbraith at the dedication ceremonies for the J. William Fulbright College of Arts and Sciences at the University of Arkansas, Fayetteville, July, 1982.

Chapter Six

The Prelude to Fulbright's Dissent
Spring, 1965

Senator Fulbright was becoming increasingly disillusioned with the American foreign aid program in the mid-1960s. Since the late 1950s he had argued against utilizing foreign aid to support corrupt, reactionary regimes whose only merit was their zealous anti-communism. In late 1964 he notified Dean Rusk of his refusal to manage the foreign aid bill in 1965. The *Washington Post* columnist William S. White denounced Fulbright's decision as "an unexampled abdication of the traditional responsibility of a chairman of the Foreign Relations Committee." Walter Lippmann's column in early March, 1965 expressed a less heated and more logical view of Fulbright's refusal to manage the bill. The fundamental issue concerning foreign aid, in Lippmann's opinion, was the dispute between Fulbright and most members of the House of Representatives, who resisted expansion of economic aid programs but consistently supported massive military assistance to oppose communism throughout the world. Lippmann believed President Johnson could not support Fulbright because of the House's adamant opposition to the Senator's position, but that the administration basically agreed with Fulbright's arguments for reduced military assistance and expanded economic assistance. The columnist concluded that Fulbright "is doing wonders to make the country and the Congress begin to re-examine the encrusted deposit of ideas and ideology and prejudices under which our foreign policy labors and groans."

Fulbright eventually acquiesced to administration pressures and agreed to manage the foreign aid bill in 1965. He had proposed the division of military and economic aid into two separate bills, the substitution of multilateral for bilateral assistance, and long-term instead of annual aid authorizations. The administration did not incorporate any of Fulbright's innovations into the aid program. This

131

rejection of Fulbright's proposals, as well as his disagreements with administration officials during the foreign aid hearings in March and April, revealed that the administration's perspective on foreign aid was much more similar to the House of Representatives' view than Lippmann had believed.

David E. Bell, the Administrator of the Agency for International Development, appeared before the Foreign Relations Committee on March 12 to discuss the foreign aid bill. At the March 12 hearing Fulbright enumerated fourteen small nations which were receiving American aid, including South Vietnam, and asked Bell if the United States had vital interests in all of those nations. Bell delivered two contradictory responses, replying first that American interests were certainly not involved in all of the countries. When Fulbright pressed him to justify aid to countries in which U.S. interests were nonexistent, the A.I.D. Administrator replied that American interests were served whenever a nation preserved its independence of communist domination. Fulbright rejoined: "Now you have come to the crux of it. We are so fascinated with communism that we are just going to keep out the communists all over the world."

Fulbright rejected Bell's contention that anti-communism was a legitimate reason for extending foreign aid to a nation and thus involving the United States in its affairs. He doubted that the United States had any vital interests in South Vietnam. In Fulbright's opinion, economic aid had gradually led to the burgeoning military commitment to South Vietnam, so that American pride and prestige had become inextricably entangled with the campaign to preserve the South Vietnamese regime. He asserted that Americans assumed the nation's interests were involved in South Vietnam simply because of the massive economic and military commitment to that nation. But in Fulbright's view, it was primarily the nebulous and emotional concept of America's "honor, pride, and prestige" which was involved in Vietnam. Bell defended his evaluation of South Vietnam as crucial to American security by quoting President Eisenhower's 1954 statement to the South Vietnamese: "We support you, we want to help you, we think it is important that your independence be sustained." Fulbright responded that if the United States defined its vital interests in terms of maintaining other nations' independence, then no region of the globe was exempt from American responsibility.

Fulbright continued to question the administration's assumptions concerning Vietnam when Under Secretary of State George W. Ball testified before the Foreign Relations Committee on April 7. The committee's chairman was gravely concerned by the negative Japanese reaction to the American military escalation. He observed that Shunichi Matsumoto, a senior Japanese diplomat, had recently challenged Washington's allegation that the Vietcong insurgency was predominantly a communist movement. Premier Eisaku Sato had sent Matsumoto to survey the situation in Vietnam. In his report to Sato, Matsumoto stated that the Vietcong had no direct connection with China or the Soviet Union. The Vietcong insurgents were basically nationalistic and would not renounce their political and military objectives in the South because of the bombing of North Vietnam. Fulbright inserted in the record of the hearings a *New York Times* article which attributed great significance to the Matsumoto report, partly because of Matsumoto's stature as the special envoy of Sato, but fundamentally because his ideas seemed to confirm a skepticism about America's role in Vietnam already evident in Japan. The *New York Times* news story concluded that despite the support for the U.S. position in the official rhetoric of the Sato government, Japanese public opinion was overwhelmingly negative in its response to President Johnson's Vietnam policy.

George Ball responded to Fulbright's pessimistic statements concerning Japanese public opinion by emphasizing the Sato regime's steadfast verbal support for the American position. Fulbright proceeded to ask Ball why the two largest Japanese newspapers were so hostile to American policy, especially the newspaper *Asahi*, which had published an article by Matsumoto summarizing his Vietnam report. Ball and Assistant Secretary of State for Congressional Relations Douglas MacArthur II attempted to denigrate the Japanese criticism by arguing that the two huge Japanese newspapers were infiltrated by communists. Fulbright interrupted this argument to assert that Matsumoto was certainly not a communist, and Premier Sato had authorized his mission. The Senator questioned Ball about the validity of Matsumoto's contention that the Vietcong would not cease their military operations because of the bombing of North Vietnam. Ball rejected Matsumoto's analysis, claiming the Vietcong were commanded by North Vietnam and encouraged by China. The bombing would bring about a cessation of the North's infiltration and control of the southern guerrillas, according to Ball, thus rendering the South Vietnamese insurrection "quite manageable."

Fulbright continued to elaborate upon the adverse foreign reaction to American policy in Asia. The chairman sardonically commented on Canada's failure to share Washington's perception of China as a malevolent aggressor: "The Canadians, as you know, among our friends have probably the best representation and best

133

reception in China than any, and we usually don't consider the Canadians Communist." Fulbright observed that a recent article from the *Toronto Globe and Mail* had failed to support American assumptions about the war in southeast Asia. The *Globe* described the escalation of the war as a "perilous course" which risked a Chinese retaliation against the inexorably expanding American intervention. Fulbright also fostered a brief discussion regarding Canadian Prime Minister Lester Pearson's critique of Johnson's Vietnam policy, apparently referring to Pearson's appeal for a termination of the U.S. bombing campaign and an immediate effort to conclude a peaceful settlement. He avoided endorsing Pearson's controversial position, but he felt the Canadian Prime Minister's proposals at least deserved serious consideration rather than an irascible dismissal. Ball averred, however, that communist propaganda had directly influenced the thinking of the Canadians, the French, and other peoples who were critical of American policy in Vietnam.

George Ball was probably the most eloquent and vigorous private critic of the military escalation in Vietnam, yet his statements at the foreign aid hearings revealed no intimation of his private dissent. He replied to Fulbright's questions concerning Japanese and Canadian opposition to the U.S. intervention by denouncing North Vietnam's aggression and by stressing the support the United States was receiving from the great majority of its allies. He recounted the Sato government's firm verbal assistance for the American cause in Vietnam. The N.A.T.O. Council had endorsed the American position a week earlier and would regard any American withdrawal as catastrophic, according to Ball. He did concede that the French government disapproved of the U.S. military involvement in southeast Asia. But the French disapprobation, no less than that of Lester Pearson, was influenced by the communist propaganda falsely portraying the Indochinese war as an indigenous revolt. Ball regretted that the complexity of the Vietnamese situation facilitated the dissemination of the communist propaganda throughout the world.

During the course of the hearings, Fulbright had generated a limited amount of constructive debate by trying to elicit from David Bell and George Ball a definition of American interests in Vietnam and an explanation of the burgeoning international opposition to President Johnson's foreign policy. It was unfortunately an atrophied debate, for there were only a half-dozen passages in the entire 650 pages of testimony in which administration witnesses were compelled to defend the Vietnam policy. Only Fulbright, Morse, and Republican Senator George Aiken of Vermont (there were nineteen members on the committee) asked a substantial number of questions about Vietnam, and much of the testimony dealt with less important issues connected with the aid program.

The 1965 foreign aid hearings might have provided an excellent opportunity to conduct a thorough investigation of the Vietnam dilemma; one year later Rusk's testimony for a foreign economic aid authorization to South Vietnam developed into the celebrated 1966 Vietnam hearings, and again in 1968 when Rusk testified for that year's foreign assistance bill the Foreign Relations Committee subjected him to a lengthy and rather hostile interrogation. But in early 1965 few members on the committee were adversaries of the executive branch. Fulbright was still attempting to demonstrate his support for President Johnson, despite his disagreements with administration officials at the hearings.

Fulbright developed several ideas during the foreign aid discussions which were central to his critique of the crusading anticommunism of American diplomacy. He recalled a theme he had been emphasizing since the late 1950s when he repudiated the A.I.D. Administrator's contention that opposition to communism constituted a legitimate basis for extending foreign aid to a government. The Senator persistently affirmed in 1965 and the later 1960s that American pride and prestige rather than any crucial national interests were involved in Vietnam. He also maintained that the aid program had acquired a momentum of its own, so that many Americans were psychologically unable to liquidate the commitment and thus admit that the billions of dollars previously channeled into support of South Vietnam had been a fatuous and futile investment. In this perspective, additional billions would have to be expended to insure that the earlier investment was not wasted.

The chairman had revealed briefly at the 1965 foreign aid hearings that administration witnesses experienced immense difficulties in presenting a persuasive defense of their policies when confronted by critical questioning. For example, the only specific argument David Bell could ultimately muster to define a concrete American interest in Vietnam was the need to uphold Eisenhower's 1954 pledge of support to South Vietnam. George Ball's basic refutation of Matsumoto, Pearson, and the French was the sterile assertion that communist propaganda had misled them. Throughout the later Johnson years the voices of dissent were strengthened by the abject failure of administration officials to present a cogent justification for President Johnson's foreign policy when they testified before the Foreign Relations Committee.

The administration was hostile to any intensive discussion of the Vietnam war. Secretary McNamara was especially disenchanted by the prospect of appearing before an open session of the

Foreign Relations Committee. He insisted that his testimony should be given at an executive session hearing. A transcript of the foreign assistance hearings was made available to the public later in 1965, but many of the statements by Bell, McNamara, and Ball were deleted "in the interest of national security." At one juncture during the McNamara hearing on March 24 Fulbright asked the Secretary of Defense ten consecutive questions about Vietnam, and nine of the responses were either evasions or security deletions. When Rusk testified there was little discussion of southeast Asia. Thus the dialogue on Vietnam at the foreign aid hearings of March and April, 1965 receded into obscurity, emasculated by the President's antipathy towards public debate and the Senate Foreign Relations Committee's reluctance to challenge the administration.

Fulbright was especially careful to avoid vehement disputes with the President's advisers in late March and early April, for he believed Johnson was finally beginning to see the validity of his arguments for a negotiated settlement. On one occasion at the end of March Fulbright privately conferred with Johnson at length, and in contrast to their earlier conversations the President seemed to be attentive and sympathetic. When the administration announced another escalation of the American military effort a few days later Fulbright eschewed definite criticism of the decision.

The President had decided at an April 2 National Security Council meeting to intensify the air attacks against North Vietnam, dispatch several thousand additional troops (there were 28,000 American soldiers in Vietnam at the time) to South Vietnam, and provide assistance for a major expansion of the South Vietnamese military forces. The administration would also increase economic assistance to Saigon. Maxwell Taylor, the Ambassador to Saigon who had recently arrived in Washington to attend the N.S.C. meeting, appeared later on April 2 before a closed joint session of the Senate Armed Services and Foreign Relations Committees. Fulbright told reporters after the joint session that he was unhappy and apprehensive about Vietnam because the war "can always escalate beyond control." He precluded an interpretation of this comment as an indictment of Johnson's policy by adding that Ambassador Taylor was "unhappy and apprehensive, too." The Senator was concerned that the administration had not defined its views of an acceptable political settlement, but he continued to profess his general support for the President.

In early April Fulbright attempted to persuade Johnson that a Titoist buffer state in Vietnam would be compatible with American interests. He summarized his ideas about Vietnam in a memorandum which he sent to the White House on April 5, two days before the President was to deliver an important address at Johns Hopkins University. Fulbright's Vietnam memorandum consisted of six basic propositions. First, it would be a disaster for the United States to engage in a massive ground and air war in southeast Asia. A prolonged war in Vietnam would be extremely costly and would revive and intensify the Cold War, which had begun to ease after the Cuban missile crisis. A large-scale air war would not defeat the Vietcong and would risk an intervention by the North Vietnamese Army or even by China. Fulbright predicted that "the commitment of a large American land army would involve us in a bloody and interminable conflict in which the advantage would lie with the enemy."

The memorandum's second point held that Chinese imperialism, and not communist ideology, represented the primary danger to peace in Asia. Fulbright's perception of China as an imperialistic power was the only serious flaw in the memorandum. A year later he would effectively refute his earlier views by writing that the Chinese tended to be introspective and were vastly more concerned with their domestic objectives of industrialization and social transformation than with supporting foreign revolutions. In 1966 Fulbright asserted that despite the ferocity of China's official rhetoric, the Chinese had made no effort to subjugate the weak and non-aligned nation of Burma, had voluntarily withdrawn from North Korea, and had failed to intervene in Vietnam. The second argument of his April, 1965 paper was accurate where it argued that Chinese ideology could not harm the United States, and the following point of the document correctly stressed the resiliency of Asian nationalism. Fulbright's third proposition stated that the smaller Asian nations were historically afraid of—and independent of—China. Thus, a communist state in Vietnam independent of China, as Tito was independent of Russia, would be far more valuable for world security than a feeble anti-communist regime dependent on American dollars and manpower.

The three remaining proposals of the memorandum dealt with Fulbright's appeal for a negotiated settlement. In order to end the war, the United States should declare a moratorium on the bombing, clarify its intentions, and initiate a campaign to persuade the Vietnamese people, north and south, of the economic and political advantages of a free, independent Vietnamese state. The United States could make its wishes known through Great Britain or Russia that it would accept an independent Vietnamese regime, regardless of political makeup, and that it would cooperate with the other great powers in guaranteeing the independence of Vietnam and the rights of minorities. America should join with the great powers in assuring that the new unified regime would not be the pawn or satellite of any great power. Finally, it would be advantageous for international stability to have a government in Vietnam oriented more toward Russia rather than exclusively toward China, since at least for the moment China was in a belligerent and resentful mood. The inaccurate perspective on China again weakened this final point, but it should be noted that there was an assumption in Fulbright's Vietnam memorandum, as there had been in his 1964 "Bridges East and West" speech, that the Chinese were not immune to the laws of change and their "resentful" attitude was not absolute or permanent.

On the day after President Johnson received the Senator's written recommendations for a diplomatic settlement he invited Fulbright and Mansfield to the White House to discuss the draft of his Johns Hopkins University speech. Fulbright's influence was partially responsible for the passage in Johnson's address proposing "unconditional discussions." After President Johnson delivered his speech at Baltimore on April 7 Fulbright complimented the President's conciliatory tone. The Johns Hopkins address was crucial in convincing Fulbright that he was persuading Johnson of the futility in escalating the Vietnam war. Fulbright's response to the speech was too sanguine, for Johnson reiterated at Baltimore the fundamental goal of three previous administrations: "Our objective is the independence of South Vietnam and its freedom from attack." Johnson regarded the American bargaining position as much too precarious to begin serious negotiations in the spring of 1965; thus the dramatic peace initiative at Johns Hopkins was primarily designed to silence international and domestic critics of U.S. foreign policy.

If the Johns Hopkins address temporarily muted Fulbright's criticism of President Johnson, it failed to prevent the Senator from offering alternatives to the escalation policy and publicly disagreeing with the President's advisers. It was not illogical for Fulbright to have made a crucial distinction between Johnson and the President's immediate entourage, because Johnson was assiduously cultivating an image of himself as a "dove" surrounded by "hawkish" advisers, particularly in his communications with Fulbright, McGovern, and Church. Fulbright provoked a brief but acrimonious controversy with Rusk and McNamara on April 18 when he advocated a cessation of the air strikes against North Vietnam in order to open an avenue towards peace negotiations. While the White House refused to comment, Dean Rusk rebuked Fulbright for proposing an action which "would only encourage the aggressor and dishearten our friends who bear the brunt of battle."

Secretary McNamara declared that terminating the bombing of North Vietnam would discourage the South Vietnamese people in their struggle to oppose Hanoi's campaign of terror, which was dependent upon the daily flow of men and military equipment from the North. Republican Senator Jacob Javits of New York joined Rusk and McNamara in rejecting Fulbright's proposal, and Senator John Stennis of Mississippi asseverated that far from halting the bombings, the United States must prepare to fight an expanded war for an indefinite period.

It was remarkable for Fulbright's mild criticism (which was expressed in an interview with Jack Bell of the Associated Press) to have provoked such vituperation from the Cabinet officials. Fulbright had merely hypothesized that a temporary cease-fire would be advisable "in the near future before the escalation goes too far" in order to allow all of the belligerents time to calmly reflect upon the situation in Vietnam. He preferred a cease-fire for all combatants, but if that couldn't be obtained then the United States should unilaterally stop the bombing. In Fulbright's opinion, the air war against the North Vietnamese might galvanize them into more determined resistance to the U.S. military effort. The North Vietnamese might react to aerial devastation as Great Britain had in World War II, when the German air raids had only strengthened British resolve to defeat Hitler. Furthermore, the Foreign Relations Committee chairman felt the Russians might cooperate in bringing about a diplomatic conference on southeast Asia if the air strikes were suspended, but would resist negotiations while the bombing continued. Fulbright approved of Johnson's proposal at Baltimore for a Mekong River Valley economic development program, but essentially his approbation was based on the belief that peace would have to be established as a precondition for inaugurating such a program. He did not think the Mekong River development project was feasible while the war continued.

Fulbright's Associated Press interview was followed by a series of speeches delivered by dissenting Senators in late April. On April 28 Senator Church praised the contributions of Fulbright, Mansfield, and Aiken to the Vietnam debate by inserting into the *Congressional Record* Arthur Krock's column in the April 22 *New York Times*. Krock complimented the three members of the Foreign Relations Committee for responsibly fulfilling their constitutional role in advising the President on foreign affairs. In Krock's opinion, Fulbright had received "unwarranted abuse" from the President's advisers for recommending a temporary suspension of the bombing. He considered the "hysterical attacks on Senator Fulbright" to be evidence that the administration refused to even consider Fulbright's idea.

Krock was complimentary of Mansfield's April 21 speech in the Senate, in which he had proposed the reconvening of the Geneva Conference on the limited basis of guaranteeing the neutrality of Cambodia. Mansfield hoped a Cambodian neutrality agreement would be the preliminary to a diplomatic solution for Vietnam. The Montana Senator's response to the Johns Hopkins address was similar to that of Fulbright in extolling the President's call for unconditional discussions. But Robert McNamara announced another expansion of the war on the same day of Mansfield's speech, prompting Arthur Krock's foreboding conclusion: "Continued escalation of the Vietnam war on a steadily rising scale is our only policy for the restoration of peace in southeast Asia."

Senator Church characterized Joseph Kraft's columns as unusually perceptive analyses of the Vietnam crisis, and placed Kraft's April 23 *Washington Evening Star* article in the *Record*. Kraft maintained that the United States must achieve a negotiated settlement immediately, before the great communist powers became directly involved in southeast Asia. He viewed the substantial reduction in Vietcong attacks during early April as a propitious development. "Taken together with the expressions of such figures as the Pope, Senator J. William Fulbright, Democrat, of Arkansas, and Prime Minister Lester Pearson, of Canada," the nascent decline in Vietcong military activity presented excellent prospects for a cease-fire and discussions. Kraft warned that if the opportunity were missed, a vicious circle of reciprocal escalation would ensue which might lead to general war. In response to the American bombing of North Vietnam the Russians had just begun to provide the North Vietnamese with antiaircraft missiles, whereupon China attempted to surpass the Soviets in demonstrating their support for Hanoi by officially recruiting volunteers, a policy the Chinese had not followed since they intervened in Korea in 1950.

On the same day Church lauded the recommendations of Fulbright and Mansfield, the Foreign Relations Committee chairman delivered a brief set of remarks on the Senate floor. Fulbright approved of Senator Aiken's recent speeches advocating a vigorous role for the United Nations in extricating the United States from the tragic predicament in Vietnam. He inserted a *New York Times* editorial into the *Record* which eulogized the "dean of Senate Republicans." The *Times* editorial criticized the State Department's refusal to encourage U.N. Secretary General U Thant in his campaign to initiate negotiations on the southeast Asian crisis. The April 28 Senate statements by Fulbright and Church, as well as the other dissenting speeches and interviews in April, offered a definite

140

alternative to the Johnson administration's course in Vietnam. In the critics' view, the United States should suspend the air war against North Vietnam as an initial step towards reconvening the Geneva Conference. They believed Secretary General U Thant should be encouraged in his efforts to arrange a diplomatic conference on southeast Asia.

It was clear in late April that an expansion of the war was opposed by several senior members of the Senate Foreign Relations Committee, columnists Joseph Kraft and Walter Lippmann, the *New York Times* editorialists, U Thant and other Asian statesmen, Prime Minister Pearson, and Charles de Gaulle. And in addition to this rather formidable array of world leaders, other prestigious statesmen were privately advising the President against escalation in Vietnam, notably Adlai Stevenson and George Ball.

The Senators and foreign policy analysts associated with Fulbright, Mansfield, and Lippmann could not match the powerful influence exerted on American diplomacy by a bipartisan political coalition which was rapidly coalescing in support of the escalation policy during the spring of 1965. William S. White, a Johnson intimate, described this "new coalition" in a *Washington Post* column at the end of April. White extolled the leadership of the Republican Party for forming an alliance with the Democratic administration and rallying to the aid of "a country called the United States of America in its terrible and thankless task of standing up all over the world against creeping Communist aggression." Senate Republican Leader Everett Dirksen and House Republican Leader Gerald R. Ford of Michigan were providing invaluable assistance for the President's resolute opposition to communist expansion. Dwight Eisenhower, Richard Nixon, and Barry Goldwater were dutifully aiding the Republican Congressional leadership in this indispensable concert for the survival of America. In contrast to White's panegyrics of the Republicans and the Johnson administration, the journalist lamented that "the chief foreign policy spokesman in the Senate, J. William Fulbright," and Senate Majority Leader Mike Mansfield were "hampering rather than supporting this Government in its all-national policy to resist Communist aggression in South Vietnam." According to White, Fulbright and Mansfield were the leaders of "a thin but vocal fringe of the Democratic Party" which invariably opposed American military actions in the Congo, Latin America, Vietnam, or any region of the globe where American power was honorably employed.

The Vietnam war was temporarily eclipsed during late April by an American military intervention in the diminutive and impoverished isle of Hispaniola in the Caribbean Sea. The eastern half of that island, the Dominican Republic, was being ravaged by a rebellion against the pro-American regime of Donald Reid Cabral. By April 28, Reid had been overthrown and civil war was being waged between the regular Dominican military leaders and the supporters of Juan Bosch, the former president. Ambassador W. Tapley Bennett sent a series of cables to Washington, the first emphasizing the need to protect American lives, the later cables predicting "another Cuba" if the military junta's forces collapsed. C.I.A. reports of communist support for the Bosch movement began to alarm Washington officials, especially Thomas C. Mann, the administration's principal Latin American specialist and a zealous anti-communist. President Johnson briefly conferred with Thomas Mann and then instructed McNamara to order U.S. Marines to the Dominican Republic.

A few hours after Fulbright delivered his April 28 Senate remarks on the U.N. and Vietnam, he was summoned to an emergency meeting at the White House. Fulbright and other members of Congress were informed of the administration's decision to land Marines in Santo Domingo for the sole purpose of protecting the lives of Americans and other foreigners. Johnson said nothing of communist infiltration. Fulbright did not express any disapproval of an intervention to save American lives. Later that evening Johnson appeared before national television cameras to report the Congressional leadership's endorsement of his actions in the Dominican crisis. He told the American people the Marines had landed "in order to give protection to hundreds of Americans who are still in the Dominican Republic and to escort them safely back to this country." Again there was no mention of communism. Yet in another televised address on May 2, the President abruptly reversed the justification for his decision and represented the intervention as a campaign to prevent communist expansion in the Caribbean: "The American nation cannot, and must not, and will not permit the establishment of another Communist government in the Western Hemisphere."

Fulbright, Morse, and Senator Eugene McCarthy of Minnesota were privately disturbed by the apparent metamorphosis of the intervention from an evacuation of American citizens to a crusade against Caribbean communism. Johnson had actually been agitated by the threat of communism on Hispaniola since late April. John Bartlow Martin, the former ambassador to the Dominican Republic, later recounted a conversation at the White House on April 30 in which Johnson proclaimed he did not "intend to sit here with my hands tied and let Castro take that island. What can we do in Vietnam if we can't clean up the Dominican Republic?" Fulbright was perplexed in late April by the conflicting reports on the revolt in Santo Domingo. The chairman and Senator McCarthy contended that the Foreign Relations Committee should conduct a thorough classified investigation of the Dominican intervention. Dodd, Frank Lausche of Ohio, Karl Mundt of South Dakota, and other members of the committee were disgruntled at the prospect of an exhaustive analysis regarding the administration's actions, but at the insistence of Fulbright and McCarthy the Dominican hearings began in the summer of 1965.

In the beginning Fulbright was not certain that the administration had committed an egregious error in landing over 20,000 American troops in Santo Domingo. But he began to doubt Johnson's judgment in May. His misgivings were intensified by the administration's failure to demonstrate that communists dominated the Dominican revolt. Fulbright became more determined to hold extended hearings after he listened to C.I.A. Director William F. Raborn's briefing shortly after the President decided to intervene. The Foreign Relations Committee chairman asked Raborn to specify the number of communists who were definitely involved in the Dominican revolution. Raborn replied, "Well, we identified three."

Fulbright devoted much of his attention to Vietnam and Europe (and also to domestic affairs) in the six weeks following the initial deployment of Marines in the Dominican Republic. In early May the President requested from Congress a $700 million supplemental appropriation, explaining that the passage of this appropriation would be considered a vote of confidence in his entire Vietnam policies. The $700 million was primarily intended to cover military expenditures for Vietnam. The Senate passed the measure by an overwhelmingly pro-administration vote on May 6, with only Morse, Gruening, and Gaylord Nelson of Wisconsin in opposition.

Fulbright was in Europe at the time of the May 6 vote, delivering speeches before the Consultative Assembly of the Council of Europe in Strasbourg. At a Strasbourg news conference on May 5, Fulbright advocated a Vietnam settlement based on the 1954 Geneva agreements. The Senator called for the United Nations to supervise the elections envisaged by the Geneva accords. He believed the elections would lead to a nationalist regime which would be determined to maintain its independence of China. A week later in a speech at Vienna he stated that the emerging reconciliation between East and West "can be arrested and reversed at any time by the spreading impact of such occurrences as the tragic war in Vietnam." In the Strasbourg and Vienna statements Fulbright did not deviate from his earlier professions of support for President

Johnson despite his appeal for a negotiated settlement.

The Johnson administration suspended the bombing from May 12 until May 18, prompting Arthur Krock to disparage the previous Rusk-McNamara invective against Fulbright's proposal for a bombing halt. Three weeks earlier Fulbright's recommendation had provoked a deluge of fiery rhetoric from the Cabinet officials portraying a bombing pause as a betrayal of America's friends and an encouragement to aggressors. Now in May the administration was experimenting with a temporary cessation of the air raids against North Vietnam. In a May 18 *New York Times* column Krock observed, "The reason why this swift turnabout has embarrassed the Administration is the round of shooting-from-the-hip which the highest officials engaged in, with Fulbright's suggestion as their target." The air strikes were resumed a few hours after the Krock column was written. Fulbright initially responded to the bombing suspension with mildly favorable comments, but in an October, 1965 *Meet the Press* appearance he argued that a bombing pause must continue much longer than six days to represent a genuine peace initiative. For Fulbright, suspension of the air attacks should have been the prelude to negotiations; for the administration, the ephemeral bombing halt of May was essentially a strategem in the campaign to silence its critics.

Fulbright delivered his last speeches in support of the Johnson administration during the first half of June. Johnson requested an additional $89 million of economic assistance to South Vietnam, Thailand, and Laos in a June 1 special message to Congress. Fulbright endorsed the proposal for expanded economic assistance in a Senate address of June 7 entitled "Political and Economic Reconstruction in South Vietnam." The June 7 speech was Fulbright's first important Senate discourse concerning Vietnam in 1965. He had been relatively quiet in the aftermath of his confrontation with Rusk and McNamara in April. Earlier in the year he had expressed his views on Vietnam in press conferences, interviews, occasional references to southeast Asia in speeches on foreign affairs, and insertions of articles and editorials into the *Congressional Record*, such as Frank Church's January *Ramparts* interview and the April *New York Times* editorial advocating a vigorous role for the U.N. in southeast Asia. But Fulbright had eschewed major Senate addresses on Vietnam until June 7, partially in order to refrain from direct public criticism of the President.

"Political and Economic Reconstruction in South Vietnam" dealt with two basic issues: Johnson's June 1 request, and the nascent nationalism of underdeveloped countries in Asia, Latin America, and Africa. Fulbright maintained that in Vietnam, as in the other emerging nations, nationalism was a far more powerful force than communist or capitalist ideology. "Communism" or "democracy" would be successful "in the underdeveloped world to the extent—and only to the extent—that they make themselves the friends of the new nationalism." In Fulbright's opinion, the Vietnamese people were not concerned with the ideological struggle between communism and democracy. He believed the Vietnamese were principally interested in tending their rice crops, educating their children, building a viable economy, and ending the violence which ravaged their land. The meeting of their human needs was "the only meaningful objective of the war and the probable condition of success in the war." Fulbright regretted that American efforts to stabilize South Vietnam's political and economic structure had been dwarfed by American expenditures for war in southeast Asia.

On June 7, Fulbright also enumerated Johnson's recommendations for additional economic assistance to South Vietnam, Thailand, and Laos. Approximately half of the $89 million would be used to finance Saigon's imports of iron, steel, and other materials necessary for industrial expansion, and another $25 million would provide electrical, agricultural, and medical services. The remaining $19 million would be utilized for the development of the Mekong River Basin. It was ironic that Fulbright was endorsing the Mekong project, for in 1965 he had been scathingly critical of such bilateral assistance programs during the foreign aid debate. He had argued that economic aid should be multilateral rather than bilateral in order to attenuate charges of American "neocolonialism" and to help prevent the United States from becoming increasingly entangled in the internal affairs of other nations. He had denied that vital American interests were involved in many of the underdeveloped nations receiving American aid, including South Vietnam.

Fulbright's June 7 endorsement of the President's Baltimore proposals for a Mekong River Basin project was partially inconsistent with his April Associated Press interview, in which he had doubted the feasibility of inaugurating the Mekong program while the war continued. Even during the June 7 Senate debate Fulbright was ambivalent about the Mekong project. Shortly after he praised Johnson's Baltimore proposals in his speech, he became engaged in a dialogue with Senator Gruening in which he said, "So long as the war is continuing as it is, what we can do in this respect [the Mekong River Basin development] will be limited." Fulbright's fundamental position was probably summarized a few moments later when he reiterated his support for a negotiated settlement as a

145

precondition for the economic development of southeast Asia. He concluded: "What appeals to me the most about the proposal is the possibility—at least, I hope it is a probability that the emphasis will be changed from escalating the war into construction or reconstruction and development in this area."

An unlikely coalition formed on June 7 to oppose the President's request for expanded economic assistance to South Vietnam. Wayne Morse and Ernest Gruening, the two most radical opponents of Johnson's Vietnam policy, were aligned with a group of Senators who had enthusiastically endorsed expenditures for military escalation in Vietnam, including Bourke Hickenlooper of Iowa and Strom Thurmond of South Carolina. The improbable Hickenlooper-Morse alliance acquired 26 total votes. Johnson's recommendations were supported by the majority of the dissenters against escalation, incuding Fulbright, Mansfield, McGovern, Nelson, and Church. Dirksen and several fervent anti-communists also voted in favor of the administration. Jacob Javits and Robert Kennedy of New York, as well as Edward Kennedy of Massachusetts and one-third of the entire Senate, abstained. The economic aid passed the Senate by a vote of 42 to 26.

An understanding of the June 7 debate is enhanced by analyzing the arguments of Hickenlooper, Fulbright, and Morse. Hickenlooper asserted that the Senate did not have sufficient information concerning the economic assistance proposal. In contrast, the Iowa Senator considered the military requests to have been quite specific. When Fulbright pressed him to define exactly what the military appropriations would be used for in Vietnam, the most specific explanations Hickenlooper could offer were "for war," "for military activity," and finally, for "victory." Fulbright challenged Hickenlooper's statements, maintaining (in a reference to the May 7 passage of Johnson's military appropriation request) "the Senate even more precipitately authorized and appropriated $700 million, and no one knew whether that was to be used for nuclear bombs for Peiping, or what it was to be used for." According to Fulbright, the Senators associated with Hickenlooper had complete trust in the military leaders and allowed them to spend billions of dollars as they pleased, but this pro-military Senate bloc would subject any meager request for economic assistance to the most rigorous and pedantic examination.

Wayne Morse represented the smallest faction in the Senate. He did not oppose all economic aid to South Vietnam, but he did oppose the addition of $89 million to the foreign aid bill, wryly observing, "We had better get the war settled first. I have a little difficulty with the paradox of pouring $89 million of aid into a country and, at the same time, destroying $89 million worth of property." Morse concluded that the Senate could never be adequately informed about the expenditure of the $89 million in a land 9,000 miles from American shores, just as it had not possessed precise information regarding the $700 million military appropriation in May.

The Oregon Senator emphasized the fact that the Vietcong would inevitably capture many of the materials sent to rural areas. Morse's perspective was accurate, for the Vietcong dominated many rural areas throughout South Vietnam and had frequently captured American commodities (and American weapons) intended for South Vietnam's development. Hickenlooper's June 7 orations on the merits of military appropriations as opposed to economic appropriations were vacuous, although he was probably correct to criticize the precipitous manner in which Johnson demanded Senate approval of his economic aid request. During the June 7 debate Fulbright had failed to explain how the United States could effectively begin an enlarged program of economic development in South Vietnam while the level of violence was expanding. Considering his colloquy with Gruening and his earlier doubts about the Mekong project, he may have actually agreed with Morse's analysis of the prospects for economic aid. But Fulbright was determined to encourage any conciliatory gestures towards the Vietnamese communists in 1965, including the Johns Hopkins proposals. In the early period of the escalation it was common for many of the dissenting Senators and other critics of the American intervention to hope that the President's Baltimore address would be an initial step towards a negotiated settlement; as late as 1966 the southeast Asian expert Bernard Fall suggested that one component of a diplomatic solution for Vietnam might be to "restate and expand the idea of a flexible area-wide rehabilitation program" on the basis of the Baltimore speech.

Fulbright's June 7 speech had not offered an alternative to the Johnson administration's policy. "Political and Economic Reconstruction in South Vietnam" dealt with the broad philosophical problem of the underdeveloped nations' responses to the West, and it described the technical points of the President's June 1 message to Congress. In a major Senate address on June 15, Fulbright attempted to clarify his position concerning the alternatives confronting American policy in southeast Asia. The June 15 speech, entitled "The War in Vietnam" was unquestionably Fulbright's most important Senate discourse on Vietnam in 1965. Johnson invited Fulbright to the White House in early June and delivered another monologue on his valiant resistance to the extremists' demands for massive expansion of the war. This conference with the President was a unique occurrence in Fulbright's career, for it was the only time he ever allowed Johnson to read the draft of one of his speeches. The June 15 address would constitute Fulbright's final effort to maintain his precarious strategy of praising the President while opposing military escalation in Vietnam.

On June 15 Fulbright rejected the arguments in favor of an intensified air war. According to the Foreign Relations Committee chairman, the bombing of North Vietnam had failed to weaken the military capability of the Vietcong. An expanded bombing campaign would invite a large-scale intervention of North Vietnamese troops, and this intervention "in turn would probably draw the United States into a bloody and protracted jungle war in which the strategic advantage would be with the other side." A decision to escalate the air war to unprecedented levels of destruction would risk Chinese intervention or nuclear war. Fulbright believed that a military victory in Vietnam could be attained "only at a cost far exceeding the requirements of our interest and honor." American policy should be based upon a determination "to end the war at the earliest possible time by a negotiated settlement involving major concessions by both sides." The Senator reiterated his appeal for a return to all the specifications of the 1954 Geneva accords.

Fulbright recited the litany of President Johnson's attempts to end the war through negotiations, above all the Johns Hopkins initiatives. The North Vietnamese and Chinese, he alleged, had repudiated the President's magnanimous offer to enter unconditional discussions for terminating the war. Fulbright admitted, however, that American policy had been characterized by serious errors in the past. In Fulbright's view, the most important mistake had been American encouragement for President Ngo Dinh Diem's violations of the Geneva accords in failing to hold the elections envisaged by the 1954 agreements. He suggested that in contemplating a new diplomatic conference it would be well for both sides to recall the destructive consequences of their past violations of the Geneva agreements. Fulbright contended American policy had erred most recently by failing to halt the bombing for more than the perfunctory six-day suspension in May, 1965.

Despite his admissions of American blunders in the past and his predictions of disaster if the U.S. military intervention expanded, Fulbright urged a restrained "holding action" in Vietnam. He explicitly repudiated a precipitous withdrawal. In a turgid, one-sentence paragraph, Fulbright delineated the justification for American involvement in the Vietnam war, the identical justification he would spend much of the next decade condemning: "I am opposed to unconditional withdrawal from South Vietnam because such action would betray our obligation to people we have promised to defend, because it would weaken or destroy the credibility of American guarantees to other countries, and because such a withdrawal would encourage the view in Peiping and elsewhere that guerrilla wars supported from outside are a relatively safe and inexpensive way of expanding Communist power." It was the most inaccurate statement Fulbright ever uttered on the subject of Vietnam, and it obviously contradicted his earlier views that the Vietnamese conflict was fundamentally a civil war. This sentence of the June 15 speech rendered Fulbright vulnerable to legitimate criticisms that he had vacillated, and it also facilitated Johnson's ad hominem charges that Fulbright's later denunciations of the Vietnam war were based on personal pique.

The vague notion that "Peiping" either was supporting or was planning to support the communist guerrillas in southeast Asia seriously weakened Fulbright's analysis on June 15. It is ironic that his opposition to the Vietnam escalation in 1965 was hampered by a perspective on China as an aggressive power, for it is clear in retrospect that one of the greatest achievements of Fulbright's 32-year career in Congress was his contribution to the improvement of Sino-American relations from 1966 to 1972. Early in 1966, Fulbright would begin to use the Foreign Relations Committee as a forum for publicizing dissident ideas about China, Vietnam, and the anticommunist ideology. The historian Daniel Yergin has described the 1966 China and Vietnam hearings as "the crucial beginning step within the United States to making a realistic appraisal of American policy in Asia." The genesis of Fulbright's criticism of Johnson's Asian policy can be traced to his January, 1965 *Time* interview (if not earlier to the "Bridges East and West" speech of 1964). In the *Time* interview, he advocated probing "for areas of peaceful contact" with China, and he expected the Chinese leadership to gradually become less hostile towards the United States. He was reading voraciously in the scholarly literature on Far Eastern politics, economics, and history, and his ideas about the Chinese communists were in flux. But his public statements on China in the first half of 1965 were erratic; at times he would revert to to the hoary platitudes of the Cold War concerning Chinese malevolence, and on other occations he would appeal for an amelioration of Sino-American relations.

Perhaps Fulbright felt that he was significantly qualifying his June 15 statement by specifying "unconditional" withdrawal as being unwise. Many other important critics of escalation opposed immediate abandonment of South Vietnam. Walter Lippmann's

June 17 column in the *Washington Post* warned against any desire to "scuttle and run." Lippmann was still trying to avoid direct personal criticism of Johnson and even complimented him in one passage of the June 17 column:

> In the task of containing the expansion of communism there is no substitute for the building up of strong and viable states which command the respect of the mass of their people. The President, of course, knows this, and has frequently said it.

Nevertheless, Lippmann joined Fulbright in adamantly opposing any expansion of the American military involvement in southeast Asia. The June 15 Senate address and the June 17 column were probably their final major efforts to conciliate the President.

Fulbright's speech fomented a debate which continued throughout the summer of 1965. The Arkansas Senator became involved in a discussion with several of his colleagues immediately after he finished speaking on June 15. Stuart Symington of Missouri commended Fulbright's address, especially the passages recounting American peace initiatives. He asked Fulbright to clarify his statement about an American holding action. Fulbright maintained that if a diplomatic conference could not be arranged immediately, then the United States should remain in South Vietnam until October and then negotiate a settlement. He thought the monsoons and the Vietcong offensive would be subsiding in October, thus making that month an auspicious juncture to end the war.

A few moments after Symington's remarks, Ernest Gruening eulogized Fulbright's exposition for opposing escalation, endorsing a return to the Geneva agreements, and reminding the Senate that U.S. policy in Vietnam had been plagued by errors in the past. Gruening observed that official U.S. pronouncements rarely admitted any American mistakes or any American violations of the Geneva accords, and he congratulated Fulbright for demonstrating that both sides had violated the 1954 agreements. No one was surprised when Fulbright agreed with Gruening's accolade of his speech.

The June 15 discussion between Fulbright and Republican Senator Leverett Saltonstall of Massachusetts was much less mellifluous than the Fulbright-Gruening dialogue. Saltonstall was disturbed by the intransigence of "the other side" in rejecting negotiations. According to the Massachusetts Republican, the North Vietnamese had transgressed against agreements in the past and might try to do so again after future negotiations. He felt that Fulbright had not adequately confronted this problem. Fulbright did not deign to repeat his arguments that both sides had violated previous agreements, and responded to Saltonstall by saying he was primarily concerned with preventing an expansion of the conflict "either of worldwide proportions or even as large as the war in Korea was. I do not think that the Korean war was beneficial to the world or to that country." A few days after the June 15 speech, the Republican Congressional leadership delivered a vigorous indictment of the Arkansas Senator's position. House Minority Leader Gerald R. Ford and Senate Minority Leader Everett Dirksen held a joint news conference to attack Fulbright's proposal for a negotiated settlement involving "major concessions by both sides." The Republican doyens averred that far from obtaining a compromise with "the Communists," the United States should specify the concessions which it would refuse to offer.

The controversy between Fulbright and important Republican politicians reverberated through the summer of 1965. In contrast to Fulbright's plea for a bombing halt, on July 7 Representative Ford called for immediate air strikes against antiaircraft missile sites in North Vietnam. Reporters asked Ford at a news conference whether he would make this recommendation if he knew Russian technicians were present at the missile sites. He replied, "If the Soviet Union wants to participate in escalating the war, I'm fearful they'll have to take the consequences." Fulbright described the Ford statement as the precise attitude which would risk a direct confrontation with the Soviet Union and possibly lead to general war.

Richard Nixon launched the most vitriolic Republican attack on Fulbright in September. While he was visiting South Vietnam on September 5, Nixon held a news conference in which he criticized Fulbright's "so-called peace feelers." Nixon accused Fulbright of advocating a "soft line" towards North Vietnam and "a major concession to the Communists in order to get peace." He pontificated that negotiations would only reward aggression, prolong the war, "encourage our enemies, and discourage our friends." The former Vice President complained that military escalation was proceeding too slowly, and a massive enlargement of U.S. ground forces in Vietnam would be necessary. In Nixon's view, the United States must prepare to fight for four more years, if not longer: "We cannot afford to leave without a victory over aggression." Nixon also warned on September 5 that if President Johnson "compromised with the Communists" the Republicans would make Vietnam a campaign issue in the 1966 Congressional elections and the 1968 Presidential election.

Immediately following Fulbright's June 15 speech, President Johnson called an impromptu press conference in which he challenged the Congressional critics of his Vietnam policies to repeal the Gulf of Tonkin Resolution. Johnson claimed that virtually all of the dissenting members of Congress had fully approved his policies by passing the Tonkin Resolution and hence could not properly oppose the escalation. Pro-administration Senators and journalists seconded the President's assertions. Senator Dodd answered Fulbright by inserting in the *Congressional Record* an endorsement of Johnson's Vietnam policy by A.F.L.-C.I.O president George Meany. On June 23 Johnson's old friend William S. White denounced the recalcitrant bloc of Senators who wistfully dreamed of rendering the communist aggressors more tractable by granting excessive concessions while requesting nothing in return. "The most important of these Senators," White affirmed, "is William Fulbright of Arkansas." According to White, the Chinese laughed at America's dissenting Senators and did not even attempt to conceal their objective of subjugating South Vietnam. The *Washington Post* columnist bemoaned the pernicious consequences of the Arkansas Senator's "appeasement": "Sen. Fulbright demanded a suspension of American bombing of the nests of aggression in North Vietnam. The predictable result was more and more aggression."

On June 16, the front-page news reports in both the *Washington Post* and the *New York Times* interpreted the Fulbright address as evidence that the President was beginning to recognize the wisdom in avoiding any expansion of the southeast Asian conflict. The *Times* reported that an increasing number of Senators shared Fulbright's disenchantment with escalation, including McGovern, Church, Morse, Gruening, Albert Gore of Tennessee, and the Republicans Javits, Aiken, and John Sherman Cooper of Kentucky. The *Post* described Fulbright's appeal for "major concessions" as an "authoritative" statement of President Johnson's position, largely because of Fulbright's extended conference with the President the day before the speech. The President's press conference dispelled this erroneous notion. Two weeks later an Evans and Novak column entitled "LBJ and the Peace Bloc" expressed a more accurate view, arguing that Johnson was conducting a June offensive to disarm his critics. He had recently persuaded Senator Church to deliver a speech praising his ceaseless efforts to restore peace to southeast Asia, and he had even convinced the "arch-critic" Wayne Morse to remain silent during much of June. Finally, Johnson had successfully beseeched Fulbright to extol the Presidential peace initiatives on June 15, although the mild criticisms in the Foreign Relations Committee chairman's address were sufficient to incur the President's wrath.

Several Senators commended Fulbright's analysis of the Vietnam crisis in the weeks following June 15. Joseph Clark of Pennsylvania endorsed Fulbright's plea for a return to the Geneva accords and placed the June 17 Lippmann column in the *Record*. Mike Mansfield opined that Fulbright's remarks "constituted a most constructive contribution to the consideration of this critical issue and were in the best traditions of the Senate." Mansfield inserted into the *Record* a June 17 *New York Times* editorial approving the Fulbright speech. The *Times* lauded Fulbright for opposing both "unconditional withdrawal" and escalation: "At a time when some military men and some Republican leaders, including Representative Laird, of Wisconsin, are returning to the Goldwater objective of total victory and calling for stepped-up bombing of North Vietnam, this re-statement of aims is invaluable." Every American, the editorial maintained, should read Fulbright's exposition that military victory could be attained "only at a cost far exceeding the requirements of our interest and our honor." The *Times* was hopeful the President agreed with Fulbright's arguments.

Senator Church addressed the Senate on July 1 and complimented Fulbright's contributions to the Vietnam debate. He placed in the *Record* an address Fulbright had delivered to the Rhodes scholars' reunion at Swarthmore College on June 19. Fulbright's caustic tone on June 19 provided a remarkable contrast to his tortured efforts to praise the President while opposing escalation only four days earlier. The Arkansas Senator contended that in the past few months the state of world politics had "taken an ominous turn," and he quoted Mark Twain's bitter "War Prayer" to illustrate the belligerent passions unleashed by the Dominican and Vietnamese interventions. Fulbright advised his fellow Rhodes scholars that "the nations are sliding back into the self-righteous and crusading spirit of the cold war" essentially because "the crises in Vietnam and the Dominican Republic are affecting matters far beyond the frontiers of the countries concerned." The Dominican intervention threatened to destroy the future of the once promising Alliance for Progress. The Vietnam war, Fulbright charged, was damaging American relations with Eastern European countries and other small nations by disseminating the belief that America was an implacable enemy of nationalism in the underdeveloped world.

Fulbright believed that the most destructive result of the Vietnamese and Dominican crises was the degeneration of Soviet-American relations. The detente which had begun to develop in 1963 was now held in abeyance, largely because of the remote involvements in Indochina and Hispaniola. Fulbright warned against the dogmatism which envisaged international relations as an immense arena of conflict between virtuous Americans and nefarious communists. It would be constructive, he observed, for Americans to realize that the Russians and the Chinese sincerely believed their policies would lead to world peace and freedom, the identical ultimate goals which Americans pursued. The remark about the Chinese was a general philosophical reflection, but it clearly bore no resemblance to Dean Rusk's specter of the Chinese conspiracy against freedom.

Fulbright's June 19 address was a harbinger of the Senator's increasingly vociferous opposition to the Vietnam war during the next decade. His rationale for giving the June 15 speech was clear; he would offer one last major effort to praise Johnson's diplomacy, and if this failed to magnify his influence he would be forced to become openly critical of the President. Frank Church recognized Fulbright's emerging role as a public dissenter on July 1, when he described the Rhodes scholars' reunion discourse as "stark, but accurate." These were the ideas, Church asseverated, of "a political philosopher and foreign affairs analyst unexcelled among those who have held political office in the modern history of our Republic." The Idaho Senator's encomium may have been exaggerated, but he obviously understood and welcomed Fulbright's burgeoning determination to publicly oppose the Johnson administration's foreign policies.

It should be acknowledged that the language of the June 19 Swarthmore address was highly generalized and theoretical. Fulbright did not refer specifically to President Johnson or any official of the executive branch. The Swarthmore address was somewhat similar to "Old Myths and New Realities" in its theoretical tenor, although "Old Myths" was optimistic about the possibility of improving Soviet-American relations, in contrast to the profound pessimism of the June 19, 1965 speech. The March 25, 1964 Senate address had endorsed the policy of supporting the non-communist regime in Saigon, while the only references to southeast Asia in the Swarthmore speech were reflections about the Vietnam war's pernicious impact upon America's relations with the Soviet Union and the underdeveloped nations of the world.

Fulbright delivered his final effort to praise Johnson's foreign policy in the June 15 Senate discourse in order to exhaust the moribund strategy of hoping to enhance his private influence at the White House by publicly supporting the President. At the time many of Fulbright's aides and several journalists were arguing that he had a responsibility to avoid an open break with the President which could destroy the Senator politically. During the next three months Fulbright would conclude that his ultimate responsibility

154

consisted of attempting to educate and marshal the force of public opinion against an anti-communist consensus which seemed invincible in 1965.

In 1964 Fulbright's fear that public criticism of Johnson's foreign policy would strengthen Goldwater had contributed to the Senator's support for the Presidential decisions on Vietnam. But in 1965 a resolve to challenge the administration's anti-communist assumptions was replacing his earlier fear that public opposition to the Vietnam policy might ignite an onslaught of McCarthyism from the radical right. During April 1965 he had publicly confronted the Secretary of State and the Secretary of Defense over the escalation of the bombings against North Vietnam, and in his June 19 speech he implied that the contemporary American policies in Vietnam and the Dominican Republic were reviving the crusading anti-communism of the early Cold War and severely damaging the prospects for Soviet-American detente. In 1965, of course, Fulbright no longer had to fear the Goldwater candidacy; but a more important reason for his nascent determination to oppose the President's diplomacy was his realization that the administration's southeast Asian and Dominican policies were displaying the rigid, global anti-communism the Senator had excoriated in "Old Myths and New Realities." There was a vital difference between Fulbright's views in "Old Myths and New Realities" and his perspective in the June 19 Swarthmore address, for in March 1964 he had directed his critique of militant anti-communism against Goldwater and the radical right; by the summer of 1965 he was beginning to direct similar criticisms against the foreign policy of President Lyndon Johnson.

Chapter Seven

Challenge to the Anti-Communist Consensus, Summer to Autumn, 1965

Senator Fulbright's first caustic criticisms of specific Johnson policies dealt with the administration's diplomacy in Europe and Latin America. It was perhaps logical that the Senator's indictment of the administration's global anti-communism was initially focused upon these two regions, because before 1965 Fulbright had primarily been knowledgeable about U.S. relations with Europe and Latin America. During July he asserted that the President was failing to resist the efforts of extreme anti-communists to sabotage American relations with eastern Europe. The dispute over eastern European policy was a comparatively minor episode; but Fulbright's opposition to the administration's intervention in the Dominican Republic precipitated an irreparable break between the Senator and the President and inaugurated Fulbright's role as a dissenter over the last three and a half years of Johnson's Presidency.

In July, 1965, Fulbright criticized the administration for failing to resist extremist pressures against the policy of "building bridges" to the communist world. The most recent example of this failure, in Fulbright's opinion, was the rupture of negotiations between the Rumanian government and the Firestone Company for the design and engineering of synthetic-rubber plants. A Firestone competitor and an extreme right-wing organization called Young Americans for Freedom had conducted an anti-communist crusade against the Firestone-Rumanian agreements, claiming that the tires which the Rumanian plants would produce would eventually be used by the Vietcong. The opponents of the Firestone contract had denounced it for indirectly supplying the Chinese communists with badly needed technical expertise. Fulbright decried the administration's curious reluctance to support Firestone against the extremists. Such stalwart anti-communists as William F.

Buckley, Jr., Strom Thurmond, and John Tower raged at Fulbright and extolled the Y.A.F. for its patriotic stand against the Rumanians who had recently joined with Russian and Chinese officials in a condemnation of American "open acts of war" in Vietnam. Joseph Kraft, Mansfield, and Morse endorsed Fulbright's position.

George Ball investigated Fulbright's allegations, and in the fall of 1965 the State Department successfully defended a group of American tobacco companies that had purchased eastern European tobacco against another series of attacks from anti-communist pressure groups. Fulbright wrote a letter to President Johnson in October congratulating the State Department for its handling of the eastern European tobacco purchases in contrast to its weak performance in the Firestone fiasco. The Senator was well aware that the Firestone affair and the tobacco purchases were quite insignificant in comparison to Vietnam. But he felt that an important principle was involved, for if extreme anti-communist organizations could influence the U.S. government then there was little hope of conducting a rational foreign policy. Fulbright believed that his criticism during the Firestone episode may have led to the more reasonable State Department response to American trade with eastern Europe in the fall of 1965. This lesson strengthened Fulbright's resolution that he could influence the Johnson administration only by public dissent, and not by private conversations and memoranda.

Fulbright's foreign policy statements in July were highly annoying to President Johnson. The President was increasingly excluding Fulbright and U.N. Ambassabor Adlai Stevenson from any significant role in the administration's deliberations on Vietnam. The responses of Fulbright and Stevenson to the Vietnam escalation in early 1965 were somewhat similar. Stevenson was favorably impressed by Johnson's Baltimore speech. The U.N. Ambassador's memoranda to the President in 1965, however, had clearly warned against a precipitous expansion of American military operations in Indochina. Stevenson was disturbed by the bombing of North Vietnam. In a March memorandum to the President, Stevenson predicted that a limited bombing campaign from the 17th to the 19th parallels would not "produce indications of a [North Vietnamese] willingness to negotiate." He speculated that an expansion of the bombing to population centers and industrial targets farther north might lead the North Vietnamese to negotiate, or it might provoke them into more extensive infiltration of North Vietnamese forces into South Vietnam via Laos; but regardless of Hanoi's reaction, world opinion would be outraged by massive American bombing of

Asian noncombatants. Thus, Stevenson concluded that "the world-wide political consequences of such action [air strikes against major population centers] would very probably outweigh any military advantages it might produce." In his view, the United States should enter negotiations even if the Vietnamese communists did not provide any favorable assurances in advance concerning the results of the negotiations.

Stevenson had been cooperating with U Thant in attempting to arrange negotiations on southeast Asia. In his April 28 memorandum to the President, Stevenson stated that U Thant was "strongly convinced that the continued use of force holds no promise for a settlement but only the ever-increasing danger of wider warfare, as well as a reorientation of Soviet foreign policy from limited detente with the West to close cooperation with Communist China." U Thant proposed a cessation of hostilities in Vietnam, followed by "immediate discussions, in whatever manner the parties prefer, designed to strengthen and maintain the cessation of military activity and to seek the basis for a more permanent settlement." Stevenson argued that a positive American response to the Secretary General's appeal would reinforce the favorable international impression created by the President's Baltimore speech. "The Secretary-General," Stevenson maintained, "by making such an appeal, would become the center of the effort to terminate hostilities in Vietnam, a fact which would facilitate a later move on our part—should we so desire—to involve the United Nations in the role of supervising or policing a negotiated settlement." Stevenson frequently advised the State Department of U Thant's proposal for discussions "with Saigon, Hanoi, and the Viet Cong seated at the table." On July 7 the Ambassador informed the Department that U Thant had recently "repeated several times that it was only realistic that the discussions of a cease-fire would have to include those [the Viet Cong] who are doing the fighting."

The U.N. Ambassador's occasional vague references to "Chinese expansionist plans" weakened the logic of his private communications to the President. Stevenson did not adduce evidence to support the allegations of Chinese expansionism. His statements on China in his 1965 memoranda were difficult to explain, especially in light of later reports by David Halberstam and other writers of his private opposition to the administration's China policy. Perhaps Stevenson believed that whatever influence he still retained as an official of Lyndon Johnson's administration would vanish if he challenged the President's view of China as an aggressor. Fulbright's private communications to the President may have been more blunt than Stevenson's in describing escalation in Vietnam as a disastrous course, but the Senator's April memorandum to the President had also suffered from the reluctance to refute the Cold War hostility toward China. Whatever the explanation for their inaccurate statements on China in 1965, the administration obviously rejected the Fulbright and Stevenson recommendations for a negotiated settlement in southeast Asia.

Stevenson's basic perspective on Vietnam may have been revealed on a July 12 British Broadcasting Corporation television program. B.B.C. correspondent Robin Day asked Stevenson to comment on a recent exposition by J. William Fulbright in which the Senator had hoped for a "greater emphasis on the political aspects of the problem" in Vietnam. Stevenson replied that all knowledgeable observers of southeast Asian affairs had always regarded the political problems as "uppermost," and "that this isn't a war that can be resolved by military means, nor can we find a solution there except by political means." A few moments later he dutifully defended American policy, reminding his interviewer that "Communist China is doing its very best to destroy the United Nations," while President Johnson had offered unconditional discussions on Vietnam. Many of Stevenson's friends later maintained that he was depressed by having to defend Johnson's Vietnam and Dominican policies and was considering resigning in early July.

Fulbright and Stevenson were also similar during 1965 in their revulsion against Johnson's policy in the Dominican Republic . The administration's Dominican intervention strengthened their suspicions that the Vietnam escalation was mistaken and precipitous. In late May, Stevenson privately remarked that "if we did so badly in the Dominican Republic, I now wonder about our policy in Vietnam." Among the major public or private critics of Johnson's foreign policy, Fulbright and Stevenson were probably the two statesmen who were most disturbed by the intervention in the Dominican Republic. Several of Stevenson's associates later said the Dominican crisis troubled Stevenson more than any other incident that occurred during his years in the U.N. The Ambassador thought the American intervention had alienated public opinion throughout Latin America and devastated the principle of peaceful international settlements. David Schoenbrun later publicly reported that Stevenson had described the intervention as a "massive blunder." The President was disgusted by the Schoenbrun story and instructed his press secretary to dismiss it as a disservice to Stevenson's memory.

The extent of the Fulbright-Stevenson communication concerning Hispaniola is not clear. In June Stevenson wrote a letter to Fulbright, his friend for thirty years, but it dealt with placing restraints on the arms race. Fulbright sent a note to Stevenson on July 13 to forward a constituent's request for an appointment, apologizing for writing about such a mundane matter during a time of crisis in southeast Asia and the Caribbean. "Now you see in action," the Senator wryly observed in a poignant admission of his lack of power, "the major function of a Senator." Fulbright's pessimism did not inhibit his determination to challenge the administration's foreign policy, for the Foreign Relations Committee investigation into the Dominican crisis was scheduled to begin in mid-July. The Senator's melancholy was deepened when Ambassador Stevenson died of a heart attack on July 14, the day the Dominican hearings began.

The decision to hold the hearings accelerated the decline in Fulbright's influence with the administration. On July 27 Johnson summoned eleven Congressional leaders to the White House to discuss the proposals for increasing the number of American ground forces fighting in Vietnam. In earlier White House meetings the President had asked Fulbright and Mansfield for their expected dissenting opinions only after all the other Congressional leaders had approved of his policies. Now in late July, Johnson's relationship with Fulbright had deteriorated to the extent that the President did not deign to invite him to the July 27 discussions. Historian George Herring has described the July deliberations as "the closest thing to a formal decision for war in Vietnam" and yet the President excluded the chairman of the Senate Foreign Relations Committee from participating in the White House discussions regarding the decision. George Smathers, who ranked tenth on the Foreign Relations Committee but was a staunch anti-communist, was asked to attend rather than Fulbright. Thus the President isolated Mansfield, who alone argued against sending more troops. And even Mansfield declared that he would loyally support Johnson's decision, despite his profound skepticism regarding expansion of the war.

The President had decided to increase the number of American troops in South Vietnam from the 75,000 already there to a total of approximately 200,000; but he publicly announced at his July 28 press conference an increase of only 50,000, although he indicated more troops would be sent to Vietnam later to halt the "mounting aggression":

> We did not choose to be the guardians at the gate, but there is no one else.
> Nor would surrender in Vietnam bring peace, because we learned from Hitler at Munich that success only feeds the appetite of aggression. The battle would be renewed in

one country and then another country, bring with it perhaps even larger and crueler conflict, as we have learned from the lessons of history . . .

I have asked the commanding general, General Westmoreland, what more he needs to meet this mounting aggression. He has told me. We will meet his needs. I have today ordered to Vietnam the Air Mobile Division and certain other forces which will raise our fighting strength from 75,000 to 125,000 almost immediately. Additional forces will be needed later, and they will be sent as requested . . .

Johnson continued to mislead Congress and the public as to the significance of his decisions, denying that he had authorized any change in policy. The United States would have to fight in Vietnam to maintain the credibility of its promises to all other nations, but the President added, "We do not want an expanding struggle with consequences that no one can perceive."

Fulbright was engrossed in his analysis of the Dominican intervention in the six weeks after the July 28 press conference. The Senator's doubts about the administration's actions had increased in May, when the executive branch exaggerated the danger of communist infiltration in Santo Domingo. Admiral Raborn had informed Fulbright on April 28 that three communists were participating in the revolt, but in May U.S. officials publicized a list of fifty-eight communists who were allegedly allied with the pro-Bosch forces. Many of the fifty-eight people on the list could not have played a role in the rebellion because they were either in prison or out of the country during April. The administration valiantly attempted to explain why fifty-eight communists represented an ominous threat to a nation of three and a half million people. Dean Rusk declared that the precise number of communists involved in the revolt was unimportant, for "There was a time when Hitler sat in a beer hall in Munich with seven people."

President Johnson was much more imaginative than Rusk in portraying the hideous specter of aggression on Hispaniola, revealing at a June 17 press conference that "some 1,500 innocent people were murdered and shot, and their heads cut off." This account mystified the President's aides, for the atrocities Johnson described never occurred. Fulbright would eventually regard the falsehood about the 1,500 decapitations as the classic example of Johnson's duplicity. During the Dominican hearings Fulbright asked Thomas Mann to explain the President's macabre assertion on June 17. Mann simply refused to believe that Johnson had uttered the statement, even after Fulbright produced the official State Department

162

bulletin of the June 17 press conference, which reprinted the President's exact words.

The Dominican hearings remained closed to the public for many years after 1965. In 1968 Haynes Johnson and Bernard Gwertzman acquired a limited amount of information concerning the hearings from an anonymous source. (The two journalists were writing a biography of Fulbright.) The most important administration witnesses were Rusk, Thomas Mann, and Cyrus Vance. The administration spokesmen argued that a military dictatorship was preferable to a communist regime. Mann contended that any popular front which included communists was "per se a dangerous thing." He conceded that Juan Bosch was not a communist, but he considered Bosch a "poet professor type" who could be controlled by the Dominican leftists, many of whom had been trained in Cuba. Mann believed that if the communists established a dictatorship in the Dominican Republic, "Haiti would fall within thirty minutes." During the course of the hearings it became clear that the administration thought the communist threat in the Dominican Republic was related to leftist subversion in Colombia, Venezuela, Uruguay, Argentina, Bolivia, Ecuador, British Guiana, Haiti, Honduras, Panama, and Guatemala.

Fulbright observed that according to Mann's analysis, the United States should intervene against any movement in Latin America which had communist support. The result of such a policy would be to restrict the alternatives for all Latin America to either communist rule or a military junta. In Fulbright's opinion, the widespread dissatisfaction with the status quo in Latin America was justified. If the policy of indiscriminate intervention persisted, then some dissident Latin Americans might conclude that they must become communists in order to change the reactionary character of their pro-United States governments. He hoped the administration would adopt a policy of encouraging changes in Latin America by aiding non-communist reformist groups. Specifically, he argued that the administration would have been wise to support the non-communist rebels in the Dominican revolt.

The Foreign Relations Committee was hopelessly divided over the Dominican controversy. Dodd, Lausche, Hickenlooper, and Russell Long assumed an aggressive anti-communist position during the debate. The largest faction on the committee did not support the "hawks," but also failed to criticize the President. Only four or five Senators supported Fulbright's resolute criticism of the administration's actions. Although the hearings were private, Dodd and others publicly accused Fulbright of being prejudiced against the administration. The dispute within the committee became so acrimonious in August that Fulbright publicly speculated about resigning his chairmanship. The committee never wrote a report on its investigation.

Johnson temporarily reversed his efforts to isolate Fulbright and instructed Rusk to begin another series of private discussions with the Foreign Relations Committee chairman. Fulbright wrote a speech in August elucidating his opposition to the intervention. His administrative assistant warned him not to deliver it, because it would precipitate an "irreparable break" with Johnson. The aide told Fulbright, "You practically call him a liar." Fulbright discussed his critique of American policy in Santo Domingo with several foreign affairs analysts, including Carl Marcy, the Chief of Staff of the Foreign Relations Committee. When Marcy and the others agreed that his analysis was accurate, Fulbright decided to deliver the address.

On September 15, 1965, Fulbright presented his conclusions concerning the Dominican crisis to the Senate. He asserted that the United States intervened in the Dominican Republic not primarily to save lives, as the administration originally contended, but to prevent the victory of a revolutionary movement which was judged to be communist-dominated. According to Fulbright, the Dominican communists did not participate in planning the revolution. Although they quickly joined the revolt after it erupted, the communists never controlled the rebel forces. The fear of "another Cuba" had little basis in the evidence offered to the Foreign Relations Committee; on the contrary, Fulbright maintained that a chaotic situation existed "in which no single faction was dominant at the outset and in which everybody, including the United States, had opportunities to influence the shape and course of the rebellion." In their apprehension lest Santo Domingo become another Cuba, American officials had forgotten that there was a crucial difference between communist support and communist control of a political movement, and that it was quite possible to compete with the communists for influence in a reformist coalition rather than abandoning it to them. The Senator argued that the policy followed in the Dominican Republic would have disastrous consequences if applied throughout Latin America:

> Since just about every revolutionary movement is likely to attract communist support, at least in the beginning, the approach followed in the Dominican Republic, if consistently pursued, must inevitably make us the enemy of all revolutions and therefore the ally of all the unpopular and corrupt oligarchies of the hemisphere.

Fulbright criticized the administration's failure to exert a positive influence on the course of events during the early days of the rebellion. On April 25, Juan Bosch's party (the P.R.D. or Dominican Revolutionary Party) had requested a "United States presence," and on April 27 the rebels asked for American mediation and a negotiated settlement. Fulbright observed that the P.R.D. entreaty presented an excellent opportunity to encourage the moderate forces involved in the coup, either by providing American mediation or officially indicating that the United States would not oppose a regime controlled by the P.R.D. But both requests were rejected on the basis of exaggerated estimates of communist infiltration into the revolutionary forces and hostility to Juan Bosch's return to power. Pedro Bartolome Benoit, the leader of the military junta, appealed for American military assistance on April 28. Only American intervention, Benoit pleaded, could avert a communist coup. Washington responded that if Benoit would say American lives were in danger the United States would intervene. Benoit then changed his rationale for needing American troops so as to conform to Washington's response, and within hours Marines landed in Santo Domingo. After an exhaustive analysis of W. Tapley Bennett's cables to Washington, Fulbright decided that the fear of communism was the Ambassador's fundamental reason for recommending the military intervention. The Senator's conclusion followed: "The danger to American lives was more a pretext than a reason for the massive U.S. intervention that began on the evening of April 28."

On September 15 Fulbright denounced the reversal in American attitudes toward Juan Bosch and the P.R.D. during the period from September, 1963 to April, 1965. Fulbright recalled that the United States had supported Bosch while he was President of the Dominican Republic during 1963. President Kennedy attributed such importance to the Dominican President's success that he sent Vice President Johnson and Senator Hubert Humphrey to Bosch's inauguration in February, 1963. Fulbright reminded the Senate that in December, 1962, Bosch had triumphed in the first free and honest election ever held in the Dominican Republic. After Bosch was overthrown by a military coup in September, 1963, the United States had not recognized the successor regime for three months. The Johnson administration had finally recognized the government which succeeded Bosch only after it began conducting military operations against a band of alleged communist guerrillas in the Dominican mountains. Fulbright strongly suspected that the successor government exaggerated the threat of the guerrillas in order to secure American recognition.

In Fulbright's view, the administration had erred in opposing the P.R.D.'s return to power after Donald Reid Cabral's regime collapsed in April. The Senator conceded Juan Bosch "was no great success as President," yet Bosch was still "the only freely elected President in Dominican history," and "the only President who was unquestionably in tune with the Alliance for Progress." Bosch himself had not been eager to return to Santo Domingo in April, 1965, but Fulbright emphasized that "the United States was equally adamant against a return to power of Bosch's party, the P.R.D., which is the nearest thing to a mass-based, well-organized party that has ever existed in the Dominican Republic." Fulbright summarized the history of American policy towards the Dominican Republic during the Johnson administration with an unequivocal condemnation: "Thus the United States turned its back on social revolution in Santo Domingo and associated itself with a corrupt and reactionary military oligarchy."

Fulbright proceeded from his indictment of the administration's actions in the Dominican Republic to a general critique of Johnson's foreign policy towards Latin America, observing, "one notes a general tendency on the part of our policymakers not to look beyond a Latin American politician's anti-communism." The Dominican crisis had severely damaged America's reputation among "our true friends" in Latin America, who had supported the ideals of the Alliance for Progress. In the opinion of many Latin American reformists, the United States had suppressed a movement which was sympathetic to the Alliance's goals. The landing of Marines in Santo Domingo violated the O.A.S. Charter's principle of non-intervention, which most Latin Americans considered the quintessence of the inter-American system. Fulbright's reference to the O.A.S. Charter was related to his only passage on Vietnam in the speech; he detected an inconsistency in the administration's zeal to uphold the "ambiguous" commitment to South Vietnam while simultaneously violating a "clear and explicit treaty obligation" in the Americas. The passage on Vietnam was brief, however, and Fulbright did not elaborate upon this argument.

In his September 15 address Fulbright attacked the global anti-communism of the Johnson foreign policies. "Obviously," the Senator concluded, "if we based all our policies on the mere possibility of communism, then we would have to set ourselves against just about every progressive political movement in the world, because almost all such movements are subject to at least the theoretical danger of Communist takeover." The rigid anti-communist approach contradicted the nation's interests, according to Fulbright. He maintained that diplomacy must be based upon developing "prospects that seem probable" rather than forever attempting to

166

anticipate possible dangers of communism.

Fulbright's final major argument on September 15 dealt with the disingenuous manner in which the administration had justified its actions to the public. "U.S. policy," he charged, "was marred by a lack of candor and by misinformation." Fulbright illustrated the lack of candor and misinformation by referring first to the initial assertions that the United States executed the intervention to save American lives, and second by quoting President Johnson's June 17 statement about the 1,500 decapitations in the Dominican Republic. The Senator tersely noted that there was no evidence to support the President's allegation. Fulbright tried to maintain in the speech, and also in a September 15 letter to Johnson, that he was not attacking Johnson personally but only the substance of the President's policies. The distinction was unimportant. As Daniel Yergin has written, "The speech was aimed at the stupidity and what he was soon calling the arrogance of American power but, though he liked to pretend it was not directed also at Johnson, Johnson rightly saw that it was."

Fulbright defined his purpose in delivering the address as an effort to develop guidelines for future policies, and not simply to lambast the administration for its previous errors. The decision to hold the hearings had apparently begun to exert a minor impact on U.S. policy by September 14, when General Wessin y Wessin, who had been one of the leaders of the military junta during late April, left the Dominican Republic under American pressure. In his speech Fulbright described Wessin's departure as "a step in the right direction." A year later in *The Arrogance of Power* Fulbright speculated about the effect of his Dominican address. His September, 1965, exposition may have been a factor, he wrote, in the administration's subsequent support for democratic government in the Dominican Republic, thus repairing some of the damage wrought by the April, 1965 intervention in support of the Dominican military. The Senator also conceded that the O.A.S. and the Inter-American Force which remained in Hispaniola until the summer of 1966 had finally restored a degree of order and stability. But Fulbright did not agree that the election of Joachin Balaguer as President of the Dominican Republic on June 1, 1966 vindicated the intervention, for the power of the reactionary military oligarchy remained unimpaired. Fulbright's skeptical attitude was accurate, especially considering the background of events before the election campaign. In December, 1965, Dominican army tanks had attacked Colonel Caamano and other leaders of the April 24 revolution while they were attending a requiem mass for one of the colonels killed in the revolt. The offices of a pro-Bosch magazine and some pro-Bosch

167

radio and television stations were bombed. The United States claimed to be neutral during the campaign in early 1966, but actually the enormous U.S. embassy provided strong support for the former Trujillist Balaguer, who had held the honorific post of President during the later Trujillo era. And the Dominican oligarchy backed Balaguer. The voting itself was reasonably fair, but the context of American support for Balaguer and the Dominican military's intimidation of some of Bosch's allies strongly influenced the results against Bosch.

In Fulbright's view, the administration's actions during the Dominican crisis had alienated virtually all the reformist movements in Latin America and weakened confidence in America's word and intentions throughout the world. He contended in both the September, 1965 speech and in *The Arrogance of Power* that the American anti-revolutionary bias might drive Latin American reformers into becoming anti-American leftists.

The administration's vehement response to his speech in 1965 shocked Fulbright. Secretary of Defense McNamara described Fulbright's criticism of Ambassador Bennett as "an unfair attack," and claimed there was "no question" that American citizens were endangered by the Dominican revolution. McNamara did not answer the Senator's assertion that U.S. officials exaggerated the communist threat. Senator Richard Russell of Georgia seconded McNamara's defense of Bennett. Bill Moyers, the President's press secretary, dismissed Fulbright's conclusions as totally unjustified. Tom Dodd led the pro-administration Senators in a counterattack against the Foreign Relations Committee chairman. According to Dodd, Fulbright suffered "from an indiscriminate infatuation with revolutions of all kinds, national, democratic, or Communist," as well as a general "tolerance of communism." Russell Long rebuked Fulbright's speech by maintaining, "We have information now that the Communists in the Dominican Republic are stronger than Castro was when he started out to take Cuba." Senator Smathers congratulated Long for his analysis of the Dominican crisis and added, "Castro proved that it was not necessary to have a large number of communists in order to deliver a country to communism." Representative Ford and Senator Dirksen joined the President's Democratic supporters in condemning the Fulbright speech.

In the first few days after September 15, the debate concerning Fulbright's Dominican address did not focus upon the substance of his analysis. Many of Fulbright's opponents argued that the chairman of the Foreign Relations Committee simply did not have the right to deliver such a scathing criticism of the President's foreign policy. William S. White epitomized this attitude when he averred

that
>it is not simply with President Johnson and Secretary of
State Dean Rusk that Fulbright has broken. He has also
broken the unwritten rule of the game, a code which demands of those holding high committee chairmanships—
and uniquely the chairmanship of foreign relations—a degree of self-restraint and personal responsibility not demanded of the rank and file.

In contrast to White, Republican Senator Margaret Chase
Smith of Maine resolutely defended Fulbright's right to dissent,
even though she supported the administration's policy in the
Dominican Republic. Similarly, Eric Sevareid's article in the October 4, 1965 *Washington Evening Star* commended the Foreign Relations Committee's investigation into the Dominican crisis for establishing lessons which would be useful in future policies. Sevareid
did not comment on the substance of Fulbright's conclusions, except
to remark he disagreed with them, but he complimented the Senator when he wrote, "the Fulbright speech was a drama simply
becuse it was unique in this period of consensus and a homogenized
Congress."

Senator Mansfield also rejected the notion that Fulbright's
criticism was irresponsible, although he publicly supported the
administration's Dominican policy. Whether Mansfield privately
agreed with Fulbright's analysis is uncertain. Mansfield had
attended only one of the thirteen Dominican hearings, and he was
reluctant to become involved in an open confrontation with the
executive branch. The Montana Senator tended to believe that he
could influence Johnson's policies more effectively through private
remonstrances rather than vociferous public opposition. Fulbright
had agreed with Mansfield's strategy earlier in 1965, but by the autumn he was convinced of his inability to influence Johnson through
private communications. After Fulbright became a public adversary of the Johnson foreign policies (including the Vietnam war) in
late 1965 and early 1966, he did not cooperate with Mansfield as
closely as he had when the two Senators were privately advising
against escalation in early 1965.

Joseph Kraft, Walter Lippmann, Morse, McGovern, McCarthy,
and Joseph Clark were among the small minority that supported
Fulbright during the Dominican furor. Kraft aptly summarized
Fulbright's position: "With the Dominican case before him, he
sensed a new disposition to identify all social protest with Communist subversion, and a connected tendency to shoot first and
think later." In Kraft's view, the administration's rancorous attacks
on the Dominican address only intensified the doubts Fulbright

raised about U.S. policy in Latin America. The administration failed to resist the extreme anti-communists who were condemning the Foreign Relations Committee chairman. In response to the Fulbright speech, the House of Representatives passed by an overwhelming vote a resolution which endorsed direct American military intervention in Latin America to prevent "subversive action or the threat of it." Armistead Selden of Alabama sponsored the resolution. According to Kraft, Selden was "wrapping himself in the mantle of anti-communism" in order to ensure his re-election. Kraft asserted that the administration had promoted Thomas Mann, Douglas MacArthur II, and other Foreign Service officers within the State Department whose ideas, careers, and reputations were permanently attached to "the era of unsophisticated, monolithic anti-communism." The State Department forces led by Thomas Mann had "practically invited the Selden resolution." Finally, Kraft concluded, "the White House itself seems to be holding anti-communism as a rod to discipline its congressional majority." If Johnson maintained this rigid anti-communist stance, it seemed doubtful that he could respond constructively to the vast social changes sweeping Latin America, Africa, and Asia. Kraft regretted that the President "has gone soft on Goldwaterism."

Walter Lippmann commended Fulbright's Dominican address in his September 28 *Washington Post* column. The amelioration of Soviet-American relations, Lippmann wrote, depended upon encouraging "the prudent and the practical to predominate over the ideological and the hot." "In this country," he continued, "the process will require the resumption of public debate—the kind of debate which Senator Fulbright has once again opened up. For the issue which he has posed in his remarkable speech is the essential issue in our attitude and policy toward the revolutionary condition of our time." Lippmann believed there was no definitive formula which could be applied to determine American foreign policy toward all underdeveloped nations. American diplomacy must be flexible in responding to the infinitely varied circumstances present in Latin American, African, and Asian revolutions. Lippmann recommended a conciliatory attitude or "some kind of accommodation" in order to avoid confrontations with the Soviet Union in the third world. He extolled Fulbright's efforts to revitalize the public dialogue between the administration and its critics. It was imperative to prevent the public debate in America from being monopolized by "the assorted hangers-on, often more Johnsonian than Johnson himself, who are presuming to lay down the rule that only those who conform with the current political improvisations are altogether respectable and quite loyal."

Lippmann had perceived the ultimate significance of the Dominican speech by analyzing it in the global context of Soviet-American relations. Fulbright had criticized far more than the American blunders on a tiny Caribbean island; he had challenged the anti-communist assumptions of an entire era. In evaluating the historical importance of the Dominican address, Daniel Yergin later wrote, "From that moment can be dated the breakup of the cold war consensus and the beginning of a meaningful dissent." As Haynes Johnson described the September speech, "Not since Borah had criticized the sending of the Marines into Nicaragua in the 1920s had the chairman of the Foreign Relations Committee directly challenged an administration of his own party," although "the circumstances were hardly comparable." The Dominican furor had a devastating impact on Fulbright's relationship with Johnson. Many years later the Senator informed an interviewer, "Never again was I consulted." Upon reflecting a moment, he added that he had never been genuinely consulted, for throughout the first half of 1965 Johnson was simply "trying to keep me in bounds, so I wouldn't take issue and embarrass him." Fulbright wrote Johnson a courteous letter in early October, explaining that his speech was intended "to help you in your relations with the countries of Latin America." "Subservience," he reminded Johnson, "cannot, as I see it, help develop new policies or perfect old ones." The President never responded to Fulbright's letter.

During the summer of 1965 Fulbright became convinced that the administration's impetuosity, duplicity, and crusading anti-communism were not confined to U.S. foreign policy in Latin America, but were fundamental characteristics of Johnsonian diplomacy. After his Senate discourse of September 15, Fulbright rapidly began to intensify his critique of the military escalation in Vietnam. In an October 24, 1965, *Meet the Press* appearance he reiterated his appeal for a suspension of the air attacks against North Vietnam, arguing that a bombing halt must continue much longer than the six day pause of May in order to represent a genuine peace initiative. When Peter Lisagor asked him if it was not the function of Republicans to dissent from a Democratic President's foreign policy, Fulbright replied that the great majority of the Republicans endorsed Johnson's actions. "I don't understand," he asserted, "why this consensus has reached such a state that people feel Senators, or particularly this Senator, should not speak about any matter in which he dissents from the current views of the administration."

Throughout the N.B.C. program Fulbright defended his analysis of the Dominican crisis. The Vietnam war was almost totally overshadowing the Dominican intervention by October, and

171

the reports in the *New York Times* and other newspapers concentrated upon Fulbright's recommendations for the Vietnam policy on *Meet the Press*. The White House issued its customary repudiation of Fulbright's Vietnam proposals.

During the fall of 1965, the discussion of Fulbright's dissenting views began to focus on the substance of his ideas, rather than the question of whether he possessed the right to openly criticize President Johnson. E.W. Kenworthy's article in the October 31 *New York Times* presented a succinct assessment of Fulbright's foreign policy positions in the early 1960s. The article was entitled, "Fulbright: Dissenter." Kenworthy recalled that in March, 1961, Fulbright's memorandum on Cuba had urged President Kennedy to tolerate the Castro regime rather than attempting to overthrow it. The Cuban memorandum obviously did not deter Kennedy from authorizing the Bay of Pigs invasion. Kenworthy affirmed that Fulbright had enjoyed a minor success in the summer of 1965, when he was "the prime mover in assembling a group of influential Senators from both parties—who must be nameless—who are credited with re-enforcing the President's growing resistance to those who advocated a call-up of reserve and national guard units last summer." Nevertheless, Kenworthy admitted, Fulbright had been advising Kennedy and then Johnson for five years, yet "much of the advice was, like Robert Frost's road, 'not taken.'" Kenworthy noted the President's hostile reactions to the Dominican address and Fulbright's statement on *Meet the Press*. The article ended with the somber observation that Fulbright's advice "has more effect after the event than on it. And so it almost certainly will be with policy on the Dominican Republic and Vietnam—if, indeed, it has any effect at all."

In retrospect, it is clear Fulbright's relationship with Johnson had been gradually deteriorating ever since the "Old Myths and New Realities" speech of March 25, 1964. A *Newsweek* article in late 1965 compared the two speeches, claiming the Dominican address "echoed his earlier salvo against U.S. foreign policy last year." Actually, there was a crucial difference between the two, for "Old Myths and New Realities" was primarily a theoretical attack on the mythical concept of a relentlessly expansionist, monolithic communist bloc. In contrast, "The Situation in the Dominican Republic" of September, 1965 constituted both a critique of America's global anti-communism and a specific denunciation of the 1965 U.S. intervention in the Dominican Republic. The March, 1964 Senate address did not, of course, criticize American policy in Vietnam. The most controversial passage of "Old Myths and New Realities" dealt with Cuba. Fulbright argued that the United States should accept the reality of the Castro regime as "a distasteful nuisance but not an intolerable danger" and stop flattering "a noisy but minor demagogue as if he were a Napoleonic menace." Throughout 1964 Johnson and Rusk had carefully disassociated the administration from the ideas expressed in "Old Myths and New Realities." Nevertheless, Fulbright's relations with Johnson had remained outwardly amicable after the March, 1964 speech.

Fulbright's objections to the foreign aid bill in late 1964 and early 1965 were a secondary annoyance to the administration. But his dissent against the bombing of North Vietnam in February and his appeal for a negotiated settlement in his April 5 Vietnam memorandum exasperated the President. From March through the June 15 Senate address Fulbright publicly supported the administration, but his proposal for a bombing halt and his resolute opposition to escalation infuriated Johnson. During the summer he began to excoriate the administration's failure to pursue the policy of "building bridges" to the eastern European nations. The process of Fulbright's alienation from President Johnson culminated in his September condemnation of the Dominican intervention. A few weeks after the Dominican controversy subsided, Fulbright decided to inaugurate an exhaustive Foreign Relations Committee investigation of American foreign policy towards Vietnam and China. There would be a vital difference between the Dominican and the Vietnam hearings, for the latter would be not only public, but nationally televised.

Walter Lippmann was Fulbright's most formidable ally in all of the Senator's major confrontations with the Johnson administration. Lippmann and Fulbright had known each other since the 1940s, and the famous columnist had often eulogized the Arkansas Senator. In a preface to Karl Meyer's 1963 collection of Fulbright's speeches Lippmann wrote, "The role he [Fulbright] plays in Washington is an indispensable role. There is no one else who is so powerful, and also so wise and if there were any question of removing him from public life, it would be a national calamity." Lippmann delivered a similar accolade to Fulbright after the "Old Myths and New Realities" speech in 1964. He endorsed Fulbright's position during the 1965 foreign aid dispute. The two men had been discussing Charles de Gaulle's neutralization plan for Vietnam at least as early as May, 1964.

During the first half of 1965 Fulbright and Lippmann eschewed direct personal criticism of President Johnson, but adamantly opposed military escalation in southeast Asia. McGeorge Bundy was having a series of private conferences with Lippmann which were similar to Dean Rusk's discussions with Fulbright. As

173

Ronald Steel has observed, Bundy did not believe that he could convince Lippmann to support military escalation, but he thought Lippmann might be "neutralized," or prevented from publicly opposing the administration's policy. Lippmann was invited to the White House on April 6, a few hours after Johnson had conferred with Fulbright and Mansfield about his Baltimore speech. The President assured Lippmann that "the war had to be won on the non-military side." Bundy hinted to Lippmann that there might be a possibility of a cease-fire. Fulbright and Lippmann later asserted that Johnson misled them about his intentions, and both men began to denounce the Johnson foreign policies in late 1965 and early 1966 when the President's duplicity had become palpable. The extensive personal communications Fulbright and Lippmann had earlier experienced with Rusk, Bundy, and Johnson had virtually ceased by December, 1965.

In 1965 there may have been a minor difference between Fulbright and Lippmann in the sense that Fulbright was incensed by the Dominican intervention, while Lippmann initially argued that the action was defensible, not on the ground that the United States was a "global fire department appointed to stop communism everywhere," but on the "old-fashioned and classical diplomatic ground that the Dominican Republic lies squarely within the sphere of influence of the United States." Later, when it became obvious there had never been a communist threat in Santo Domingo, Lippmann expressed his dismay that Marines had restored the power of a reactionary military dictatorship. And after the Dominican address in September, Lippmann congratulated Fulbright for generating a public dialogue concerning American foreign policy.

In evaluating Fulbright's analysis of the Vietnam war in early 1965 Daniel Yergin has written, "history shows that Fulbright's private arguments to Johnson were perceptive." The Senator had predicted in his April memorandum that "the commitment of a large land army would involve us in a bloody and interminable conflict in which the advantage would lie with the enemy." It is precisely because Fulbright's prediction was so perspicacious that some foreign policy analysts have criticized him for not being more aggressive in opposing the war. Johnson deceived Fulbright in early 1965, but that did not absolve the Senator from the responsibility of exhausting all methods of resistance against a policy he detested, especially in the years 1965 to 1968. Fulbright and the minority of dissenting Senators might have introduced an amendment to terminate the funds for the war during the Johnson administration. Albert Gore later contended that such an action would have "destroyed us and the movement politically." Fulbright reluctantly agreed with Gore's argument in the early period of the war, for he did not sponsor legislation cutting off funds for military operations in southeast Asia until the Nixon administration began.

Fulbright would sponsor an amendment to a defense appropriations bill in 1969 which prohibited the President from using American money to support military operations in Laos and Cambodia. The Fulbright amendment did little or nothing to inhibit Nixon's military incursions into those two countries. Yet it served as the model for the McGovern-Hatfield amendment to end the war and the Cooper-Church amendments restricting military operations in Laos, Thailand, and Cambodia. The Fulbright amendment may have been similar to many of the Arkansas Senator's foreign policy initiatives; in the beginning it appeared to be a failure, but from a long-term perspective it may have strengthened other dissenters in their determination to oppose the war. One should hasten to add that it was late in the Nixon administration before the Congressional movement to cut off funds for the war in Cambodia succeeded in ending the American military involvement in southeast Asia. Perhaps if the movement had begun in 1965 or 1966 its success might not have been so belated. Senator Gore argued, to the contrary, that opposition to the military expenditures would have simply destroyed the anti-war forces before they could gather political momentum. It is clear that the opponents of the war were a small minority in 1965. But perhaps Fulbright offered the most accurate answer to the question of how to oppose the Vietnam war in his 1972 book, *The Crippled Giant*. "In our system," Fulbright maintained, "withholding funds is a legitimate, appropriate—and, all too often, the only effective—means of restraining the executive from initiating, continuing, or extending an unauthorized war, or from taking steps which might lead to war." Fulbright's conclusion might provide a fitting epitaph for an era of Congressional impotence: "It is not a lack of power which has prevented the Congress from ending the war in Indochina but a lack of will." Many opponents of the Vietnam war might have wished Fulbright had arrived at this conclusion in 1965, rather than 1972.

If Fulbright's performance in the arena of direct legislative action was belated, it was nevertheless true that during late 1965 Fulbright began to revitalize the process of public debate concerning American foreign policy. The initial reaction to Fulbright's dissent revealed the potentially repressive nature of the American anti-communist consensus. In the first six months of 1965 Fulbright's efforts to foster an open dialogue with the administration had been sporadic, and his statements had often been inconsistent. During the period when he was largely confining his opposition to

175

private remonstrances, his influence on U.S. foreign policy was negligible. After he became one of President Johnson's foremost adversaries in late 1965, Fulbright's admirers attributed a panoply of magnificent achievements to the Senator: supposedly, he had marshaled the forces of public opinion against a disastrous war, he had restrained the crusading anti-communism of American diplomacy, and he had led Congress' struggle to arrest the expansion of the administration's power. It is doubtful that one Senator could have immediately produced all of these alleged triumphs. Yet Fulbright's dramatic emergence as a dissenter represented a historic accomplishment, for he had demonstrated that an American statesman could repudiate the dogmas of militant anti-communism and retain, or even enhance his public prestige.

Chapter Eight
Fulbright's Opposition to the Vietnam War, 1966-1968

In the aftermath of the Dominican controversy, President Johnson attempted to ostracize Senator Fulbright from Washington's social and political life. A minor example of the administration's bitterness occurred in December, 1965, when the executive branch rejected the Senator's routine request for a jet to fly to a parliamentarian's conference in New Zealand, causing him to make a tedious four-day journey by a propeller plane. The President no longer permitted Fulbright to engage in lengthy private conversations with him at the White House, and an increasing hostility replaced their earlier friendship. In contrast to the President's repudiations of the Foreign Relations Committee chairman's ideas concerning American foreign policy, Johnson began to praise Governor Orval E. Faubus, a zealous anti-communist who was Fulbright's principal critic in Arkansas.

Johnson's efforts to denigrate Fulbright's foreign policy positions did not deter the Senator from fostering a public debate on the Vietnam war in 1966. During early January he reflected upon the most effective strategy to employ in restraining the administration's Far Eastern policy. The President "takes actions," Fulbright informed a constituent in a January 13, 1966 letter, "in the Dominican Republic and in Viet Nam of which I do not approve. Under a strict interpretation of the constitution it would appear that he should request a declaration of war or some other form of approval by the Congress." He observed that Congress possessed the "constitutional recourse" of impeaching the President, but he apparently regarded impeachment as extreme and quixotic, and he did not recommend it. His response to the dilemma of how to oppose the Vietnam war constituted an attempt to mobilize public opinion against the escalation policy, an attempt which Fulbright inaugurated with the Vietnam hearings.

177

The Senate Foreign Relations Committee's nationally televised investigation of the Vietnam war in January and February, 1966 was the first organized forum for dissent against America's involvement in the southeast Asian conflict. There had been sporadic anti-war demonstrations, speeches, and teach-ins in 1965, but there was no genuine, sustained dialogue between the administration and the opponents of the American intervention in Vietnam until 1966. During the 1966 Vietnam hearings the Foreign Relations Committee transferred its respectability to the opposition against the Vietnam war, and began the discrediting of President Johnson's policies which eventually contributed to his decision not to seek reelection in 1968.

In preparation for the Foreign Relations Committee's analysis of the Johnson administration's Asian policy, Fulbright continued to educate himself about Far Eastern affairs. During the December trip to New Zealand he read Han Suyin's *The Crippled Tree*, a Chinese engineer's poignant critique of Western imperialism in early twentieth-century China. He was also reading the works of Jean Lacouture, Philippe Devillers, and Bernard Fall during late 1965 and 1966. He began to regard China's official anti-Western rhetoric as an understandable reaction to Western intervention in Chinese internal affairs from the Opium Wars to the 1940s. The Senator agreed with Lacouture's arguments stressing the autonomy of the Vietcong and deprecating Rusk's perspective on the southeast Asian conflict as "a war of aggression, mounted in the North against the South."

On January 28, 1966, the Foreign Relations Committee scheduled Dean Rusk to testify in support of a bill authorizing a supplemental $415 million in foreign economic aid, most of which would be used in Vietnam. There were 180,000 American soldiers in South Vietnam at the time. Three days earlier the Foreign Affairs Committee in the House of Representatives had responded favorably to the Secretary of State's testimony. Rusk's dialogue with the Senate Foreign Relations Committee was not to be so harmonious. Fulbright's opening statement at the Vietnam hearings revealed that the Senate committee would analyze the central issues of the Vietnam war and would not confine its investigation to the specific proposal for supplemental assistance: "These requests for additional aid cannot be considered in a vacuum, but must be related to the overall political and military situation in Vietnam. I am sure that this hearing will be helpful to the committee and to the public in gaining a better understanding of fundamental questions concerning our involvement in the war."

On the first day of the hearings Fulbright and Senator Albert

Gore questioned Rusk's contention that the administration's massive escalation of the war was justified by the Gulf of Tonkin Resolution. Senator Gore claimed that he had voted for the resolution because he had interpreted it as approving the "specific and appropriate response" [the August 5, 1964 air raid] to the alleged North Vietnamese attacks on the American ships in the Gulf of Tonkin. Rusk replied to Gore's statement by simply reading verbatim the two crucial sections of the resolution. The first section authorized the President to take all necessary measures to prevent aggression. The second stated that since the peace and security of southeast Asia were vital to American national interests, the United States was prepared, as the President determined, to assist any member or protocol state of the Southeast Asia Collective Defense Treaty requesting assistance in defense of its freedom.

Fulbright inserted excerpts from the record of the Senate's August, 1964 debate over the Tonkin Resolution into the transcript of the hearings in order to show that Congress had not intended the resolution to be a blank check for the expansion of the military effort in Indochina without the consent of Congress. These excerpts included the passage (which is discussed in the chapter on 1964) where Fulbright and Senator Gaylord Nelson had agreed that the resolution was "aimed at the problem of further aggression against our ships." During the August, 1964 debate Fulbright and other Senators had rejected the strategy of a massive deployment of ground forces in Vietnam. Rusk responded to Fulbright's assertions concerning the Tonkin Resolution with platitudes about the perfidy of the North Vietnamese and the need to uphold the credibility of America's commitments. The sterility and evasiveness of Rusk's answers at the hearings strengthened the administration's adversaries; as David Halberstam has written, "From that time on, dissent was steadily more respectable and centrist," primarily because of "the failure of the Administration under intense questioning to make a case for the war."

Fulbright asked Rusk to explain why the administration's stated reason for intervening in Vietnam and its terms for withdrawing seemed to be contradictory. American forces were fighting in southeast Asia, according to Rusk, to help the independent sovereign nation of South Vietnam resist the foreign aggression of its neighbor to the north, and the Geneva Agreements of 1954 were an adequate basis for peace. The fallacy in Rusk's argument was that the Geneva Agreements had stipulated that the 17th parallel was "provisional and should not in any way be interpreted as constituting a political and territorial boundary." If one accepted Rusk's doubtful assumption that there were two legitimate states in

Vietnam, the conflict was still basically a civil war, for even according to Rusk's estimates eighty percent of the Vietcong were South Vietnamese and there were no Chinese soldiers in South Vietnam.

Fulbright's crucial question about the Geneva Accords concerned the provision for holding elections by 1956. The United States had not signed the Accords, but Undersecretary of State Walter Bedell Smith had issued a unilateral declaration stating that the United States would refrain from the threat or use of force to disturb the Agreements, and would seek to achieve the unification of Vietnam through free elections. In 1955 Eisenhower had acquiesced as John Foster Dulles supported Diem's refusal to hold the elections which would have, in the opinion of all knowledgeable observers, unified Vietnam under Ho Chi Minh's rule. Rusk stressed the continuity of the Eisenhower, Kennedy, and Johnson policies, and asserted that the United States had failed to honor its commitment with respect to the Geneva Agreements because the prospects for free elections were poor in 1955. Fulbright described this explanation as a "device to get around the settlement" and asked if the prospects for free elections had ever been favorable in 2,000 years of Indochinese history. Rusk then referred to the elections of 1965, which were local elections held only in the areas controlled by the South Vietnamese government, and were irrelevant to the provision for national elections of the Geneva Agreements.

The administration blamed the North Vietnamese for the failure to reconvene the Geneva conference and bring about a cessation of hostilities. According to Rusk, China and North Vietnam had repeatedly stated that negotiations would be possible only when the United States recognized the National Liberation Front (the communist political organization in South Vietnam) as the "sole representative of the South Vietnamese people." Fulbright argued that the NLF's statements were conflicting and that on numerous occasions the NLF had called for free elections to create a coalition government. The administration's position was more bluntly affirmed by retired General Maxwell Taylor, the President's Special Consultant, who informed the Committee in February that the administration intended to achieve sufficient military successes to force the communists to accept an independent, non-communist South Vietnam. When Fulbright asked Taylor if the Vietcong might be included at a diplomatic conference and if a compromise might be reached on the basis of the existing political and military strength, Taylor dramatically replied, "How do you compromise the freedom of 15 million South Vietnamese?"

Thus, for the Johnson administration the corrupt, authoritarian regime of Nguyen Cao Ky and Nguyen Van Thieu was a valiant defender of freedom. As the Vietnam hearings began Johnson flew to Honolulu to confer with Thieu and Ky. Partly this meeting was a successful effort to dominate the news as the Vietnam hearings were opening. The Honolulu conference was probably Johnson's most spectacular justification for the war; the principal administration officials were present, photographs were taken of Johnson embracing Ky, and Johnson delivered an exuberant declaration pledging America's everlasting friendship to the South Vietnamese people. The South Vietnamese, he pronounced, "fight for dreams beyond the din of battle. They fight for the essential rights of human existence—and only the callous or the timid can ignore their cause." Johnson could not accept the logic of the "callous and the timid" "that tyranny 10,000 miles away is not tyranny to concern us—or that subjugation by an armed minority in Asia is different from subjugation by an armed minority in Europe." The President proposed a comprehensive program for development of South Vietnam's economy, medical and educational facilities, and agricultural system which Vice President Hubert Humphrey soon began describing as an Asian or Johnson Doctrine which would, in Humphrey's words, realize "the dream of the Great Society in the great area of Asia, not just here at home."

The Honolulu conference caused considerable dismay among the opponents of the war, partly because General Ky had recently expressed his admiration for Adolf Hitler. More importantly, the Honolulu conference created grave doubts about Johnson's sincerity in claiming that the United States was seeking a political settlement, for the President had solidified the alliance between his administration and the government of Ky and Thieu, who were intransigent in their demand that the National Liberation Front be excluded from all negotiations. When the Secretary of State made his second appearance at the Vietnam hearings in February, Fulbright described the administration's attitude as "adamant" and asked Rusk if the U.S. government supported Ky and Thieu in their refusal to accept a coalition. Rusk evaded the question by relating that Ky had called the NLF the "national enslavement front" at Honolulu.

Johnson revealed that he considered the alleged North Vietnamese-Chinese aggression in southeast Asia to be analogous to the Soviet threat to Europe in the late 1940s by his statement at Honolulu that it was as essential to help "free men" resist "subjugation by armed minorities" in Asia as it was in Europe. "Subjugation by armed minorities" were the famous words of President Truman in the March, 1947 Truman Doctrine speech. When Rusk testified at the hearings in January, he elaborated upon the administration's intention of devising a containment policy for Mao Tse-tung and his presumed surrogate Ho Chi Minh in southeast Asia similar to the containment policy directed against Stalin in Europe.

Rusk began his opening statement at the Vietnam hearings by quoting the basic formula of the Truman Doctrine: "I [Truman] believe that it must be the policy of the United States to support free peoples who are resisting attempted subjugation by armed minorities or by outside pressures." "That is the policy we are applying in Vietnam," Rusk proclaimed. For Rusk, the Vietnam war was ultimately a clash of ideologies, in which the Truman Doctrine must triumph over the Chinese dogma of "wars of national liberation." In 1968 the Foreign Relations Committee again held televised hearings on Vietnam, and Fulbright then questioned Rusk as to whether China or North Vietnam represented the threat to American security. Rusk replied that the danger emanated from the Chinese doctrine of world revolution. Fulbright responded by stating the fact that Lin Piao, the Chinese theorist and politician who was the author of the doctrine, had written that if a war of national liberation fails to "rely on the strength of the masses, but leans wholly on foreign aid, no victory can be won, or consolidated even if it is won."

Thus the Chinese dogma of supporting wars of national liberation emerges to a large extent as an expression of sympathy for third world revolutions rather than a declaration of an intent to sponsor worldwide subversion and guerrilla warfare. The absence of a Chinese military presence in Vietnam was palpable evidence of this fact. Yet at one point in the 1966 hearings Rusk asserted that the struggle in southeast Asia was not the United States' war, but "Mao Tse-tung's war" because of China's support for Ho Chi Minh.

George F. Kennan challenged many of the administration's basic assumptions concerning Vietnam when he testified at the hearings in February. Kennan was a former Ambassador to the Soviet Union and Yugoslavia, and had been chairman of the State Department's Policy Planning committee in the late 1940s. In contrast to Rusk's opening statement that the Truman Doctrine must be applied to southeast Asia as it had been applied to Europe in the 1940s, Kennan began his presentation by calling Vietnam an area of minimal military and industrial importance and asserting that "if we were not already involved in Vietnam I would know of no reason why we should wish to become so involved." Kennan refuted Rusk's contention that a communist Vietnam would be a Chinese satellite, stating that nationalism is a universal human phenomenon and does not magically desert men when they become communists. In the opinion of Fulbright and Kennan, Yugoslavia was an example of a communist country which had followed a neutral course in the East-West rivalry and which certainly was not a puppet of either of the great communist powers. The existence of the Soviet Union as an alternative ally within the communist world rendered it unnecessary for a communist Vietnam to become merely an extension of Chinese power.

The question of whether China was an expansionist state was one of the fundamental issues debated at the Vietnam hearings. Fulbright and Kennan doubted the validity of the popular view of China as a relentlessly aggressive power, observing that there was a significant disparity between the Chinese leaders' violent rhetoric and their actions. Neither Fulbright nor Kennan expressed the opinion that China was not a difficult nation to deal with. Fulbright described their conduct as "outrageous"; Kennan stated that the idea that China was the center of the universe had always presented problems in China's relations with other countries. But the Senator regarded the arrogant anti-American statements of the Chinese as an understandable reaction against the century or more of humiliation inflicted upon China by the West from the Opium Wars to the 1940s. In late February General Taylor conceded in testimony before the Committee that the Chinese had been justified in their grave concern and military response to the possibility of an American invasion in1950, when MacArthur was rapidly advancing towards the Yalu. Fulbright noted that according to Taylor the Indian troops had started the brief war with China in 1962 by moving forward into the disputed territory along the Chinese border. Kennan did not excuse the Chinese aggression in seizing Tibet in 1959, but he pointed out that Chiang Kai-shek was fully in agreement with Mao Tse-tung in considering Tibet to be an integral part of China. Thus,many of the international controversies involving China in the postwar years would have existed even if China had not been a communist country, in Kennan's judgment, for the problems originated in traditional emotions of Chinese nationalism and xenophobia.

Kennan's basic critique of the American policy in Vietnam focused upon his conviction that the Johnson administration had "become enslaved to the dynamics of a single unmanageable situation" and had thereby caused a "grievous disbalance" in the entire global structure of American diplomacy. The administration's escalation of the war had violated one of the cardinal precepts of American foreign policy since the Korean war, which was never to risk a military confrontation with China on the Asian land mass.

Moreover, the Vietnam war forced Russia to compete with China in vilifying the American imperialists, for Chinese propaganda had consistently accused the Russians of somehow being in collusion with the United States in southeast Asia. The central issues of international relations, such as nuclear armaments control agreements, the problems of Germany, and the future of the United Nations and China had all been placed in abeyance in deference to this one remote involvement.

Retired General James Gavin presented the "enclave theory" as an alternative to the escalation policy when he appeared at the hearings in February. In 1954 General Gavin and General Matthew Ridgway had helped persuade President Eisenhower to reject the plan of Admiral Radford, Dulles, and Nixon to intervene in Vietnam to rescue the French from military disaster. Gavin had believed that an intervention would have been a tragic mistake because of the difficulties in the terrain and the possibility of a Chinese intervention. The General reiterated his basic argument in 1966.

Gavin suggested that the United States should confine its military activities to enclaves along the coast or other areas where American air and sea power could be decisive, cease enlarging its ground force, and desist from the bombing of North Vietnam as an initial step toward achieving a diplomatic solution. He urged the administration to renounce its infatuation with the air war, for it was in his estimation one of the greatest illusions of modern times that air power could win a war. The bombings were not "psychologically punishing" the North Vietnamese as Chairman of the Joint Chiefs of Staff Wheeler claimed, but were largely only succeeding in seriously damaging America's image before the court of world opinion.

The American bombing campaign had been utterly futile. Johnson began the systematic bombing of North Vietnam shortly after the Vietcong killed nine Americans at the U.S. base in Pleiku in February, 1965. Apparently the air strikes galvanized the North Vietnamese into even more frenzied military resistance against the Americans, for North Vietnamese infiltration into the south had increased from 800 men per month in the summer of 1965 to 4,500 men monthly in early 1966. Gavin believed that if the Johnson strategy of aerial devastation combined with ever-expanding ground combat forces continued for a substantial length of time, the Chinese would re-open the Korean front and invade South Vietnam. The Chinese, with their virtually limitless supplies of manpower, could probably only be defeated through the use of nuclear weapons in Gavin's opinion. Some of the Chinese leaders were saying at the time that even if China suffered 200 or 300 million casualties from a nuclear attack, they would still have several hundred million people with whom they could win any war. This was perhaps the ultimate fear of the opponents of the Vietnam war; that America had "become enslaved to the dynamics" of a situation which might lead to a nuclear war with China.

Fulbright believed China would intervene in southeast Asia only if the Chinese political leaders concluded that the United States was planning to expand the war into a conquest of North Vietnam or an invasion of the Chinese mainland. The Senator repudiated the view of China as an aggressive power after the pattern of Nazi Germany. The Johnson administration, however, seems to have equated Nazi aggression in Europe with the alleged North Vietnamese and Chinese threat in southeast Asia; those who called for an American withdrawal from Vietnam were advocating appeasement. Rusk replied to the question of whether the Vietnam war presented a situation different from Hitler's expansionism in Europe by saying, "There are differences but there are also enormous similarities." When Rusk spoke of "this phenomenon of aggression" he did not draw a significant distinction between the Vietnam dilemma in the 1960s and German aggression in the 1930s. At one point during the Vietnam hearings Rusk proclaimed, "Hitler could see the Japanese militarists were not stopped in Manchuria. Now, what happens here in southeast Asia if Peiping discovers that Hanoi can move without risk?" Henry Cabot Lodge, the Ambassador to South Vietnam, sent a telegram to the Foreign Relations Committee as the Vietnam hearings were opening declaring: "We, Vietnamese and Americans, are doing in Vietnam in 1966 what the free nations failed to do in 1936 when Hitler went into the Rhineland."

Fulbright tried to refute the notion that there was a basic similarity between the China of Mao Tse-tung and the Germany of Hitler in his book *The Arrogance of Power*. This book was based on the Vietnam hearings and a series of lectures the Senator delivered in April, 1966 at Johns Hopkins University. "China," the Senator wrote, "is not judged to be aggressive because of her actions; she is presumed to be aggressive because she is communist." The ferocity of Peking's language had obscured the fact that China had allowed her neighbors to remain independent. China had withdrawn her troops from North Korea in 1958 although there was no external pressure to do so, and had not attempted to dominate the weak and non-aligned nation of Burma. Fulbright agreed with Kennan that even though North Vietnam was to some extent dependent on China for economic and logistical support to prosecute the war, North

185

Vietnam remained substantially in control of its own affairs.

Fulbright did not romanticize China. He stated that the Chinese would have to abandon their ancient image of China as the celestial empire in a world of barbarians and their more recent role as the nominal champion of world revolution before an amelioration of American-Chinese relations could occur. But Fulbright depicted the basic American perspective on the Vietnam war as the consummate example of the ideological prejudice which had distorted the judgments of Americans since the 1940s. Ho Chi Minh was the hated tyrant, while Ky and Thieu were valiant democrats fighting for their nation's freedom; North Vietnam was China's puppet while South Vietnam was America's stalwart ally; and China was the true aggressor in southeast Asia despite the fact that there were no Chinese troops on the soil of China's southern neighbor, whereas the hundreds of thousands (over 200,000 in 1966, over 500,000 in 1968) of American soldiers in a land 8,000 miles from America's shores were resisting foreign aggression.

If the United States considered it vital to its national interests to construct a bulwark against the alleged "Chinese imperialism" in Vietnam, Vietnamese nationalism alone could have provided that bulwark. Americans must acknowledge, Fulbright wrote, that Ho Chi Minh and his communist allies in South Vietnam represented the genuine nationalist movement of Vietnam, which was the only nation in the world which won its independence from colonial rule under communist leadership.

Fulbright argued that the unilateral nature of the American intervention in Vietnam indicated that America's allies did not share the Johnson administration's view of the conflict as a manifestation of international communist aggression. He believed any political settlement would have to be only tolerable and not satisfactory, such as the 1962 Geneva Accords providing for the neutralization of Laos. Fulbright admitted at the Vietnam hearings that it was true, as Rusk never tired of asseverating, that the North Vietnamese had consistently violated those agreements by infiltrating troops and equipment through Laos to assist the communists in South Vietnam. But as unsatisfactory as the 1962 Accords were, Fulbright asserted that they were diplomatic triumphs in the sense that hundreds of thousands of American soldiers were not engaged in the Sisyphean task of eliminating the communist guerrillas from the jungles of Laos.

The Foreign Relations Committee succeeded in strengthening the opposition to the war in 1966 despite several difficulties during the hearings. Fulbright could not persuade General Matthew Ridgway to testify before the Committee. Ridgway held profound doubts about the war and might have powerfully reinforced Kennan's views, but he could not bring himself to publicly criticize a war while American troops were still fighting. Senator Mansfield did not make a significant contribution to the Committee's investigation of the Vietnam policy, atttending only one of the six hearings. A minority of hawks on the Committee continued to praise the administration and disparage Fulbright's foreign policy positions. Nevertheless, Fulbright was receiving far more support from the members of the Foreign Relations Committee in 1966 than he had a year earlier. During the Dominican controversy probably only four or five Senators supported Fulbright; by the time of the Vietnam hearings and the "Arrogance of Power" speeches of early 1966, approximately ten of the nineteen members of the Committee agreed with Fulbright's critique of America's crusading anti-communism.

The Fulbright hearings gradually produced a crucial and salutary change in television coverage of Vietnam, despite the failure of C.B.S. to carry the Kennan hearing. C.B.S. would have absorbed a financial loss if it had covered the Kennan hearing, and some of the C.B.S. executives were reluctant to publicize the controversial ideas of an intellectual who was not an administration witness. However, N.B.C. televised the Kennan hearing, and C.B.S. televised four of the six hearings, including Gavin's testimony. Before the Vietnam hearings, television had been a reliable ally of the administration, usually reporting pro-war goals and statements without criticism. The fact that administration witnesses, and especially Dean Rusk, delivered the builk of the testimony legitimized the Vietnam hearings to the public. But it was obvious that Rusk's answers to the difficult questions at the hearings had not been convincing. During the Vietnam hearings, for the first time national television reported in detail the dissenting views of critics such as Fulbright, Morse, and Gore. After the hearings, the television networks exhibited an increasing tendency to report both pro-war and anti-war analyses of the southeast Asian conflict.

In Fulbright's "Arrogance of Power" speeches of April, 1966 the Senator intensified and elaborated upon his indictment of the Johnson administration's foreign policy. The speeches formed the nucleus of his book *The Arrogance of Power* (published several months later) in which Fulbright summarized the basic foreign policy proposals he had advocated in 1964, 1965, and 1966. One part of the book reiterated the theme of his "Old Myths and New Realities" and "Bridges East and West" speeches of 1964 in appealing for the policy of "building bridges" to the communist world. Another chapter reiterated the thesis of Fulbright's September, 1965

Dominican address. The most detailed sections of the book dealt with the controversies over America's Asian policy which Fulbright, Rusk, Taylor, Gavin, and Kennan had debated at the Vietnam hearings.

In *The Arrogance of Power* Fulbright delineated a program for the eventual restoration of peace in Vietnam. The initial point in his program was a recommendation that the South Vietnamese government should seek negotiations with the National Liberation Front. The United States should remind the contemporary regime in Saigon, the Senator maintained, that America would not become committed to the objective of complete military victory for the government of Ky and Thieu or any successor government. "At the same time," he continued, "as the Saigon government makes direct overtures to the National Liberation Front the United States and South Vietnam together should propose negotiations for a cease-fire among military representatives of four separate negotiating parties: the United States and South Vietnam, North Vietnam and the National Liberation Front." While the United States was inaugurating these peace initiatives, it should terminate the bombing of North Vietnam and pledge to withdraw American military forces from Vietnam.

According to Fulbright, the four principal belligerents should direct their negotiations toward organizing a national referendum acceptable to the South Vietnamese government and to the National Liberation Front. The United States should commit itself explicitly to accept the results of the national referendum in order to allay suspicions that America and the South Vietnamese government would repeat the error of 1956, when the Diem regime failed to hold the elections envisaged by the Geneva Agreements. In Fulbright's opinion, "the outcome of a referendum in South Vietnam cannot be predicted," but he observed that elections might reveal "the full diversity of South Vietnamese society, with the National Liberation Front emerging as a major political force in the country but with the Buddhists and Catholics, the Cao Dai and the Hoa Hao also showing themselves to be important forces in their respective zones of influence."

After the principal belligerents arranged a cease fire and a national referendum for South Vietnam, Fulbright proposed that "an international conference should be convened to guarantee the arrangements made by the belligerents and to plan a future referendum on the reunification of North Vietnam and South Vietnam." All of the great powers, including the Soviet Union and China, should participate in this conference. In addition to the plans for the reunification of Vietnam, the international conference

188

should negotiate a multilateral agreement for the neutralization of all southeast Asia.

If the negotiations failed, Fulbright conceded that the United States should retire to General Gavin's "enclave theory," although the Senator did not refer to Gavin's theory by name. One should emphasize that Fulbright proposed the coastal enclave strategy only if determined, constant, and sincere American efforts to negotiate a peaceful settlement failed. The administration, of course, repudiated Fulbright's peace program.

The Senator concluded his plea for the restoration of peace in southeast Asia by quoting a speech Charles de Gaulle delivered in Cambodia on September 1, 1966. De Gaulle predicted a triumph for American diplomacy if the United States followed a course of accommodation and neutralization in Vietnam: "In view of the power, wealth, and influence at present attained by the United States, the act of renouncing, in its turn, a distant expedition once it appears unprofitable and unjustifiable and of substituting for it an international arrangement organizing the peace and development of an important region of the world, will not, in the final analysis, involve anything that could injure its pride, interfere with its ideals and jeopardize its interests. On the contrary, in taking a path so true to the Western genius, what an audience would the United States recapture from one end of the world to the other, and what an opportunity would peace find on the scene and everywhere else."

In a memorable passage of *The Arrogance of Power*, Fulbright defended the right of a patriot to advocate dissident ideas concerning American diplomacy. "Gradually but unmistakably," he wrote, "America is showing signs of that arrogance of power which has afflicted, weakened and in some cases destroyed great nations in the past. In so doing we are not living up to our capacity and promise as a civilized example for the world. The measure of our falling short is the measure of the patriot's duty of dissent." Fulbright urged Americans to eschew "the arrogance of power, the tendency of great nations to equate power with virtue and major responsibilities with a universal mission."

In reminding the republic that foreign adventurism had frequently wrought the decline of great nations in the past, Fulbright often compared the American crusade in southeast Asia to the disastrous Athenian expedition against Syracuse in ancient history. At a hearing during the spring of 1966, the Senator reflected:

> It seems to me the best we could get out of it, if we were to have a total victory, would be another authoritarian regime, which would not be much to show for billions for dollars and thousands of lives, and, I think, the loss of the

confidence of our important allies.

I keep having this persistent thought that some historian in the year 3000 will be comparing our exploit in southeast Asia to Athens' attack on Syracuse. It is the classic case of a misjudged situation . . .

I have made a suggestion, a very feeble one, for which I am sure I will have very few followers. I think it was in accordance with the views of General Ridgway, General Gavin, and Mr. Kennan, that we should de-escalate this war and seek a conference in the nature of a compromise, because it is not an issue which warrants enormous sacrifice of life and money. I said it reminded me of Syracuse. In that case they also had a debate, and there was a great division of opinion, and the side that finally decided it won by a very narrow margin,but it was a disaster and a catastrophe that we have been paying for ever since.

President Johnson interpreted the Senator's "arrogance of power" rhetoric as a personal attack upon his administration. Fulbright continued to argue that his criticisms were directed against the substance of Johnson's foreign policy, and were not accusations that Lyndon Johnson was an arrogant politician. In a May, 1966 letter to the President, Fulbright attempted to clarify the thesis of his speeches: "Greece, Rome, Spain, England, Germany, and others lost their pre-eminence because of failure to recognize their limitations, or, as I called it,the arrogance of their power; and my hope is that this country, presently the greatest and the most powerful in the world, may learn by the mistakes of its predecessors." He added the he was confident America would not succumb to the "arrogance of power" under President Johnson's leadership. This additional comment was not consistent with some of the more critical passages in Fulbright's speeches; it was part of a forlorn effort to deter Johnson's tendency to personalize their conflict. The Senator had written a somewhat similar letter to the President in March, 1966, requesting that the administration should at least devote careful study to his proposal for the neutralization of Vietnam "before it is discarded as unreasonable." The Department of State, he observed, had recently rejected the neutralization idea "as being quite unthinkable." He respectfully recommended that the Policy Planning Staff conduct a thorough investigation of the neutralization proposal.

The President's remarks at a Chicago fund-raising dinner in mid-May, 1966 delineated his response towards Fulbright's attempt to restore a modicum of direct communication between the Foreign Relations Committee chairman and the administration. Johnson disparaged the opponents of the Vietnam war with the following animadversions: "I do not think that those men who are out there fighting for us tonight think that we should enjoy the luxury of fighting each other back home. There will be Nervous Nellies and some who become frustrated and bothered and break ranks under the strain and turn on their leaders, their own country, and their own fighting men."

Fulbright and four other Senators displayed impressive political courage when they voted in favor of an attempt to repeal the Gulf of Tonkin Resolution on March 1, 1966. The Senate rejected the repeal of the Resolution by the overwhelming margin of ninety-two to five, and the administration cited this triumph as evidence of Congress' supposedly enthusiastic support for Johnson's escalation policy. Fifteen Senate critics of the war failed to vote for such a politically dangerous, direct confrontation with the administration. The five Senators in dissent were Fulbright, Morse, Gruening, Eugene McCarthy, and Stephen Young of Ohio. In their biographies of President Johnson and Fulbright, Doris Kearns and Haynes Johnson neglected to mention the dissenters' effort to repeal the Gulf of Tonkin Resolution. This omission was unfortunate, because the abortive repeal attempt was an important demonstration of Fulbright's relentless determination to oppose the escalation policy. Haynes Johnson and Kearns do not even seem to have known about the March 1 Senate vote on repeal. Kearns contended that the Foreign Relations Committee hearings were not related to any direct legislative challenge to Johnson's Vietnam policy, but this contention was incorrect, for the repeal movement clearly constituted a direct challenge to the administration's policy and it was related to the hearings, which were constantly referred to during the Senate debate over repeal. The Vietnam hearings ended a few days before the vote, and other hearings on the war and U.S. policy in Asia resumed a few days after the March 1 vote. After the debacle of the ninety-two to five re-affirmation of the Resolution, Fulbright did not advocate any additional attempts to obtain repeal until the dissenters could expect to gain substantially more than five votes; in 1966 such attempts had no chance of winning a majority, and the administration publicized such results as the March 1 vote as endorsements of escalation. Nevertheless, Fulbright had shown that he was not afraid to publicly repudiate the Gulf of Tonkin Resolution.

By the spring of 1966, a pattern had emerged which would persist, with minor variations, for the remainder of Johnson's Presidency. Throughout the interminable period of American military escalation during 1966, 1967 and early 1968, Fulbright repeatedly urged a cessation of the military intervention and pleaded for the

191

neutralization of Vietnam. The administration incessantly reiterated its position and dismissed the Foreign Relations Committee chairman's recommendations.

During the last three years of the Johnson administration Fulbright argued that the Tonkin Resolution did not provide any legal justification for the war in Vietnam. Fulbright emphasized Johnson's almost pacifistic rhetoric during the 1964 Presidential campaign and the assurances given by the administration at the time of the resolution's passage that it was intended to prevent a war by demonstrating to the Chinese and North Vietnamese that America was determined to oppose aggression. The Tonkin Resolution, Fulbright continued to maintain, amounted to Congressional acquiescence in the executive's exercise of the war power, which the Constitution vested in Congress and which Congress had no right to renounce.

The significance of the August, 1964 resolution lies in its symbolic nature as evidence of Congress' willingness to allow the President to acquire virtually complete control of foreign policy. Senator McGovern later stated that the momentum in favor of escalation in the Johnson administration was already so powerful by August, 1964 that the Gulf of Tonkin crisis had no real effect on the administration's thinking concerning Vietnam. McGovern's contention may have been accurate; as early as February, 1964, the President authorized the "34A" program of clandestine military operations against North Vietnam. Although Johnson referred to the Gulf of Tonkin Resolution in justifying his Vietnam policy during the early period of his Presidency, he often avoided doing so after 1966. The fact that Fulbright and other dissenting Senators were publicizing the doubtful circumstances surrounding the resolution's passage may have contributed to the President's reluctance to rely on the resolution in defending his policies during 1967. In an August, 1967 press conference Johnson described the resolution as a courtesy extended to Congress to permit them to "be there on the takeoff as well as on the landing. We did not think the resolution was necessary to do what we did and what we're doing."

President Nixon continued his predecessor's policy of disregarding Congress' views concerning the resolution. When in 1971 Fulbright and other opponents of America's Vietnam policy finally succeeded in repealing the Gulf of Tonkin Resolution, the only legislative instrument which provided some facade of constitutional legitimacy for the Vietnam war, Nixon continued the war as if nothing of consequence had happened.

Fulbright later wrote that the Congress thought it was acting to help prevent a large-scale war in southeast Asia by passing the

Tonkin Resolution. Actually, there was considerable confusion in Congress over precisely what the resolution signified. Senator Nelson offered his amendment (which declared it to be the policy of the United States to avoid a military intervention in Vietnam) in order to clarify the meaning of the resolution, for he claimed to be "most disturbed to see that there is no agreement in the Senate on what the joint resolution means." The Pentagon Papers stated that beyond the central belief that "the occasion necessitated demonstrating the nation's unity and collective will in support of the President's action and affirming U.S. determination to oppose further aggression, Congressional opinions varied as to the policy implications and the meaning" of the almost unanimous support for the resolution. According to the Papers, "several spokesmen stressed that the resolution did not constitute a declaration of war, did not abdicate Congressional responsibility for determining national policy commitments and did not give the President carte blanche to involve the nation in a major Asian war."

The Johnson administration claimed that the American commitment to Vietnam centered upon the SEATO treaty. Fulbright argued that the SEATO treaty did not commit the United States to defend member nations against internal revolts. In case of a threat of internal subversion, the only obligation of the SEATO treaty was to consult; in the event of encountering an act of internal aggression, the members were to "meet the common danger" in accordance with their constitutional processes. Even if Johnson had been correct in his view of the conflict as a war of foreign aggression mounted by the North against the South, the war would still have been unconstitutional. Fulbright (a former constitutional law professor) and legal authorities agreed that Congress' power to declare war, as stated in Article I, Section 8 of the U.S. Constitution, cannot be discharged either by a treaty, in which the House of Representatives does not participate, or by provision of appropriations for a war initiated by the President on his own authority.

In addition to his indictment of the war's unconstitutionality, the Arkansas Senator increasingly decried the domestic repercussions of America's intervention in southeast Asia. He began describing Johnson's "Great Society" as a "sick society" in 1967. At an American Bar Association meeting of August, 1967 Fulbright sadly enumerated the statistics on the American death toll during a single week of July, 1967: 164 Americans were killed and 1,442 were wounded in Vietnam, while 65 Americans were killed and 2,100 were wounded in urban riots in the United States. The war not only diverted resources from health, education, and welfare programs, but perhaps even more seriously, it disseminated the idea that violence was an effective means of solving social and political problems.

There was a total dichotomy between the perspectives of Fulbright's August, 1967 address, entitled "The Price of Empire," and the Senator's January, 1965 speech at Miami. In January, 1965, he had believed President Johnson would concentrate on domestic reconstruction and end America's preoccupation with opposing communism abroad. By 1967, he was convinced that Johnson's foreign policy had grievously exacerbated America's domestic maladies. Administration officials produced impressive statistics concerning the gross national product to demonstrate that the United States could afford both the Vietnam war and the Great Society. But the statistics, in Fulbright's view, could not explain

> how an anxious and puzzled people, bombarded by press and television with the bad news of American deaths in Vietnam, the 'good news' of enemy deaths—and with vividly horrifying pictures to illustrate them—can be expected to support neighborhood anti-poverty projects and national programs for urban renewal, employment and education. Anxiety about war does not breed compassion for one's neighbors; nor do constant reminders of the cheapness of life abroad strengthen our faith in its sanctity at home. In these ways the war in Vietnam is poisoning and brutalizing our domestic life.

Fulbright responded to the administration's economic statistics with a brief comparison of defense and social spending in recent American history. Since 1946, he observed, 57 percent of the expenditures in the regular national budget had been devoted to military power, whereas 6 percent was spent on education, health, labor, housing,and welfare programs. The Johnson administration's budget for fiscal year 1968 was consistent with the postwar trend, calling for $75 billion in military spending and only $15 billion for "social functions." According to Fulbright, Congress had not been reluctant to reduce expenditures on domestic programs, but was much too willing to provide virtually unlimited sums for the military.

"The Price of Empire" was not entirely negative. The Senator eulogized the burgeoning protest movement against the Vietnam war. He dismissed the notion that the young idealists who opposed the war were radical. He predicted that the regenerative influence of the younger generation would eventually prevail over the truly radical super-patriots who were attempting to transform the United States into the self-appointed gendarme of the world. The struggle between these "young idealists" and the advocates of the

Vietnam war, Fulbright asserted, was a conflict between "two Americas." The modern ultra-patriots represented an emerging imperial America which contradicted the ideals of the "traditional" America, the America of Jefferson, Lincoln, and Adlai Stevenson. In Fulbright's view, the opponents of the Vietnam war were remaining true to the traditional American values in their desire to abandon the quest for empire and devote the nation's energies to achieving freedom and social justice at home, and the "fulfillment of our flawed democracy."

Domestic opposition to the Johnson administration's southeast Asian policy increased rapidly during the summer and fall of 1967. By August, 1967, draft calls were exceeding 30,000 per month, and more than 13,000 Americans had died in Vietnam. The President announced a 10 percent surtax to cover the spiraling costs of the war. In August, public opinion polls revealed that for the first time a majority of Americans believed the United States had been mistaken in intervening in Vietnam. Public approval of Johnson's handling of the war plummeted to 28 percent by October.

The opposition to the war increasingly focused on the bombing, which many dissenters regarded as futile and immoral. By 1967 the United States had dropped more bombs in southeast Asia than in all theaters during World War II. The President expanded the number of sorties in 1967 and authorized air attacks on steel factories, power plants, and other targets around Hanoi and Haiphong, as well as on previously restricted areas along the Chinese border. Civilian casualties mounted as high as 1,000 per week during periods of heavy bombing. The air war inflicted severe damage on North Vietnam's raw materials, vehicles, and military equipment, but these losses were offset by increased Soviet and Chinese aid to North Vietnam. The Soviet Union assisted North Vietnam in the construction of a powerful antiaircraft system centered around Hanoi and Haiphong. Nine hundred and fifty American aircraft were destroyed over Vietnam from 1965 to 1968. As George Herring has described the futility of the air strikes, "The limited success of air power as applied on a large scale in Korea raised serious questions" about the military effectiveness of bombing, "and the conditions prevailing in Vietnam, a primitive country with few crucial targets, might have suggested even more." North Vietnamese infiltration into South Vietnam increased from roughly 35,000 men in 1965 to about 90,000 in 1967 despite the intensification of the bombing.

American officials asserted that the United States was "winning" the war, claiming that 220,000 enemy soldiers had been killed in "search and destroy" missions in South Vietnam by late 1967. These figures were based on "body counts" which were notoriously unreliable, since it was not possible to distinguish between Vietcong and noncombatants. Moreover, approximately 200,000 North Vietnamese reached draft age every year, and Hanoi was able to replace its losses and match each American escalation. If the North Vietnamese and Vietcong began to suffer unusually severe casualties in a particular military engagement, they would often simply disappear into the South Vietnamese jungle or retreat into North Vietnam, Laos, or Cambodia. Although 450,000 American soldiers were in Vietnam by mid-1967, General Westmoreland urged the President to send 200,000 additional troops. The General conceded that even with 650,000 men the war might last two more years; with only a half million troops Westmoreland believed the war could last five more years or longer.

Political, social, and economic conditions in South Vietnam were rapidly deteriorating. American spending had a devastating impact on the fragile economy of South Vietnam, where prices increased 170 percent from 1965 to 1967. The expansion of Vietcong and American military operations had driven four million South Vietnamese (about one-fourth of South Vietnam's population) from their native villages. These refugees drifted into the already overcrowded cities or were herded into refugee camps. The United States furnished $30 million per year to the Saigon government for care of the displaced villagers, but much of the money never reached the refugees. A large portion of South Vietnam's population thus became rootless and embittered, and the refugee camps were often infiltrated by Vietcong fifth columns. In *The Arrogance of Power* Fulbright lamented the "fatal impact" of American economic and military power on South Vietnam and other underdeveloped countries. "With every good intention," he wrote, "we have intruded on fragile societies, and our intrusion, though successful in uprooting traditional ways of life, has been strikingly unsuccessful in implanting the democracy and advancing the development which are the honest aims of our 'welfare imperialism.'" The Senator doubted "the ability of the United States or any other Western nation to go into a small, alien, undeveloped Asian nation and create stability where there is chaos, the will to fight where there is defeatism, democracy where there is no tradition of it, and honest government where corruption is almost a way of life."

Nguyen Cao Ky candidly admitted that "most of the generals are corrupt. Most of the senior officials in the provinces are corrupt." But Ky excused the corruption by claiming that it "exists everywhere, and people can live with some of it. You live with it in Chicago and New York." The September, 1967 elections in South Vietnam again revealed the weak and corrupt nature of the Thieu-

Ky regime, for even after the Saigon government disqualified many opposition candidates and fraudulently manipulated some of the election returns, the Thieu-Ky ticket received only a plurality of 35 percent of the vote. The chaos and corruption in America's South Vietnamese ally contributed to the American public's disillusionment with the war.

By late 1967 there was an increasingly vociferous and expanding bloc of Senators who agreed with Fulbright's indictment of the war. According to a majority of the members of the Senate Foreign Relations Committee, Dean Rusk should have defended the administration's southeast Asian policies in a public hearing. In December, 1967, Rusk rejected the Committee's invitation to testify at an open hearing. Fulbright renewed the Committee's request in early 1968 shortly after the Vietcong launched the Tet offensive, a massive assault against the major urban areas in South Vietnam. "What is now at stake," the chairman contended in a February 1968 letter to President Johnson, "is no less urgent a question than the Senate's constitutional duty to advise, as well as consent, in the sphere of foreign policy." The members of his committee, Fulbright maintained, were anxious to clarify for the American people the implications of U.S. policy in Vietnam. In the midst of widespread disenchantment with the administration's southeast Asian policies, President Johnson acquiesced to Fulbright's request, and a few weeks later Rusk testified before the Committee.

The day before Rusk's testimony in 1968, the *New York Times* published reports of General William Westmoreland's proposal for 206,000 additional troops in Vietnam. The Pentagon Papers described the publication of the Westmoreland recommendation as a "focus" for political debate which intensified public dissatisfaction with the war. Rusk appeared before the Foreign Relations Committee on March 11, 1968, ostensibly for the purpose of discussing foreign aid. Instead the televised hearings became a two-day grilling of the Secretary on Vietnam, with Fulbright sharply questioning Rusk over the Tonkin crisis and the administration's interpretation of the Tonkin Resolution, Rusk's views on Lin Piao's doctrine of world revolution (see page 182) and the reports of Westmoreland's requests for more troops. Rusk refused to discuss possible troop increases, though he confirmed that an "A to Z" policy review was being conducted by the President and his advisers.

During the hearings Fulbright stressed the irrelevance of Indochina to America's vital national interests. The administration described the conflict in Indochina as an "exemplary war" which was discouraging the communists from promoting subversive activities in other third world nations. Fulbright execrated this notion as a reversion to the crusading anti-communism of the earlier postwar years and averred that far from proving to the communist powers that wars of national liberation could not succeed, the Vietnam war was demonstrating to the world that even with an army of a half million men and expenditures of $30 billion per year America could not win a civil war for a regime which was incapable of inspiring the patriotism of its own people.

Fulbright bluntly dismissed the administration's version of the Gulf of Tonkin incidents as untrue. He stated that if the United States would begin bombing North Vietnam in retaliation against doubtful skirmishes which had not damaged the U.S. armed forces, then the North Vietnamese must have understandably concluded in 1964 that America was determined to attack them regardless of their actions. By March 1968, of course, the Arkansas Senator had criticized the Gulf of Tonkin Resolution on innumerable occasions. The dialogue between Fulbright and Rusk at the 1968 hearings was essentially a repetition of the opposing arguments they had been advancing since 1966. Rusk's sterile, evasive answers did not differ significantly from the testimony he had delivered at Foreign Relations Committee hearings throughout the Johnson Presidency.

If the 1968 Fulbright-Rusk confrontation was not different in substance from earlier debates between the chairman and the Secretary, it was nevertheless true that the political atmosphere in which the debate occurred had changed dramatically. Walter Cronkite had eloquently summarized the prevailing public mood in his widely publicized television broadcast on February 27: "To say that we are closer to victory today is to believe, in the face of evidence, the optimists who have been wrong in the past." "We are mired in stalemate," Cronkite pronounced. Public opinion polls in March indicated that approximately 75 percent of the American people believed U.S. policies in Vietnam were failing. The March 11 and 12 Foreign Relations Committee hearings reinforced Secretary of Defense Clark Clifford's nascent conviction that major actions must be taken to reduce America's military involvement in Vietnam.

Immediately after Rusk's testimony Fulbright asked Secretary Clifford, formerly a "hawk" on the Cold War, to testify before the Foreign Relations Committee. The President and Clifford were concerned about the prospect of the Secretary testifying in the hostile Senate forum on national television; therefore, they decided that Clifford's assistant Paul Warnke should testify. In stating that he did not wish to appear before the Committee, Clifford informed Fulbright that he needed to devote more time to a review of the Vietnam policy because he was "too new in office," having only recently replaced Robert McNamara (who had earlier become disillusioned with the escalation policy). But Fulbright insisted that either Clifford or Paul Nitze, Deputy Secretary of Defense, must testify, and that the Committee would wait until either Clifford or Nitze was prepared to testify. Nitze had previously indicated to Clifford that he would refuse to appear before the Committee because of his private opposition to the administration's Vietnam policy. At this juncture, according to Nitze, Clifford's growing but inchoate doubts about U.S. policy crystallized into a definite conviction that the United States must de-escalate the war and move towards a disengagement from southeast asia. Clifford was influenced in his burgeoning dissent by the private arguments of his assistants Warnke and Nitze, by the weakness of the Joint Chiefs of Staff's pleas for additional escalation, and by the disaffection of the Congressional critics. In Nitze's analysis, the final deciding factor in Clifford's decision in favor of de-escalation was the Secretary's antipathy to the idea of having to defend the Johnson policies before a committee of well-informed and assertive Congressional dissenters: "When Clark Clifford had to face up to the possibility that he might have to defend the administration's policy before the Fulbright committee, his views changed," Nitze recalled. William Bundy also later agreed with Nitze's assessment of Clifford's views.

Nitze's emphasis upon Fulbright's influence on Clifford may or may not have been accurate; but clearly the arguments and pressures from the Congressional critics were among the important considerations leading to Clifford's change of mind. In March Clifford held a private conference with Fulbright and informed the chairman of his profound doubts concerning Johnson's policies. Fulbright agreed that Clifford could testify somewhat later rather than immediately, provided that Clifford (who had known Fulbright well for many years) pressed his views concerning the futility of further escalation during the administration's review of the Vietnam policy. In the next few weeks, Clifford was indeed successful in refuting the military's appeal for continuing the escalation policy. As Clifford later explained his perspective, "I was convinced that the military course we were pursuing was not only endless, but hopeless. A further substantial increase in American forces could only increase the devastation and the Americanization of the war ... Henceforth, I was also convinced, our primary goal should be to level off our involvement, and to work toward gradual disengagement."

Shortly after the conclusion of the second Rusk hearing, the returns from the Presidential primary in New Hampshire revealed surprisingly strong support for the President's challenger, Senator Eugene McCarthy. On March 16 Senator Robert Kennedy declared that he would seek the Democratic Presidential nomination on a platform of opposition to the war. Clifford advised Johnson to consult with the Senior Informal Advisory Group—the famous "Wise Men," for he believed that many of them were beginning to harbor doubts about the war. A few days later the Senior Informal Advisory Group, consisting of Dean Acheson, George Ball, Matthew Ridgway, Cyrus Vance, McGeorge Bundy, and others advised the President to order a reduction in the bombing. In a shocking, nationally televised address on March 31, the President announced his withdrawal from the Presidential campaign, a token troop increase, and the de-escalation of the air war against North Vietnam in order to obtain Hanoi's entry into negotiations.

The March 10 *New York Times* publication, the Foreign Relations Committee hearings, and the apparent political strength of the anti-war candidates Kennedy and McCarthy clearly demonstrated that significant and growing elements of the American public believed that the costs of the war had reached unacceptable levels. According to the Pentagon Papers, the President's dramatic change in tactics was based upon two major considerations. One was the opinion of his principal advisers, especially Secretary of Defense Clifford, that the troops General Westmoreland requested would not make a military victory any more likely. The revelation of the Vietnamese communists' power during the Tet offensive was crucial in Johnson's belated acceptance of Clifford's evaluation of the military realities. The Pentagon study described the second major consideration leading to Johnson's March 31 speech as "a deeply felt conviction of the need to restore unity to the American nation."

The March, 1968 decisions constituted an end to the Johnson administration's escalation of the Vietnam war. But the administration did not alter its fundamental goals, for Johnson remained determined to secure an independent, non-communist South Vietnam. Fulbright quickly recognized the limited nature of the President's changes. On April 2, he registered his disillusionment with Johnson's address: "Today, within 48 hours, it appears that it [the March 31 de-escalation of the air war] was not a significant change at all." He publicized the disturbing fact that on April 1 U.S. planes bombed North Vietnamese targets 205 miles north of the Demilitarized Zone. On April 1, administration spokesmen revealed American planes could still strike targets only 45 miles from Hanoi under the terms of Johnson's bombing pause. Fulbright believed a total and unilateral cessation of the bombing would be necessary as a significant inducement towards a cease-fire. The Senator refuted the notion that he and Wayne Morse were somehow endangering

American lives in Vietnam by their adamant opposition to Johnson's southeast Asian policies, stating "the idea that what the Senator from Oregon and I and others who seek an end to the war advocate is not protecting the lives of our boys is absurd. What we advocate, is, really, the only effective way to protect their lives; namely, stop the war."

Lyndon Johnson complained in his memoirs that the media devoted considerable attention to Fulbright's views on Vietnam but virtually ignored the pro-administration positions of Frank Lausche and Mike Mansfield. Johnson was correct in arguing that Mansfield approved of the March reductions in the bombing campaign. But the Montana Senator had also implied that the bombing halt should have been more extensive, and he described Fulbright's April contributions to the Vietnam debate as "worthwhile." The President claimed in his memoirs that Fulbright's persistent opposition to the war during 1968 interfered with the administration's negotiating efforts at the Paris peace talks, which began on May 13. Johnson lamented that the North Vietnamese could quote the anti-war statements of Charles de Gaulle, Robert Kennedy, and J. William Fulbright in an attempt to "turn the Paris talks into a propaganda sideshow."

Johnson's innuendo concerning the Paris deliberations was obviously an effort to blame the failure of his diplomacy on his domestic critics and Hanoi. Fulbright was deeply interested in the success of the Paris negotiations, as he indicated in a May 7 letter to the President. He vaguely but approvingly referred to "a very cordial and reassuring visit" he had recently enjoyed with his old friend Clark Clifford, one of the primary architects of the de-escalation policy (he did not mention any details of the Clifford conversation.) "I am so pleased," Fulbright informed Johnson, "that Paris was agreed upon, and you certainly have the best wishes of all of us for success. If we could only get a general cease-fire, then the pressure would relax and perhaps a reasonable compromise might be developed."

Unfortunately, the President's inflexible attitude towards the Paris discussions was not conducive to a "reasonable compromise." The interminable quarreling at Paris in 1968 seems to have confirmed Fulbright's April 2 prediction that Johnson's tactical changes would not lead to constructive negotiations. Walt Rostow and other advisers to the President persuaded him that the enemy forces had exhausted their military strength during the Tet offensive and the United States could therefore afford to be demanding at Paris. The North Vietnamese were equally intransigent. By the end of Johnson's Presidency in January, 1969, the nominal achievements of the Paris negotiations consisted of an agreement on a speaking arrangement which enabled the United States and Saigon to claim a two-sided conference, and a seating arrangement which permitted Hanoi to claim the presence of four delegations, including the National Liberation Front.

Throughout much of 1968, Fulbright was engrossed in his re-election campaign, which attracted significant national attention. Three Democratic candidates opposed the Senator, and all three attacked his foreign policy positions. One opponent, the right-wing political veteran Jim Johnson, repeated the hoary charge that Fulbright was "giving aid and comfort" to America's communist enemies. The Senator vigorously maintained his indictment of the Vietnam war during the campaign and defeated his three challengers in the Democratic primary. His right-wing Republican opponent in 1968 was Charles Bernard, a wealthy businessman and landowner. Bernard also utilized the strategy of condemning Fulbright's ideas concerning American foreign policy. Republican Presidential nominee Richard Nixon, John Tower, California Governor Ronald Reagan, and the reactionary millionaire H. L. Hunt opposed Fulbright's re-election. Senator Edward Kennedy endorsed Fulbright. The chairman of the Foreign Relations Committee relentlessly advanced his critique of America's crusading anti-communism to the Arkansas electorate (Fulbright also discussed many domestic issues during the 1968 campaign) and eventually defeated the Republican candidate by 100,000 votes.

There had been a dramatic reversal in Fulbright's political fortunes since 1965. When Fulbright emerged as an adversary of Johnson's foreign policy in late 1965, many political analysts regarded him as a maverick who had wrought his own destruction through his heretical dissent. In February, 1966, President Johnson privately boasted that he would destroy the political careers of Fulbright, Robert Kennedy, and other Senate "doves" within six months. By 1968, the public had repudiated Johnson's Vietnam policies so thoroughly that he no longer dared to travel openly around the country. Kennedy was demonstrating impressive political strength at the time of his assassination in June, and Fulbright won a triumphant re-election after reiterating his opposition to the Vietnam war throughout 1968.

Fulbright was far from optimistic at the end of 1968, despite his electoral victory. There were still a half million American soldiers in Vietnam. During the Presidential campaign, Richard Nixon proclaimed that "Those who have had a chance for four years and could not produce peace should not be given another chance," but he had carefully avoided any explanation of how he planned to end the war.

Early in the Nixon Presidency Fulbright would correctly conclude that Nixon was determined to pursue Johnson's fundamental goal of establishing an independent, non-communist South Vietnam. The chairman of the Foreign Relations Committee would oppose Nixon's Vietnam policies at least as adamantly as he had opposed the Johnson escalation policies.

Four years after the Republican Presidential candidate had lambasted the Democrats for failing to bring peace to southeast Asia, the deluge of American bombs upon Indochina continued on an ever more destructive scale. By 1972 Nixon had succeeded only in establishing himself as "the greatest bomber of all time," in the words of the *Washington Post*. In Fulbright's scathing indictment of recent U.S. foreign policy, *The Crippled Giant*, the Senator lamented President Nixon's failure to deviate from the fundamental objectives of the Johnson administration despite the palpable weakness of Thieu's regime, the military resilience of the Vietnamese communists, and the burgeoning domestic opposition to America's futile crusade in Vietnam: "Employing the insane anti-logic which has characterized this war from its beginning, the Nixon Administration pointed with pride to its troop withdrawals, as if the substitution of a devastating, permanent air war for large-scale American participation in the continuing ground war represented the course of prudence and moderation as between the radical 'extremes' of expanding the war and ending it."

Chapter Nine
The Nixon Years

The central theme of Richard Nixon's 1968 campaign was a vague promise to restore the unity of the American people after the war and the divisiveness of the Johnson years. For the first few months of the Nixon administration, Fulbright did not aggressively criticize the new President (although Fulbright opposed Nixon on the National Commitments Resolution debate of early 1969) in order to give him time to "bring the American people together" and to show that he had rejected the Johnson strategy of establishing an anti-communist American client state in South Vietnam. When in October of 1969 Nixon made the unprecedented request for a 60-day moratorium on criticism of the President, Fulbright responded with a plea for a moratorium on killing. The response came in a Senate speech in which Fulbright emphasized the continuity of the Johnson and Nixon policies. Although Nixon professed to support self-determination for South Vietnam, he had recently praised Thieu as "one of the greatest politicians of the present day." It was contradictory to support Thieu and South Vietnamese self-determination, for Thieu had adamantly refused to permit any communists to participate in a coalition government even through a free election. Fulbright pointed out that it was not exactly a triumph for Nixon's policy that he had been President nine months and withdrawn 60,000 troops, for at that rate there would be an American presence in Vietnam for the next ten years.

The Presidency's tendency to conduct foreign policy with the utmost secrecy and to usurp Congress' war power reached its apogee on April 30, 1970 when Nixon sent American troops plunging into Cambodia without the consent or even knowledge of Congress. On April 17, 1970 Secretary of State William Rogers conferred with the Foreign Relations Committee on foreign policy with respect to Cambodia, but failed to inform the Committee that the Nixon administration was planning to invade Cambodia in the next week. No effort was made to justify the invasion on any legal grounds other than to vaguely refer to the President's authority as Commander-in-Chief. Nixon claimed that his authority to wage the war in Indochina was based upon the need to protect the lives of American personnel. The United States must invade Cambodia to prevent a North Vietnamese attack upon the dwindling numbers of American troops. This pretext was flimsy even by Nixonian standards, for the North Vietnamese had offered to refrain from attacking American troops if the United States would set a withdrawal date.

The demonstrations against the expansion of the war were so vehement that Nixon withdrew the troops from Cambodia in July, 1970. In the aftermath of the Kent State University demonstrations, where four students were killed by the Ohio National Guard, Fulbright lamented the precipitous decline of America's world image. Fulbright publicized the reaction of western European opinion to the Cambodian invasion at the Foreign Relations Committee's hearings on the moral aspects of the war in southeast Asia in May, 1970. He recounted Arnold J. Toynbee's recent statement that the world's phobia concerning CIA subversive activities or direct military interventions by the United States was becoming as "fantastically excessive" as America's phobia about world communism. Toynbee believed the "roles of America and Russia have been reversed in the world's eyes." He considered the Cambodian incursion to be "a second Vietnam" which had confirmed the prophecy of an anonymous Pentagon representative who said in 1968, "There are going to be many more Vietnams."

At the May, 1970 hearings Fulbright and General James Gavin discussed the reaction of Chancellor Brandt's Social Democratic Party to the Cambodian intervention. Many Social Democrats denounced Nixon's imperialistic policy which had escalated the "Vietnam war" into the "Indochina war." Several speakers at the Party's May 11 national convention spoke of "creeping fascism" in American foreign policy (although Brandt thought the phrase was objectionable). Fulbright described it as a "terrible tragedy of history" that the Germans were accusing the United States of engaging in "what we have accused and reminded them of for 25 years." General Gavin agreed, saying "as a veteran of over three years in Europe, and one who participated in the liberation of the concentration camps, it is a sad, sad day when such an analogy must be drawn by the Germans."

In the early 1970s Fulbright supported a series of Congressional measures to prevent the President from expanding the war in southeast Asia. The most significant legislative achievements were the two Cooper-Church amendments, the first prohibiting the use of

American ground combat forces in Laos and Thailand, the second prohibiting the use of American ground combat forces or military advisers in Cambodia. Fulbright's amendment to the Defense Appropriation Act for fiscal year 1970 would have prohibited the U.S. government from extending financial aid to foreign forces in Laos and Cambodia, but the Nixon administration continued to finance Thai units in Laos and evaded the law by pretending that the Thai soldiers were "volunteers." The first binding legislative proposal for ending the war was the McGovern-Hatfield amendment, which would have cut off funds for the war after December 31, 1971 subject to recovery of American prisoners of war. This amendment was defeated twice, in 1970 and 1971. According to a view McGovern later stated, the sentiment in Congress that the President must be supported in his foreign policy was still so strong that the most surprising fact about the amendment was that it received as many as 42 votes.

The day before the first vote on McGovern's amendment, Fulbright and McGovern appeared together on a televised rebuttal to Nixon's Indochina policy. Fulbright deplored Nixon's attempt to invoke "the specter of a first American defeat," saying that to rectify an error was "not a humiliation but a rational and honorable way of coming to grips with reality." The Senator considered "Vietnamization" to be "only the latest in a series of military strategies which would not extricate us completely" but would "keep us involved indefinitely." Fulbright objected to Nixon's contention that our choice is between Vietnamization and "precipitate withdrawal," and offered the alternative of a negotiated settlement based on a "total American military withdrawal from Vietnam to be completed by a specified date."

The Fulbright-McGovern telecast was the first broadcast in compliance with a Federal Communications Commission regulation requiring networks to allow prime-time exposure to critics of the administration's policy because of five Presidential speeches on Vietnam in the ten-month period preceding the vote on the "end the war" amendment. Despite the preponderance of Nixon's television exposure over that of his adversaries, F.C.C. Chairman Dean Burch rejected any interpretation of the F.C.C. ruling as establishing the principle of "equal time" for leaders of the Congressional opposition to match Presidential appearances. The day after the Fulbright-McGovern telecast (September 1, 1970), McGovern's amendment was defeated in the Senate by a vote of 55 to 39.

In late 1971 Congress finally enacted a measure in favor of ending the war, although without specifying a withdrawal date. The Mansfield amendment declared it to be "the policy of the

207

United States to terminate at the earliest possible date all military operations of the United States in Indochina." Thus the President was at last confronted with a binding provision of law to change his bankrupt policy. Nixon simply defied the Congress, saying the amendment was "without binding force or effect," and the Congress rather obsequiously failed to take any official action regarding the President's intention to violate the law. Fulbright explained Congress' unwillingness to withhold funds for the war by referring to the Nixon administration's success in representing the issue as not being "whether you approve or disapprove of the war, but of whether you wish to support or abandon our boys out there on the firing line and in the prisoner of war camps."

It became apparent during the Nixon administration that Congress lacked the power, and also possibly the will, to stop the Presidential war in Vietnam. Nixon's opponents in Congress thus attempted to legislate a generalized reassertion of Congress' authority in foreign affairs in the later 1960s and early 1970s. Fulbright was the floor leader for the National Commitments Resolution of 1969, which expressed the sense of the Senate that no foreign commitment should be made without the prior consent of Congress. This resolution did not deter Nixon in his determination to ignore Congress in the conduct of foreign policy, for the Cambodian invasion occurred a year after its passage. The most important legislative enactment directed at preventing "future Vietnams" was probably the War Powers bill adopted by the Senate in April, 1972 and eventually passed over Nixon's veto. This bill confined unauthorized use of the armed forces by the President to specified conditions of emergency. Even in an emergency the President could not continue hostilities beyond sixty days unless Congress authorized him to do so. Senator Sparkman and Senator Cooper, both of whom supported the bill, privately expressed doubts about its constitutionality during the debate over the bill. The Foreign Relations Committee reported that such legislation would not have been necessary if Congress had defended and exercised its constitutional responsibilities in war and foreign policy.

In his book *The Crippled Giant* Fulbright excoriated Nixon's justifications for continuing the war. Nixon had argued that an American withdrawal would precipitate a "blood bath" in South Vietnam and plunge America from the "anguish of war into a nightmare of recrimination" from the radical right. Fulbright charged that it was absurd to sacrifice thousands of American soldiers and the peace of Indochina to the appeasement of the lunatic fringe in the United States. And the administration had failed to explain why it was better for South Vietnamese civilians to be incinerated by American napalm or "blown to bits by American fragmentation bombs" than to confront the hypothetical threat of a future communist blood bath.

Fulbright believed that Nixon's Vietnam policy was the consummation of the ideological anti-communism of the Truman Doctrine. Nixon claimed that he had renounced the international communist conspiracy theory of Dulles and the earlier Cold Warriors, but his contention was belied by many of his statements on Vietnam. By the early 1970s, the Nixon policies were becoming totally contradictory, with the administration's diplomacy towards the great communist powers beginning to display the emphasis upon detente advocated by Henry Kissinger, while the Nixon southeast Asian policies continued in the ideological tradition of the Truman Doctrine. Early in his administration Nixon had spoken of "great powers who have not yet abandoned their goals of world conquest," referring to China and Russia. As late as Nixon's speech of April, 1972, the President had repeatedly denounced "communist aggression" in Indochina, not North Vietnamese aggression, in a manner reminiscent of Dean Rusk's view of Ho Chi Minh as a Chinese agent in the grand communist strategy for the conquest of Asia. The thesis of Chinese proxy war should have been discredited long ago, Fulbright held, if not by the evidence of North Vietnamese nationalism then by the fact that no Chinese combat forces ever participated in the war in Vietnam.

Fulbright considered Nixon's "Vietnamization" to be a euphemism for the substitution of an air war of unprecedented dimensions for Johnson's tactics of large-scale American involvement in the ground war. The build-up of the South Vietnamese army and the gradual withdrawal of American forces had reduced American casualties, but Nixon's aerial devastations maintained the total death toll. Thus Fulbright described "Vietnamization" as having succeeded only in "changing the color of the corpses." Nixon had intensified the bombing campaign to the extent that from 1969 to the middle of 1971, the United States had dropped more bombs on Indochina than it had in both the European and Pacific theaters during World War II.

By mining the North Vietnamese harbors and expanding the air war to unparalleled heights of devastation in 1972 Nixon raised the level of violence in the war beyond any of Johnson's successive acts of escalation. Fulbright listed the sordid record of destruction in Vietnam during the years since Nixon had promised to end the war in 1968: 3.2 million tons of bombs dropped on Indochina, (the figure Fulbright cites here was already greater than the total tonnage dropped during the Johnson administration, with the infamous Christmas bombings of 1972 not included) 20,000 American deaths, 110,000 Americans wounded, 340,000 Asian deaths, and the creation of four million new refugees. In the spring of 1972 Fulbright wrote that the Nixon policy "had come back full circle" to that of Johnson four years before; Johnson had partially suspended the bombing of North Vietnam and initiated the Paris peace talks in April, 1968, while in April, 1972 Nixon suspended the peace talks and resumed massive bombings of North and South Vietnam.

On May 9, 1972 the Foreign Relations Committee hearings on the "Causes, Origins, and Lessons of the Vietnam War" began. Fulbright learned of Nixon's decision to mine the entrances to the ports of North Vietnam against all shipping, including Russian and Chinese shipping, on the afternoon of May 8, a few hours before Nixon's speech that night. It was purely a coincidence that the hearings began the day after Nixon's decision. Fulbright issued an invitation for any member of the administration to appear before the Committee, although he did not expect his invitation to be accepted. Kissinger had been asked to testify innumerable times, but he steadfastly refused on the grounds of "executive privilege." Most of the members of the Foreign Relations Committee did not attend the three sessions of the public hearings. The topics which were most frequently discussed were the origins of the American involvement in Vietnam in the 1940s. Thus, while four Senators in the half-empty chambers of the Senate Office Building held their dialogue with the past, the President precipitated a crisis which apparently risked a nuclear war with Russia or China.

Three days later the fact that Nixon, Kissinger, Ambassador Dobrynin, and Soviet Minister of Foreign Trade Nikolai Patolichev were photographed together smiling broadly in the White House seemed to indicate that there had been an understanding between the Soviet Union and the United States, whereby the Russians would accept an ostensible humiliation (the mining of the entrances to North Vietnamese ports) in return for American wheat and tractors at low prices. Nixon's May 8 speech was, of course, mentioned at the hearings. Fulbright deplored the President's action. Clearly Congress and the public had been notified of decisions already made during the crisis while the President and his men manipulated the entire scenario.

The most important witness at the May, 1972 hearings was Frank White, who had been an O.S.S. officer in Hanoi in 1946 and had talked at length with Ho Chi Minh. Fulbright asked White if there was any evidence that Ho had been an ally or representative of "international communism." White replied that Ho believed the Russians had been so devastated by World War II that they would

210

be unable to supply Vietnam with "moral, political, or economic aid." Ho did not mention Mao Tse-tung, and when he did speak of the Chinese he elaborated at "extraordinary length" on the ancient hostility between the Vietnamese and Chinese peoples. According to White, Ho believed that the United States would be the great power most likely to assist Vietnam because of the American tradition of support for national self-determination. Ho concluded, however, that he did not expect the United States to concern itself with southeast Asia in the postwar era, for Vietnam was "a small country and far away."

Abbot Low Moffat, chief of the Division of Southeast Asian Affairs at the State Department from 1945 to 1947, discussed the reason for the failure of the Truman administration to reply to the eight communications Ho addressed to President Truman between October, 1945 and February, 1946 asking America to intervene in favor of Vietnamese independence. Moffat informed the Committee that he had written a memorandum arguing against any reply to Ho, for if the President had officially answered him this would have violated international protocol, (and would have been tantamount to a recognition of Ho as a head of state) and infuriated the French. Anti-communism was not a factor until late 1946, according to Moffat,who stated that by February, 1947 the Cold War mentality had begun to permeate the world view of the State Department so thoroughly that speculation about Ho's "direct communist connection" became common, even though in Moffat's opinion there never was any evidence that such a connection existed. Moffat was generally accurate in asserting that the Cold Warriors triumphed in the debate within the Truman administration concerning southeast Asian policy; the State Department's debate in the late 1940s was eventually won by Dean Acheson and those advisers who contended that the Cold War would be won or lost in Europe, and hence the United States could not risk losing France's cooperation by opposing French colonialism in southeast Asia. Thus far had American diplomacy evolved since President Roosevelt's 1944 memorandum to Cordell Hull had denounced the French for "milking" their colonies and proposed an international trusteeship for Indochina.

At the close of the hearings Moffat mentioned a theory of America's involvement in Vietnam which stressed economics. He claimed that he had supported the Open Door policy because he considered "international trade to be one of the big facets of peace." The State Department was never interested in opening Vietnam to American investors. Insofar as there was an economic motive, Moffat said that the Department was concerned with southeast Asia as a source of two raw materials: tin and rubber.

If Moffat intended to refute the economic interpretation of recent American diplomacy, he had not focused his criticism upon the most plausible economic arguments advanced by Walter La Feber and other scholars. Some of the radical revisionists alleged that America's dependence on raw materials in the third world had forced the United States into the role of the global defender of the status quo, but the scholars who have most convincingly stressed the importance of economics in American interventions have not argued that America became involved in Vietnam in order to protect American investments, which in fact were quite meager in South Vietnam. Walter LaFeber has written that the Eisenhower and Kennedy administration emphasized the significance of the domino theory largely because of its economic implications for Japan, a nation which was crucial to the American strategic policy in the Far East, if southeast Asia fell to communism and hence deprived the Japanese of important markets and sources of raw materials. The weight of the evidence, however, indicates that these economic considerations exerted only a secondary influence upon the U.S. officials who determined the early postwar policies in Vietnam.

Fulbright conceded at the hearings that the economic interpretation based upon America's determination to promote the Open Door policy and the domino theory's economic repercussions for Japan had "a certain consistency," although he was inclined to think that "it was much more complex than just being economics." In his books which deal with Vietnam, the Senator has not argued that the United States held any significant economic interests in South Vietnam; and, of course, he constantly reminded the American public that the war had inflicted massive damage upon the U.S. economy. Moffat's statements about the State Department's concern with southeast Asian raw materials and the domino theory's hypothetical implications for Japan's economy seem to demonstrate that economic motives were not entirely non-existent in the American commitment in Vietnam (at least in the 1940s and 1950s) and should not be totally ignored. The domino theory, however, was ultimately based on the ideological assumption that the communist bloc was inherently expansionist and monolithic, an assumption belied by the Chinese-Vietnamese border skirmishes of the mid and late 1970s. Relations among the Far Eastern communist states after the American withdrawal from Indochina were clearly dominated by the traditional national rivalries which Ho Chi Minh had so eloquently lamented in placid conversations with his American friends at the Hanoi Palais du Gouvernement in 1946.

Fulbright convened a brief set of hearings in early 1972 on American policy with respect to China shortly before Nixon's visit to Peking. John Stewart Service appeared before the Committee to discuss his recent trip to China. Service had been a Foreign Service officer in the Far East in the 1940s and had predicted a communist victory in the Chinese civil war at least as early as 1944. His accurate prognostications had led to his dismissal in the McCarthy era. The state of the communist world at the time Service testified revealed once again the absurdity in the Cold War mythology of the "monolithic" communist bloc. The Soviet press condemned Nixon's negotiations in Peking as a "dangerous plot." According to Service, the North Vietnamese were extremely suspicious that the Chinese might conspire with the Americans to betray North Vietnam. And in China, Service reported that "the central part of Shanghai is torn up with digging air raid shelters. In Peking they are digging air raid shelters. Every school, every factory has air raid shelters." When Service asked people in Shanghai and Peking "the defense is against whom?" the Chinese replied, "the Russians, the Soviets."

The Foreign Relations Chairman held the 1972 Vietnam and China hearings in an effort to provoke thought concerning the origins and lessons of the Vietnam war, and he described the sessions as "educational." But the hearings did not attract as much attention or promote as much reflection as Fulbright would have liked. In the early and mid-1970s, unfortunately, most Americans were simply growing weary of thinking about the deeper issues involved in America's tragic experience in Vietnam. The U.S. military involvement in southeast Asia continued for over a year after the 1972 hearings, and the public's attention continued to be focused on the ongoing conflict rather than efforts to analyze and understand the history of the Vietnam war.

In 1972-73 the anti-war movement inexorably gained strength, but not until the summer of 1973 did the Congressional opponents of the war succeed in defeating Nixon's policy of military intervention in southeast Asia. The Paris cease-fire agreements of January, 1973 terminated the American phase of the ground warfare by providing for the return of American prisoners in exchange for the withdrawal of U.S. military forces in 60 days. But massive American bombing of Cambodia continued in an effort to uphold the fragile pro-American regime of Lon Nol against the Hanoi-supported Khmer Rouge insurgency, and also to maintain what Kissinger called Nixon's "reputation for fierceness." Fulbright was one of the leaders of the movement to cut off funds for the bombing of Cambodia. Public opinion polls in May revealed that 60 percent of the public opposed the Cambodian bombing, and 75 percent believed that the President should seek Congressional approval before executing additional hostilities in southeast Asia. During the summer, Congress approved an amendment to end the use of funds for the Cambodian bombing after August 15; the vote in the Senate was 63-19 in favor. In the Senator's correspondence in 1973, he explained how the embattled Nixon had used every resource of his dwindling power to prolong the conflict, even though it was obvious that the policy of intervention was politically doomed by that late date. Fulbright explained to a constituent in July:

> If I could have had my way, the U.S. bombing of Cambodia certainly would not have been continued after June 29. Unfortunately, the President had the upper hand and the votes were simply not available to over-ride his veto. That being the case, we did the best we could which was to write an August 15 cut-off date into a piece of legislation which the President had to sign. Although I regret the prolongation of the bombing, I believe that in finally compelling the President to accept the authority of the Congress in matters pertaining to the use of U.S. military forces we have taken a major step toward the restoration of a proper constitutional balance.

The power and prestige of the Nixon administration was severely weakened by the Watergate crisis. Watergate had the effect of discrediting in the public mind virtually all of Nixon's policies; the discrediting of Nixon's Vietnam policies was fortunate for the opponents of the war, but Fulbright would later observe that the eventual popular disillusionment with Nixon's detente policies towards the Soviet Union held highly damaging implications for the future of Soviet-American relations. The Senator would have preferred that each of Nixon's policies should have been judged on its own merits, rather than allowing Watergate to foster a popular revulsion against all of Nixon's undertakings. While Fulbright always argued that the Nixon administration's crusade in southeast Asia was disastrous, he supported the 1972 Moscow summit and the Kissinger-Nixon detente approach. However,the Foreign Relations chairman was certainly encouraged by the reality that Watergate had weakened Nixon's power to execute his policies in southeast Asia. "In regard to the Watergate affair and related developments," Fulbright informed a constituent in the summer of 1973, "I believe this is indicative of what can happen when too much power is concentrated in the Executive. People in the Executive Branch become so concerned with the preservation and enhancement of their power that they feel above the law. It could, however, be beneficial in the long run by helping to restore some perspective and reestablish the balance between Congress and the Executive."

During the late Nixon administration, the brilliant U.S. Representatives Ray Thornton of Arkansas and Peter Rodino of New Jersey, North Carolina Senator Sam Ervin, and others led the investigations revealing the massive scope of the Watergate scandals. The 1972 burglary of the Democratic National Committee headquarters was only a part of an immense effort to influence the results of the 1972 election through covert and illegal activities; eventually the various investigations of the scandals established that the Nixon administration had been engaged in a systematic attempt to "cover up" its involvement in Watergate. Fulbright was not as vigorously involved in the Watergate inquiries as Thornton, Ervin, and several other members of Congress. When Thornton, Rodino, and others were attempting to gain evidence from the White House as part of the impeachment inquiry in 1974, Fulbright made public statements rejecting Nixon's attempted use of executive privilege to deny Congress the evidence. "I think the Constitution gives the Congress the right," Fulbright argued, "to have all the relevant information of any kind. I think all this parrying and delay by the President is quite unjustified." Fulbright differed from many critics of the Watergate affair in arguing that the proper Congressional response to an "arrogant" administration should have been a censure of the President, as Joe McCarthy had been censured twenty years earlier. Although Fulbright was not one of the principal leaders of the Watergate investigations, during the late 1960s and early 1970s he had played an essential role in beginning the movement to halt the expansion of the executive's power. The Cold Warrior mentality that bred the American intervention in Vietnam also promoted the excessive growth of executive power which culminated in Watergate, for the anti-communist crusaders believed that unethical or even illegal activities were justified in order to ensure that the administration overcame both domestic and foreign foes in its struggle with a supposedly fiendish, global, and totalitarian enemy. One of the important motives leading to Watergate was the administration's effort to defend the Vietnam war against its critics during the 1972 Presidential campaign. In 1973-74, the Watergate investigations and the anti-Vietnam war movement had combined to check the excesses of the executive branch; the future would show whether other leaders in other generations might attempt to resurrect the "imperial Presidency."

By 1973, Fulbright was in the unfamiliar position of enjoying the support of a majority in Congress and in public opinion. After many years of suffering overwhelming defeats in his efforts to end the U.S. military involvement in southeast Asia, Fulbright and his allies had achieved a momentous victory of their own in the 63-19 Senate vote to cut off funds for the Cambodian bombing. Although the Senator would have greatly preferred that the air war had ended much earlier, he was nevertheless encouraged that the military crusade in Indochina was at last coming to an end. After a seemingly endless era of public allegiance to Presidential domination of foreign policy, opinion polls and other measures of the public's views revealed widespread support throughout the nation for Fulbright and the Congressional critics of Nixon's southeast Asian policies. Thus, in 1973, in the Senator's eighth year of public opposition to the war, the mainstream of America had finally rejoined Fulbright.

Chapter Ten
Epilogue and Conclusion

Fulbright's opposition to the obsessive anti-communism of recent American diplomacy was not an abject failure, despite the interminable and disastrous intervention in Vietnam. The Arkansas Senator had contributed to the creation of a general American consensus against military expeditions into regions of the globe where vital American interests were not involved; by the late 1970s, pulbic opinion polls revealed that the vast majority of the American people opposed U.S. military involvement in the third world and believed that the Vietnam war was "more than a mistake, it was fundamentally wrong and immoral." Whether a large majority of Americans agreed with Fulbright's dissent against the anti-communist ideology by the 1970s was not clear. However, his constant appeals for the amelioration of American relations with the great communist powers throughout the 1960s foreshadowed and facilitated the detente policies which National Security Adviser Henry Kissinger pursued in the early 1970s.

Fulbright maintained in *The Crippled Giant* that by the time of the President's journey to China in February, 1972, Nixon's foreign policy was no longer dominated by the rigid anti-communism of the Truman Doctrine. Henry Kissinger had persuaded Nixon by the early 1970s that China's policies in Indochina were no more than conventional great-power maneuverings in a region the Chinese had always considered to be their "sphere of influence." Fulbright was not optimistic about the prospects for establishing a permanent foundation of international peace and security on the basis of Kissinger's "geopolitical or balance of power approach," for he believed the nineteenth century European "balance of power policies" had culminated in the first world war. Yet Fulbright supported the Kissinger foreign policy (except in Indochina), which was based upon a scholarly, dispassionate analysis of specific advantages and threats to America's vital national interests. The Foreign Relations Committee chairman described the geopolitical diplomacy of Dr. Kissinger as an "enormous improvement" upon the policies of the Cold War crusaders, whose ideological prejudices led them to imagine that all communist states were aggressive and united in their determination to destroy the free world.

During Nixon's visit to China he declared it to be the objective of the United States to withdraw its soldiers from Vietnam (the 1973 cease-fire agreements would provide for the withdrawal of the last 27,000 American troops from South Vietnam), and at some unspecified date in the future to remove its military installations from Taiwan. Both the Chinese and American governments agreed to seek to achieve "normalization of relations." Nixon did not attempt to explain why it was necessary for thousands of Americans to continue risking their lives in Vietnam to "contain" the alleged Chinese imperialism when the President could drink toasts of friendship with the Chinese leaders in Peking. Fulbright continued to denounce the administration's "unreconstructed" policies in Vietnam.

Fulbright's defeat in his 1974 re-election campaign cannot be interpreted as a repudiation of his opposition to the Vietnam war. The Senator's opponent, Governor Dale Bumpers, agreed with his dissent against the war. No differences concerning Vietnam emerged during the nationally televised debate between Fulbright and Bumpers just before the May, 1974 Democratic Primary. During the debate, Bumpers agreed with Fulbright that the United States should not have intervened in Vietnam, asserting that "I didn't think that it was a moral war for us to be involved in." Bumpers' only sharp disagreement with Fulbright during the May debate focused on the Senator's defense of the seniority system, which the Governor claimed had prevented Congress from responding to "the grass-roots problems in this country." Fulbright countered by observing (and his observation was accurate) that he and the other senior members of Arkansas' Congressional delegation had used their seniority to obtain federal government funds to assist the economic development of Arkansas, which had enjoyed substantial economic progress over the previous 30 years. Bumpers' overwhelming margin of victory (approximately 2 to 1) in the election was difficult to explain. A few political observers argued that some Arkansans regarded Fulbright as a foreign affairs specialist who did not devote sufficient attention to the domestic concerns of his constituents; this argument was speculative, however, and Fulbright actually devoted great amounts of time and energy to Arkansas affairs. One reason for the primary's denouement was simply the talent of Bumpers, who in some ways was as gifted as Fulbright. Bumpers had fashioned a successful and constructive record in his two terms as Governor. 1974—a year of inflationary troubles and the height of the Watergate crisis—was an exceedingly unfortunate time for any national incumbent to seek re-election, even though Fulbright had absolutely nothing to do with the Nixon administration's domestic wrongdoing. The Senator attempted to disassociate himself from the administration, and one of his campaign slogans proclaimed that "Nothing would make Richard Nixon happier than a Fulbright defeat." In the televised debate Bumpers acknowledged that "Senator Fulbright is a man of integrity who has disagreed very vigorously with the President." However,the voters displayed a somewhat illogical mood of resentment against all national incumbents in that year; Daniel Yergin described Fulbright as the major political casualty of "the Incumbents Syndrome of 1974."

In one sense, the Senator was identified with the administration, since he continued to encourage Kissinger's detente with China and the USSR. During the election year, Kissinger rather ostentatiously visited Arkansas to confer with Fulbright about U.S. diplomacy. At a Little Rock press conference with the Foreign Relations Committee chairman, Secretary of State Kissinger first evaded reporters' suggestions that his conference with Fulbright had political implications by joking that "I am not in my job for my competence in domestic politics," but he added that he had always respected Fulbright's advice, and claimed that during his years at Harvard "When I was a professor, I used to assign his books in my courses." The Senator's identification with the Kissinger policy was not necessarily a political disadvantage, since there was little strong evidence that detente was highly unpopular in Arkansas; and Bumpers was also a moderate in foreign policy. Whatever the explanation for the Fulbright defeat, it is clear that his dissent on Vietnam and his support for detente had no extensive impact upon his 1974 contest with Bumpers.

During his career as a Senator, Bumpers adopted a moderate, realistic approach to international issues that was reasonably similar to Fulbright's, although for obvious reasons the two men rarely acknowledged the similarities in their foreign policy positions. The 1974 election provoked bitter animosities among admirers of the two candidates, for Fulbright had assisted Bumpers' 1970 gubernatorial campaign and Bumpers had previously supported Fulbright. Admirers of Fulbright argued that Bumpers should have waited for future opportunities to run for the Senate. The Bumpers camp would respond that there was a traditional resistance in Arkansas to third gubernatorial campaigns, so that if the Governor's political career was to continue then he had no choice but to declare his candidacy in the Senate election of 1974; the Bumpers partisans also contended that Fulbright, who was 69 in 1974, should have retired. The Fulbright admirers would answer that the Senator was perfectly alert and capable of serving brilliantly for one last term at the prestigious post of Foreign Relations Committee chairman. Indeed, Fulbright was still remarkably perspicacious as late as ten years after 1974. The debate between the Fulbright and Bumpers advocates was endless; an objective observer could only regret the unfortunate situation in which two of the most eloquent and enlightened statesmen in recent American history had campaigned against each other.

In later years, Senator Bumpers opposed President Ronald Reagan's military interventionism abroad, although by 1984 he was not yet as prominent a critic of the Cold Warriors as Fulbright had been. Bumpers criticized the expanding U.S. involvement in Central America in 1983, stating that many Americans feared that Reagan "may be heading us into a war in Central America that they don't want." The Senator was even more outspoken in his dissent from the President's decision to deploy Marines in Lebanon in a quest to uphold the tottering government of Amin Gemayel. In September, 1983, Bumpers was among the minority of the members of Congress voting against a measure to allow the President to keep the Marines in Lebanon for another 18 months. During the Senate's emotional debate over Lebanon, Bumpers announced, "The people in this country do not want another 55,000 dead sons for something they do not understand . . . The parallel is not perfect, but there are enough lessons to be learned from Vietnam that we ought not to do what we are about to do." The Senator maintained that most Americans did not believe U.S. national security was endangered by the civil war in tiny Lebanon. He also opposed the measure in part because Reagan had not fulfilled his obligation under the War Powers Resolution "to tell Congress and the American people the conditions under which we will leave Lebanon." Bumpers warned his colleagues not to be influenced by a recent announcement of a cease-fire, for "This is the 172nd cease-fire in Lebanon since 1975." Arkansas' junior Senator David Pryor joined Bumpers in attempting to prevent the United States from becoming entangled in a Vietnam-like quagmire in the Middle East.

In addition to the two U.S. Senators, U.S. Representative Bill Alexander in Arkansas continued in the Fulbright tradition in opposing the Reagan administration's inverventionism. Alexander's criticisms of Reagan's policies in Lebanon and Central America were surprising, for in his early career he had not chal-

lenged the Cold Warrior approach to foreign policy; but during the
Reagan Presidency he charged that the President was speaking
publicly about negotiation while quietly continuing to escalate
hostilities in Nicaragua. When a reporter asked Alexander if he
sought to emulate Fulbright's former role as an advocate of the
amelioration of U.S.-Latin American relations, Alexander first
avoided the question by remarking, "This is a different day and
generation," but then added, "It's already done, don't you think?"
The Representative supported Congressional efforts to prohibit the
administration from supplying covert aid to the Nicaraguan rebels.
Alexander observed that most Latin Americans envisaged the 1980
Nicaraguan revolution in which the leftists came to power as the
beginning of a historic rebellion against the oligarchy, oppression,
and right-wing dictatorships that had previously dominated most
Latin American governments. In the Arkansas Congressman's
view, Latins were being united against U.S. policy by the administration's actions in Nicaragua and El Salvador, which they
regarded as "Yankee imperialism." Alexander proposed a plan for
peace in Central America, beginning with a hemispheric peace
conference including Cuba and four countries—Colombia, Mexico,
Panama, and Venezuela—that had offered to help negotiate a settlement. According to Alexander, the United States should concentrate on food and economic aid rather than military aid in Latin
America.

Alexander developed themes reminiscent of Fulbright's career
when he professed that even if his constituents displayed no concern
about Central America, he would feel obligated to educate them: "I
think I can convince my people it's in their best interest to pursue a
rational policy in Latin America. It's a [political] risk but I see it as a
challenge." In making this statement, Alexander appeared to be
pursuing the fundamental attitude advocated by Fulbright in *The
Arrogance of Power*, where the Senator explained the educational
motivations behind the decision to hold the Vietnam hearings. "The
hearings were criticized," Fulbright observed, "on the ground that
they conveyed an 'image' of the United States as divided over the
war." But the country clearly was divided, so that the hearings conveyed a fact rather than an image. The Vietnam hearings were
undertaken, Fulbright declared, "in the belief that the best way to
assure the prevalence of truth over falsehood is by exposing all
tendencies of opinion to free competition in the marketplace of
ideas. They were undertaken in something of the spirit of Thomas
Jefferson's words:

I know no safe depository of the ultimate powers of the society but the people themselves; and if we think them not

enlightened enough to exercise their control with a whole-some discretion, the remedy is not to take it from them, but to inform their discretion.

Alexander joined Fulbright (then of counsel to the Hogan and Hartson law firm in Washington) in opposing President Reagan's policies in Lebanon. Fulbright was more sharply critical of the President's intervention and placed great emphasis upon the danger that crises might erupt from the war in Lebanon that could precipitate a clash between the superpowers. In February, 1984, Alexander asserted that "the American Marines have been viewed by the majority Moslem population as the enemy because of the American support of a minority Christian government that has not shared power with a majority Moslem population." Alexander approved of the President's February decision to move the Marines from Beirut to U.S. naval vessels near the Lebanon coast, but he predicted that the ground forces' redeployment was a "prelude to a major escalation" of U.S. air and naval assaults against the enemies of the Gemayel government.

As the removal of the Marines began, American naval vessels bombarded Moslem positions east of Beirut in the most massive U.S. naval barrage since the Vietnam war. The bombardment provoked warnings by pro-Syrian factions that they would retaliate if the shelling continued. Thus, by early 1984 it was not yet clear whether the movement of the Marines would be followed by naval and aerial warfare which could heighten international tensions and risk a conflict between the superpowers. It was clear, however, that public opinion opposed the American military involvement in Lebanon; in September, 1983 a public opinion poll indicated that 58 percent of the Americans surveyed thought the Marines should be withdrawn in six months or less, and public opposition to intervention in Lebanon increased after terrorist attacks and other hostilities led to the deaths of over 260 soldiers in the last months of 1983. By early 1984, it was uncertain whether the dissent in Congress and the public would succeed in pressuring Reagan into reversing his policies in Lebanon.

A minority of Arkansas politicians, including the Republican U.S. Representative Ed Bethune, supported Reagan's crusading approach to international controversies. However, most of the major Arkansas politicians dissented from Reagan's policies. (One might also mention that Governor Bill Clinton had worked for the Foreign Relations Committee during the latter part of Fulbright's chairmanship, and most Arkansans generally regarded him as a Fulbright protege; of course, as a Governor, Clinton's attention was primarily focused on Arkansas rather than diplomatic issues.)

Thus, in the years after Fulbright's defeat,the former Senator's plea for moderation and realism was sometimes echoed in the statements of Alexander, Bumpers, Pryor, and other Arkansas figures, although by 1984 these younger men had not yet attained the international stature of Fulbright.

Fulbright was unquestionably one of the historical giants of his time. One measure of his stature was the praise he received from intellectuals and politicians of widely divergent philosophies. For example, John F. Kennedy lauded the Fulbright exhange program as "the classic modern example of beating swords into plowshares." Edward Kennedy once said of the Arkansan, "Only a small handful of Senators in our history have even begun to rival his stature in foreign affairs and his impact on the conduct of U.S. foreign relations ... From the Fulbright scholarship program to his unflagging courage and insight during the national trial of Vietnam, to divining a new course for America in the post-Vietnam era, Senator Fulbright has set the highest standards for wisdom, statesmanship, and leadership. One cannot travel anywhere without hearing him spoken of as the personification of what is best in America and best in our foreign policy." Walter Lippmann praised Fulbright as "the bravest and wisest of advisers," and John Kenneth Galbraith described him as "perhaps the most diversely intelligent legislator" of the post-World War II era. It was not surprising that Lippmann and Galbraith honored Fulbright, since they agreed with his basic perspective on American diplomacy; but perhaps the most impressive tributes to the Senator were delivered by men who had usually disagreed with him during most of his career. For example, Fulbright and Henry Kissinger, though basically in agreement concerning detente, had assumed totally antagonistic positions regarding the Vietnam war and U.S interventionism in the third world. Yet in the second volume of Kissinger's memoirs, the former Secretary of State wrote, "I greatly respected Senator Fulbright across the chasm of our policy differences for his erudition, fairness, and patriotism." At the opposite end of the philosophical spectrum from Fulbright was John McClellan, a "hawk" and a hard-line anti-communist. Yet near the end of his career, McClellan once conceded that Fulbright had "gained the recognition of being regarded as a prophet in his own time. Often in defiance of conventional wisdom he has taken a sometimes lonely and unpopular stand on some of the great issues of our day. Often, it has turned out that his position was correct."

Perhaps the man who was the most unlikely admirer of Fulbright was Dr. Martin Luther King, Jr., who wrote an encomium to Fulbright in 1965 when the Senator had just begun his historic opposition to Johnson's foreign adventures in southeast Asia and the Caribbean. The famous civil rights leader and the Southern Senator obviously held divergent views and different constituencies in the realm of civil rights; nevertheless, King had encouraged the Arkansan to continue publicizing his dissenting ideas concerning foreign policy:

> In many respects the destiny of our nation may rest largely in your hands. I know the tremendous price you pay for your outspoken critique of administration policy, and I write to you these few words simply as personal encouragement and to let you know that there are many of us who admire and respect your role in our nation's international affairs ... Yours is one voice crying in the wilderness that may ultimately awaken our people to the international facts of life. I trust that you will not let any pressure silence you.

The Senator had responded to King's epistle by confessing that "my influence is not sufficiently strong in the highest echelons of our Nation's Government to do much about the policy which is now being followed" in 1965. It was not unusual for famous Senators to receive panegyrics; but only a unique statesman could have been praised by such heterogeneous leaders as Kennedy, John McClellan, Walter Lippmann, Henry Kissinger,and Martin Luther King.

There were other leaders, of course, who denounced the Arkansas Senator during the course of his career. Joe McCarthy had lambasted him as "Halfbright." President Nixon's private denunciations of the Arkansan were reportedly too profane to be printed by most writers, while in the early 1970s General Alexander Haig privately told his associates that Fulbright was a "traitor" because of his opposition to the Vietnam war. President Johnson delivered some of the most abrasive criticisms of his former colleague, charging that Fulbright had opposed his Vietnam policies merely to attract publicity; or, in Johnsonian language, "even a blind hog can find an acorn once in a while." The President attempted to discredit Fulbright's motives, explaining to Doris Kearns that the anti-war movement was

> Nothing but a lot of sound and poppycock stimulated by the personal needs of William Fulbright ... Fulbright's problem is that he's never found any President who would appoint him Secretary of State. He is frustrated up there on the Hill. And he takes out his frustration by making all those noises about Vietnam. He wants the nation to stand up and take notice of Bill Fulbright, and he knows the best way to get that attention is to put himself in the role of

critic. He would have taken that role whichever way I moved on Vietnam.

The charge that Fulbright was frustrated because he had not been appointed Secretary of State was incorrect, for Johnson himself had complained in December, 1960, that Fulbright had made no effort to persuade President-Elect Kennedy to select him for the State Department post. Ironically, in 1960 Johnson had been one of the most vigorous advocates of the idea of appointing Fulbright to be Secretary of State. The truth seems to have been that the Senator would have accepted the Cabinet post if Kennedy had offered it to him, but that he was also quite happy to remain as Foreign Relations Chairman. In any event, Johnson was obviously vindictive and emotional in accusing Fulbright of opposing the war because of alleged frustrations over his career, for Fulbright never displayed any great zeal to become Secretary of State.

In the late 1970s and early 1980s, Fulbright enjoyed the relatively quiet role of an elder statesman. (He continued to encourage the growth of the Fulbright Scholarship program; he also agreed to the establishment of a Fulbright Institute of International Relations at the University of Arkansas and the naming of the College of Arts and Sciences at the University as the J. William Fulbright College of Arts and Sciences.) The former Senator usually did not actively involve himself in controversies over U.S. diplomacy during this period. However, Fulbright once again began to receive national attention in 1982-83 when journalists frequently sought his opinions concerning President Reagan's attempt to revive Lyndon Johnson's approach to foreign policy. Perhaps the most memorable single episode in his post-1975 career occurred in the autumn of 1983, when the Illinois Republican Charles Percy, chairman of the Senate Foreign Relations Committee, invited Fulbright to testify on the future of Soviet-American relations. Fulbright's testimony promised to be dramatic; at a time of escalating tensions between the superpowers, he was returning to the chamber where the Vietnam hearings had been held and appeared before the Committee he had led from 1959 until the end of his Senate career—the longest chairmanship over the Foreign Relations Committee of any Senator in American history.

"Perhaps I should preface my remarks with the personal observation that I am an old man of 78 years," Fulbright announced in his opening statement, "forty of which have been intimately connected with public affairs. I have witnessed many hopeful events which, with only a few exceptions, have been frustrated, so that I well may be more pessimistic than one should be." According to Fulbright, one of the greatest disappointments was the abandonment of the Nixon-Kissinger detente approach before it gained a fair trial. The former Senator emphasized that Nixon's 1972 policy eventually lost the support of Congress "for causes quite irrelevant to the validity of the process initiated and the agreements [SALT I and the "confidence-building" joint ventures for cooperative research in medicine, pollution control, space, and cultural exchange] made at that time. The failure of the President's policy was influenced by the circumstances of Watergate and the disastrous Vietnam War, which undermined the power and prestige of that administration." Fulbright observed that "some of the most disturbing aspects of our present condition are that the rhetoric of our government is so ideological and so hostile toward the Soviet Union that an objective and reasoned discussion of our relations seldom takes place." In his view, the arms race had developed a dangerous momentum propelled by vast economic power and heated ideological rivalry. Although he believed that the horror of a nuclear war acted as a restraining force upon both Russia and America, the former Senator warned that "Crises are likely to arise out of the ongoing war in the Middle East, which could lead to a clash between the Super Powers."

Fulbright contended that Reagan's interventionism in Lebanon, Grenada, and Central America was escalating the superpowers' "dangerous game of 'Tit for Tat,'" in which "a move by one calls for a response from the other." The Reagan administration frequently attempted to justify its interventions by claiming that agents of what the President had called the "evil empire" of the Soviet Union were the real enemies the United States was fighting in Central America and the Middle East. Reagan's justifications were obviously similar to the preachments of John Foster Dulles in the 1950s when Dulles portrayed Ho Chi Minh and other anti-Western third world leaders as puppets of the Soviet bloc. Fulbright warned Reagan, just as he had warned Dulles a quarter of a century before, that military crusades in the third world would wreak havoc upon the prospects for a peaceful international order. The former Senator noted several volatile regions where great power confrontations might occur: "For example, in case of a conflict between Israel and Syria and the occupation of Damascus, the Soviets may come to the aid of Syria, and the U.S. is not likely to stand aside;" or, he observed, in response to the administration's decision to invade Grenada the U.S.S.R. might accelerate its military aid to Nicaragua and Cuba. He also reminded the Committee that the Soviets might "increase the number of submarines off our coast ready to send missiles to Washington as quickly as our Pershings can reach Moscow from Germany. Such a game is likely to end in a conflict." The former Senator advocated a reduction in

Soviet-American tensions by negotiating and ratifying strategic arms limitation treaties (such as SALT II, which the Senate never approved) and other cooperative agreements, and by ending the reckless game of intervening against leftists or alleged Soviet agents anywhere in the world. Such moderate and realistic policies, Fulbright contended, would affect the climate of hostility which contributed to the outbreak of violence by both superpowers in crises such as "the Korean plane tragedy, the Grenada affair, and the ongoing conflict in the Middle East."

Fulbright quoted several famous statements by historical figures in an effort to support his plea for an end to the rigid and chronic American animosity towards the Soviet Union. He asked the Committee to remember that in Washington's Farewell Address, the first President had counseled his countrymen to avoid indulging in ideological or emotional biases towards other nations: "A nation which indulges toward another an habitual hatred, or an habitual fondness, is in some degree a slave. It is a slave to its animosity or to its affection, either of which is sufficient to lead it astray from its duty and its interest." Fulbright compared the Soviet-American arms race to the militaristic rivalries that had afflicted Europe before World War I. He recalled that after the First World War, Lord Grey (British Foreign Minister before and during World War I) had analyzed the origins of that war in these words: "Every country had been piling up armaments and perfecting preparations for war. The object in each case had been security. The effect had been precisely the contrary." The perfecting and stockpiling of armaments, Fulbright asserted, "is exactly what we are doing today." The former Chairman argued that a more enlightened approach to international relations was suggested in Freud's celebrated 1932 letter to Einstein: "Anything that creates emotional ties between human beings must inevitably counteract war . . . Everything that leads to important shared action creates such common feelings, such identifications. On them the structure of human society in good measure rests." In Fulbright's view, these sentiments in the Freud-Einstein correspondence were consistent with the policies advocated by the supporters of detente in 1972.

During his November, 1983 testimony, the former Chairman implored the Committee members to acquire a sense of empathy for the Soviets' world view. The United States had never been invaded and enjoyed borders with two friendly and comparatively weak nations, while the great Russian plains, Fulbright reminded the Senators, "have throughout history been tempting to foreign invaders, and since the 13th century, they have succumbed to that temptation on numerous occasions. We should recognize that these

227

experiences have affected and do affect the Soviets' point of view." He suggested that the members of the Committee might reflect upon the thought that if they were members of the Politburo, they would probably be "deeply disturbed by the installation of Pershing missiles in Germany and Western Europe, and by the congressional appropriations of $250 billion for armaments." He believed the Politburo would probably be even more disturbed by the prospect that in a future war, the Soviets might be opposed not only by its traditional enemies to the west and south, but also by Britain, France, and the United States—nations which had been Soviet allies in the previous World War—and by some of the disaffected Soviet satellites. According to Fulbright, any nation would be anxious about its national security when confronted by the possibility of facing such an unprecedented combination of power.

Fulbright proposed that Reagan should reverse the direction of his Soviet policies, just as Presidents Kennedy and Nixon had during the course of their administrations. Nixon had been a zealous Cold Warrior throughout most of his career, Fulbright recalled, until he displayed the flexibility to change his policies towards the great communist powers in the early 1970s. The former Chairman did not state the obvious point, which all the Senators were aware of, that he had always been an ardent critic of Nixon's dogged adherence to military intervention in southeast Asia in the early 1970s; Nixon's southeast Asian policies remained the central blot on the former President's diplomatic record.

Fulbright regarded President Kennedy's emergence as an advocate of stable and normal Soviet-American relations in 1963 as an even more impressive example of intellectual growth and flexibility than Nixon's reversal of his Soviet policies in 1971-1972. He observed that Kennedy had pursued "a very hard line indeed with the Russians" during the years 1960-1962, pledging to end the "so-called missile gap," authorizing the Bay of Pigs debacle, and threatening war over the Berlin crisis and over Russian missiles in Cuba. "However," Fulbright concluded, "after looking 'down the abyss,' as it is said, at the time of the missile crisis in October, 1962, Kennedy abruptly changed course and negotiated the Test Ban Treaty in August of 1963, after making the most enlightened and conciliatory speech about the Soviet Union of any President in June, 1963, at American University. It was the hope for the establishment of more normal relations with the Soviet Union aroused by that speech and the treaty that, in my opinion, accounts for much of the faith in and respect for what is often called the Kennedy 'Legend' or Camelot."

Fulbright did not argue that in 1963 Kennedy had attempted to alter the Cold War policies of interventionism in Vietnam. Several months before his assassination, Kennedy asked Canadian Prime Minister Lester Pearson for his advice concerning U.S. policy in southeast Asia, and Pearson answered, "Get out." The President bluntly replied, "That's a stupid answer. Everybody knows that. The question is: How do we get out?" Mike Mansfield and White House official Kenneth O'Donnell later contended that the President had privately informed them in 1963 that he planned to withdraw the U.S. military presence from South Vietnam, but he would have to wait until 1965 to do so in order to avoid right-wing charges of "appeasement" in his 1964 re-election campaign. At a high-level administration policy meeting in the autumn of 1963, Robert Kennedy noted the chaotic nature of the Saigon regime and the devastating impact of the war upon the Vietnamese people; he then proposed that the United States should consider withdrawing from Vietnam. Robert Kennedy was the first powerful Presidential adviser to privately suggest the possibility of a withdrawal as a solution to the American dilemma in southeast Asia. There was no public reversal of U.S. southeast Asian policy in 1963, of course, and it will never be known whether President Kennedy would have changed America's course in Vietnam if he had lived to serve a second term.

Senator Percy or one of the other Senators who attended the November, 1983 hearing might have asked Fulbright if he felt that the changes in the Kennedy foreign policy in 1963 were confined to the arena of the direct relationship between America and Russia, or if he believed that Kennedy had also considered changing the policy of interventionism in the third world. No Senator asked Fulbright this fairly obvious question, even though the Arkansan had stressed in his statement that military interventionism by the superpowers in favor of their respective third world clients had frequently damaged Soviet-American relations. In fact, Percy and his colleagues generated very little debate at the hearing with the former Chairman. Percy had been a member of the Foreign Relations Committee during the last few years of Fulbright's Senate career, but as Chairman he did not follow in Fulbright's tradition of utilizing hearings to promote a candid national discussion of American diplomacy. In the early 1980s the Foreign Relations Committee was a shadow of what it had been at the height of Fulbright's Chairmanship. For example, a clear majority of the Committee members had attended each of the Vietnam hearings; and at most of the important hearings during the late 1960s and early 1970s several Senators, notably Fulbright, Morse (until his defeat in 1968), Gore, McCarthy, Church, and (after 1967) John Sherman Cooper had consistently promoted an extensive and perceptive dialogue with the wit-

229

nesses. In contrast, only four Senators attended the November, 1983 hearing, and only Percy and ranking Democrat Claiborne Pell of Rhode Island asked a few perfunctory questions.

No one asked Fulbright for his thoughts concerning the recent Soviet shooting of a Korean airliner (although he had briefly mentioned it in his statement), and other important questions were not raised by the Senators. The exchange between Fulbright and Percy was amicable: Fulbright commended the Committee for holding the hearing and Percy praised Fulbright's record as Chairman, stating "The longer I serve in this chair, the more I realize the burden and load that you carried and the greatness and the dignity with which you carried this gavel." But Percy was a supporter of the administration, and he clearly did not wish to encourage and prolong a dialogue in which the former Chairman was trenchantly pointing out the dangerous flaws in Reagan's foreign adventures. During the early 1980s, the Republican Mark Hatfield of Oregon, Edward Kennedy, the Arkansas Senators, and others promoted educational discussion of and debate over U.S. foreign policy, but the Senate Foreign Relations Committee under Percy did not provide vigorous leadership in this discussion.

Percy was pleased by the former Chairman's observation that "if President Reagan would change course, revive the spirit of detente, negotiate a significant agreement with the Russians, stop and reverse the arms race in a credible manner, that confidence in peace would be restored, the budget could be balanced, interest rates would come down, and the economy of the world, certainly including that of the United States, would revive, and he would be elected next year by a landslide. If he did such things, I surely would be tempted to vote for him." The Illinois Senator chuckled at the notion that Fulbright might vote for Reagan, whereupon Fulbright asserted that Reagan was not serious about arms control and a reversal in his policies was unlikely. According to the Arkansan, the President was interested not in arms control but in achieving military superiority for the United States. He maintained that from the beginning of the Reagan administration the President had demanded a $1½ trillion arms program and that after "he gets that $1½ trillion and he has what he considers superiority over the Russians," then he might attempt to freeze the strategic arms ratio at a level of U.S. superiority. An obvious difficulty with the Reagan approach was that the Soviets had always attempted to match the Reagan arms escalation, and they could not be expected to acquiesce in their own strategic inferiority.

One might also argue that the entire concept of strategic superiority was chimerical in an age when both superpowers could destroy each other many times over. Fulbright observed that Dean Rusk had proclaimed after the Cuban missile crisis that the Americans and Russians were "eyeball to eyeball, and the Russians blinked first." "But it was rumored," the former Chairman informed the Senators, "that Mr. Khrushchev said after that, 'Yes, but the next time we won't be the one to blink first.' I think that next time may well have arrived. In other words, they have enough weapons now that they won't be bluffed as easily as then [1962] because they obviously were inferior." Fulbright regarded the relative military power of America and Russia in the 1980s as "a condition of parity, or as near parity as you are likely to get." In a condition of inferiority on the part of one of the powers, the superior side usually attempted to preserve its advantage, while the inferior side tended to engage in feverish efforts to expand its strategic arsenal; hence Fulbright envisaged the contemporary situation of relative strategic parity as providing a historic opportunity for progress in arms control.

Most of Fulbright's conclusions were generally supported by retired Admiral Noel Gayler, one of the other witnesses at the November, 1983 hearing; while two bitterly anti-Soviet witnesses, especially Reagan's former National Security Adviser Richard Allen, sharply disagreed with the former Chairman. In contrast to Fulbright's perspective, Richard Allen used phrases redolent of John Foster Dulles' pronouncements in condemning the Soviet Union as an allegedly fiendish threat to the peace and civilization of the world. According to Allen, Reagan was not a "gun-slinging Western cowboy," but rather a thoughtful man who believed that the Soviets respected only military strength in their rivals. The President's former adviser alleged that ultimate Soviet objectives encompassed the control of the Panama Canal and the Marxist "liberation" of Mexico, and that the Soviets were constantly engaged in revolutionary warfare and "the unbridled use of terrorism as a destabilizing force throughout the world." Allen did not adduce any evidence to prove that the Soviets intended to control Mexico and the Panama Canal, he merely asserted it; he also implied that the Russians were basically responsible for all revolution or terrorism throughout the globe, ignoring the reality that much of this subversion and violence emanated from indigenous sources in the third world.

The hearing was not long enough for Fulbright to answer all of Allen's allegations, but he did respond to the complaint that Reagan sincerely desired arms control but had been frustrated by Soviet unwillingness to end the arms race. The former Senator recalled that the Soviets had offered to reduce their SS-20s to 140, if the

Reagan administration would not deploy Pershing missiles in Europe, but the administration dismissed the Soviet proposal "as of no consequence." In Fulbright's opinion,the President had agreed to the INF (intermediate nuclear force) talks in Geneva only after the nuclear freeze movement had acquired an imposing momentum within the United States,when there were "stories in the paper, bills in the Congress, and people like Kennedy and Hatfield, the chairman of the Appropriations Committee, and others, very prominent Senior Members, who were beginning to show an interest and get a following." Fulbright argued that the Geneva talks were charades, which Reagan had undertaken to "pull the teeth" of the domestic nuclear freeze movement, so that the President "said we will go to Geneva. It did have that effect. People thought, well after all, he has made a gesture." But Fulbright could not detect any evidence of a genuine negotiating effort by the President, and he pointedly noted that Reagan had appointed as leader of the Geneva talks a General, Edward Rowny, who had not demonstrated a serious concern for arms control.

The Arkansan generally avoided attempts to predict specific future events, but he did maintain that the Russians would leave INF if the administration deployed the Pershing missiles in western Europe. Allen had prophesied that the Soviets would be impressed by Reagan's "toughness" and begin to negotiate after the deployment occurred. When the Pershings were deployed shortly after the November, 1983 hearing, Allen was proven to be somewhat lacking as a prophet, as the Soviets at least temporarily withdrew from INF and warned that they would escalate their build-up and deployment of nuclear weapons in response to the President's action.

Senator Pell's questioning fostered the most acid exchange of the hearing between Allen and Fulbright. Pell complimented Fulbright's achievement in influencing many Americans to question the "hawkish" consensus which had dominated U.S. foreign policy before the mid-1960s. "Looking back at the Vietnam war," the Rhode Island Senator said, "I think it was thanks to Senator Fulbright and the committee that public opinion got turned around." Pell hoped that the advocates of a moderate American foreign policy in the 1980s would continue to attempt to encourage an enlightened public dialogue, just as the opponents of the Vietnam war had done. He asked Allen to respond to a report Pell and several other Senators (including Bumpers) had written after they had conferred with Soviet leader Andropov in August. The report concluded that both the Reagan administration and the Soviet leadership had failed to advance constructive proposals for nuclear arms control, and that many Soviet leaders "believe that the U.S. Government has no interest in better relations with the Soviet Union." As Allen conceded, Reagan had been one of the vociferous critics of SALT II and contributed to the eventual demise of that treaty, and by early 1984 he had not fulfilled his 1980 campaign pledge to negotiate arms reduction agreements with the U.S.S.R. Nevertheless, Allen simply argued that Reagan's opponents were irresponsible and the American people should trust their President. Allen assured the Committee that he had known the President for years and understood Reagan's intentions: "I am going to continue to believe him as long as he gives his word that he does want such an agreement." Fulbright disagreed with the notion that Americans should dutifully trust Reagan's intentions; in his view, Presidents and their policies should be judged by their effects and actions, not by their promises. "With regard to what Mr. Allen just said," Fulbright countered, "in my position I do not have to believe the President, and in my experience with former Presidents, I know they don't always tell the truth. There is no reason why anybody has to believe any President. You have to judge him by circumstances, by what he actually does and the effect of it. I used to believe President Johnson until I learned better."

Allen condemned as "an abysmal failure" the detente policy Fulbright had supported. Instead of exerting a moderating effect on Soviet behavior, Allen asserted that detente had led to a massive Soviet military build-up and the brutal communist conquest of Cambodia, South Vietnam, and Laos in the years after America withdrew from southeast Asia. He neglected to mention the American failure to give detente a fair trial. And he did not explain how the detente policies of the early 1970s had supposedly caused the results of the Indochina wars.

Allen ignored the reality that southeast Asia has always been outside the range of vital American interests. If the United States constantly followed Allen's suggestion that America must halt all repression, then the United States should intervene to stop the brutal actions of regimes in South Africa, El Salvador, Guatemala, Iran, Vietnam, Chile, and dozens of other repressive nations in every corner of the globe; but such a policy was clearly beyond the power of America or any other nation to enforce. Allen's argument was disconnected and vague on this point, but he seemed to be arguing that detente had caused the fall of South Vietnam and Cambodia to the communists and that the United States should have prevented the violence that occurred in southeast Asia after the fall of Saigon in 1975. The obvious question arises as to how the United States could have done this, unless Allen meant that another massive U.S. military expedition should have been dispatched to Vietnam and Cambodia in the late 1970s. One wonders how many more billions of dollars, and how many more tens of thousands of American lives Allen might have wished that the United States had hurled into the maelstrom of southeast Asia. The violence and repression in southeast Asia after 1975 were brutal, but the entire history of the U.S. involvement had demonstrated the virtually insurmountable difficulties America experienced in its futile quest to control events in far-away Indochina. Neither the United States nor any other nation possessed the power to eradicate all brutality from the world. If the republic continued to dissipate its resources on adventures such as the Vietnam war, then America might find itself too over-extended and exhausted to confront a genuine threat to its vital interests at some time in the future.

American public attitudes towards interventionism had changed in the years from the height of the Cold War until the post-Vietnam era. However, many of the Richard Allens, Ronald Reagans, and other rigid anti-communists had not changed their views. Reagan had been a supporter of the Vietnam war, and in 1980 he called the war a noble cause that failed. Although the Cold Warriors had not altered their basic assumptions even in the aftermath of Vietnam, it was nevertheless true that in the 1980s Reagan's attempts to escalate U.S. involvement in Lebanon and Central America encountered greater resistance from the public and Congress than earlier Presidents had faced in executing interventions in the 1950s and 1960s. Johnson had received massive Congressional and public support for his Vietnam policy in 1964 and 1965. In contrast, in the 1980s opinion polls and other indications of public attitudes registered extensive opposition to escalation in Lebanon and Central America. By early 1984, the administration had ordered a military withdrawal, at least temporarily, from Lebanon. Richard Allen claimed that Reagan had been elected because of his "tough" anti-Soviet stance in foreign policy, but this assertion was inaccurate. Reagan was elected primarily because of some of his domestic positions, his promises in 1980 to reduce the federal deficits (a promise much further than ever from fulfillment by 1984), popular dissatisfaction with the incumbent administration, and a variety of other reasons; but one of his greatest political disadvantages was the widespread misgiving that he was reckless in foreign policy. By early 1984, this misgiving remained one of the most serious of Reagan's political liabilities. It was always possible that the crusading militarism of the 1950s and 1960s might revive at some point in the future, of course. But in the late 1970s and early 1980s the political environment had changed (not necessarily perm-

234

anently) since the earlier epoch, when Presidents could wield a virtually unrestricted anti-communist consensus in support of their decision for intervention. To a certain extent, this change emanated from the military labyrinth which had frustrated America in Vietnam; but in addition to the obvious military difficulties of the southeast Asian conflict, an enlightened group of intellectual and political leaders had educated most thoughtful Americans regarding the fallacies and prejudices that led to the disastrous Vietnam war. In that endeavor, no one exercised more vigorous leadership than J. William Fulbright.

Conclusion

During the Nixon Presidency Fulbright had been active in the Congressional movement to terminate funds for the war. His reluctance to sponsor legislation ending appropriations for the war had probably been the only significant flaw in his opposition to the Vietnam war in the later years of the Johnson administration. Fulbright believed that the Senators who would have voted for an amendment cutting off the war funds would have been a small minority, and President Johnson would have claimed such an amendment's resounding defeat as another triumphant Congressional endorsement of his Vietnam policy. The anti-war forces, in Fulbright's view during the Johnson years, would have to change public opinion concerning the war and gather strength in the Senate before introducing amendments to terminate the funds. Yet it might also be argued that if Fulbright had voted against the appropriations in the early years of the escalation, he might have established the precedent that no member of Congress should ever feel obligated to support funds for a war he detested. A dissenting vote by Fulbright might have encouraged other Senators to become more resolute in opposing the Vietnam war. These arguments are conjectural, however, and one could easily sympathize with Fulbright's perspective, since the dissident bloc of Senators constituted a small minority throughout most of the Johnson Presidency.

It is clear that Fulbright was dilatory in publicly challenging the escalation policy in Vietnam during 1964 and 1965. The crucial reasons for his indecisive public responses to Johnson's Vietnam policies in late 1964 and early 1965 were his conviction that Johnson was moderate and reluctant to use force, his fear of the Goldwater Presidential candidacy, his inaccurate view of China as an aggressive power, and his belief until the summer of 1965 that he could influence Johnson through private communications. Fulbright envisaged his emerging adversary role with distaste, for in the years before 1965 he had usually preferred to exert influence quietly within the policy-making process. The Senator's scholarly approach to foreign policy controversies also tended to delay the presentation of his public positions, for he would deliver important statements on U.S policies only after extended periods of laborious research. His careful strategy, however, had the salutary effect of convincing many Americans that Fulbright was not an irresponsible radical, but that he was a moderate who had arrived at his adversary role only after a painful and judicious re-evaluation of American diplomacy.

Frequently during the Senator's career, one sensed the tension within Fulbright created by pressures to remain in the mainstream and cultivate his ties to the Establishment, and the conflicting pressures to speak for the dissenters and those who believed that the republic was abandoning the profound, realistic diplomatic tradition established by the Founding Fathers. Fulbright's greatest accomplishments would come when he assumed the duties of the dissenter and eschewed the dream of influencing the panorama of events by private remonstrances through the elite, as he had devoted much time and energy in doing in the early 1960s until mid-1965. Under Fulbright's leadership in 1966, the Senate Foreign Relations Committee had indeed embarked upon the historic task of educating the nation concerning the realities of Asia and American foreign policy; but the program of enlightening and changing public opinion through speeches, books, and hearings was an arduous, time-consuming struggle that would require years to complete its full effects. For years after the vast American armies began to enter the rice paddies and elephant grass of Vietnam in 1965, critics of America's lost crusade would be haunted by somber reflections about the delay in the Senate's challenge to the intervention. If there was any possibility that the dissenters might have prevented the escalation, that possibility may have existed in inaugurating the campaign of enlightenment concerning the Far East in the early 1960s, before hundreds of thousands of American soldiers had arrived in Vietnam, before many Americans imagined that the national honor and prestige were in peril, and before the Vietnam policy had become enshrouded in the flag. Whether these disturbing doubts embraced the truth can never be determined.

Fulbright's record after 1965 is much more difficult to criticize (with the possible exception of the controversy over termination of the war appropriations.) The journalist I. F. Stone, an early critic of

America's involvement in the southeast Asian conflict who had disparaged Fulbright's views on Vietnam in 1964-1965, argued that Fulbright's opposition to the Vietnam war after 1965 was so courageous and eloquent "that it makes much that went before forgivable." According to Robert Beisner, Fulbright and other dissenters directed an attack on the Vietnam war which was among "the most comprehensive, meticulously detailed, merciless and unremitting ever to be directed at a government of the United States in its conduct of foreign affairs." David Halberstam described the Senate Foreign Relations Committee and its chairman as "the center of opposition" to the war. The historian Daniel Yergin delivered an unusually perceptive assessment of Fulbright's opposition to the Vietnam war: "What is most important to say about Fulbright and Vietnam is that, though he was not the first Senator to oppose the United States involvement in war there, he, more than any other politician except perhaps Eugene McCarthy, made opposition respectable, even possible. His example seemed to say that you could still be a loyal American and not subscribe to the militant anti-Communist creed."

During the later 1960s, Fulbright used his position as chairman of the Foreign Relations Committee to disseminate the knowledge that China was not a relentlessly expansionist power and North Vietnam was not a Chinese satellite. Fulbright further attempted to argue that the Vietnam war was not simply a unique aberration arising from the dynamics of an incredibly complicated situation, but was a manifestation of a historical phenomenon which had afflicted all the great nations of the past. The United States was exhibiting in Vietnam "the arrogance of power," the tendency of nations at the apogee of their power to see their economic and political ascendancy as proof of their national virtue and to confuse their immense responsibilities with an obligation to eradicate evil from the universe. If the United States hoped to avoid allowing "the arrogance of power" to dominate its foreign policy, the people of America must recognize that communism might be a harsh system for organizing society, but it is not a nefarious conspiracy to banish freedom from the earth.

It should be acknowledged that some Americans remained hostile to Fulbright's ideas concerning U.S. foreign policy. The Congressional movement to terminate funds for the war did not succeed until late in the Nixon administration. Many of the more zealous anti-communists remained unrepentant, lamenting that America had failed to unleash sufficient violence against the Vietnamese communists. In the late 1970s the scholar Guenter Lewy, the columnist George Will, and others began an intellectual counter-offensive against the "no more Vietnams" consensus. Will vaguely asserted that a failure to intervene in future foreign crises could lead to the "loss" of the Middle East and the collapse of N.A.T.O. In contrast to Fulbright's "arrogance of power" theses, McGeorge Bundy contended that Vietnam was unique, and therefore no lessons could be learned from America's tragic experience in southeast Asia.

It is likely that from the perspective of the small group of elitists who essentially directed American diplomacy during the 1960s, the American withdrawal from Vietnam did not symbolize the repudiation of the policy of enhancing America's credibility in the role of the global anti-communist gendarme. McGeorge Bundy, one of the principal architects of America's strategy in Vietnam, had written in 1965 that the plan of "sustained reprisal against North Vietnam may fail. . . . What we can say is that even if it fails, the policy will be worth it"; the implication being that even a disastrous war effort would strengthen American credibility by demonstrating that the United States was not only a powerful nation but was utterly determined to exercise its power. America evacuated Vietnam after the terror bombings of North Vietnam completed the most massive campaign of aerial devastation in the history of warfare. This senseless paroxysm of violence in 1972 could only be explained as one last, defiant affirmation by the United States that even after the expenditure of over $200 billion, after the "roles of America and Russia have been reversed in the world's eyes" in Arnold Toynbee's words, and after decades of war in which as many as 2 million people may have been killed in Indochina, America remained undaunted in its will to use it matchless power, in its resolve to confront what Kissinger had called "the risks of Armageddon." Six years after the Foreign Relations Committee hearings on Vietnam had revitalized the essential process of serious, sustained dialogue between the public and the policy-making elite, the United States was not only still fighting in Vietnam, but the quest for upholding America's "credibility" had attained its frenzied zenith.

Nixon's tactics of escalating the air war, expanding the South Vietnamese ground forces, and withdrawing American troops were clearly effective in delaying the success of the Congressional movement to end the war. Yet when Richard Nixon, the infamous anti-communist of the 1950s, could visit Peking and drink toasts to Mao Tse-tung in February, 1972, then travel to Moscow in May and simultaneously address the Russian and American peoples on international television, Fulbright was not naive when he approved of the "welcome reversal" in American diplomacy with respect to the great communist powers. The improvement of American relations with the Soviet Union and China rendered the U.S. involvement in Vietnam completely irrational, for the United States had originally intervened in southeast Asia to block the expansionism of an allegedly Soviet-controlled communist monolith across Asia, and America had enlarged its commitment to South Vietnam to halt the presumed aggression of China. Nixon evaded charges of pursuing contradictory foreign policies by increasingly referring to Vietnam as a test of American determination to maintain world order, but Fulbright dismissed this nebulous concept as no more convincing than the earlier rationalizations for the Vietnam war. Nevertheless, Fulbright continued to support the Kissinger-Nixon detente policies unti the end of his Senate career in 1975.

President Johnson's diplomacy had not deviated from the post-war anti-communist dogmas, either in Vietnam or in his policies toward the great communist powers. E. W. Kenworthy had obviously been correct when he predicted in 1965 that the Johnson administration would repeatedly reject the Arkansas Senator's advice regarding the southeast Asian conflict. Fulbright's influence upon public opinion constituted the basic significance of his opposition to the Vietnam war. The chairman of the Foreign Relations Committee had gradually changed the ideas of many Americans concerning U.S. foreign policy; if the public opinion polls and foreign affairs analysts such as Daniel Yergin and David Halberstam were correct, then by the mid-1970s the vast majority of the American people belatedly endorsed Fulbright's dissent against the war. Whether Fulbright and the other major critics of the war had fostered a permanent re-evaluation of public attitudes toward American foreign policy was uncertain, however, and it was clear that even in the 1970s the Senator's plea for an amelioration of American relations with the Soviet Union frequently encountered hostility.

Yet it is true that many Americans eventually recognized the validity in Fulbright's indictment of anti-communist military expeditions abroad, especially when he appealed for a return to the "traditional America" of Jefferson, John Quincy Adams, Lincoln, and Adlai Stevenson, the America which abhorred the dream of a militaristic destiny for the United States. Any claim of a partial and belated victory for the Vietnam war's adversaries must be juxtaposed, of course, with the Johnson and Nixon administration's long succession of political "triumphs" in escalating and prolonging the tragic American military commitment to South Vietnam. Nevertheless, Fulbright and the other antagonists of the rigid anti-communist world view had helped to create a general consensus against "future Vietnams" by the mid-1970s, so that the opponents of the Vietnam war may have achieved a certain limited (and not necessarily permanent) victory in the political struggle which began in 1965-1966 and continued through the 1970s. Perhaps this limited victory of the dissenters had been assured, in a symbolic sense, from the day at the 1966 Vietnam hearings when George Kennan and J. William Fulbright endorsed the proposition that John Quincy Adams' famous pronouncement of July 4, 1821 had directly addressed the America of the latter twentieth century: "Wherever the standard of freedom and independence has been or shall be unfurled, there will be America's heart, her benedictions, and her prayers. But she goes not abroad in search of monsters to destroy."

Biographical Sketch of J. William Fulbright

James William Fulbright was born in Missouri in 1905, and a year later his family moved to Fayetteville, Arkansas. His family owned a number of business enterprises and a newspaper. His mother, Roberta Fulbright, was one of the most prominent journalists in Arkansas.

Fulbright graduated from the University of Arkansas and subsequently held a Rhodes Scholarship. After he graduated from Oxford in 1928, he spent one year traveling on the continent of Europe. In the early 1930s he attended George Washington University Law School. He married Elizabeth Williams of Philadelphia. After graduating from law school, he served from 1934 to 1935 as a special attorney in the Justice Department's Anti-Trust Division. From 1935 to 1936 he was a law professor at George Washington University. In 1936 he returned to Fayetteville to become a law professor at the University of Arkansas. He also helped manage the Fulbright businesses.

From 1939 to 1941 Fulbright was the president of the University of Arkansas. He was the youngest university president in the United States. During his presidency, he supported William Allen White's Committee to Defend America by Aiding the Allies. In 1941, Arkansas Governor Homer Adkins engineered the young president's dismissal as a part of a vendetta against the Fulbright family for Roberta Fulbright's editorial criticisms of Adkins. Fulbright's opponent in his 1942 campaign for the U.S. House of Representatives was an ally of Adkins. In the 1944 U.S. Senate campaign in Arkansas, Fulbright and Adkins received the largest number of votes in the primary election, and Fulbright defeated his family's old adversary in the run-off election. See Haynes Johnson and Bernard Gwertzman, *Fulbright the Dissenter*.

There are hundreds of important facts concerning Fulbright's career after 1945; a list of a few of them follows:

1946 - President Harry S. Truman signed the Fulbright Act, creating the Fulbright Scholar Program.

1949 - Fulbright became a member of the Senate Foreign Relations Committee.

1951 - Fulbright supported Truman in the MacArthur-Truman controversy during the Korean War.

1954 - Fulbright cast the lone dissenting vote against the appropriations for Senator Joseph McCarthy's Permanent Investigations subcommittee.

1957 - Fulbright opposed the Eisenhower Doctrine.

1959 - Fulbright became the chairman of the Senate Foreign Relations Committee. He was chairman of the Committee from 1959 until January, 1975, the longest chairmanship over Foreign Relations of any Senator in American history.

1961 - In March, Fulbright delivered his Cuban memorandum to President John F. Kennedy, arguing against the Bay of Pigs invasion.

1963 - Fulbright supported the Nuclear Test Ban Treaty.

1964 - Fulbright supported President Lyndon B. Johnson in the election of 1964.

1965 - On September 15, Fulbright delivered his Senate speech opposing the U.S. intervention in the Dominican Republic.

1966 - The Vietnam hearings were held, followed by an extensive program of hearings on the crucial issues involving U.S. foreign policy during the remaining years of Fulbright's chairmanship.

1966 - In the spring, Fulbright delivered his lectures on "The Arrogance of Power" at Johns Hopkins University.

1968 - Fulbright gained re-election to the Senate after emphasizing his opposition to the Vietnam war throughout his campaign.

1973 - In the summer, Fulbright supported the movement to cut off funds for the bombing of Cambodia.

1974 - Fulbright was defeated for re-election by Governor Dale Bumpers; afterwards he became counsel to a famous Washington law firm.

1983 - Fulbright testified before the Senate Foreign Relations Committee concerning the future of Soviet-American relations.

Bibliographical Notes

In writing this book I have relied upon a wide variety of sources. Scholars interested in doing research on Senator Fulbright's foreign policy positions may wish to read my entire manuscript, which includes 75 pages of footnotes and bibliography. The manuscript is in the Special Collections Room at the University of Arkansas Library in Fayetteville.

The sources I have used are too numerous to discuss in their entirety. However, I might note the most important sources, especially the J. William Fulbright Papers at the University of Arkansas. This book makes extensive use of the correspondence, memoranda, and the large collection of various other types of documents in the Fulbright Papers. Almost all of the correspondence I have discussed refers to documents in the Fulbright Papers.

Transcripts of Senate Foreign Relations Committee hearings were important sources. Fulbright was involved in an extraordinarily large number of important hearings. A list of a few of them follows:

> U. S. Congress. Senate. Committee on Foreign Relations. *Military Situation in the Far East.* May-August, 1951. Washington: Government Printing Office, 1951. (All the hearings listed here were published by the Government Printing Office.)
>
> _____. Subcommittee. *Nomination of Philip C. Jessup to be United States Representative to the Sixth General Assembly of the United Nations.* September-October, 1951. Washington: 1951.
>
> _____. *Mutual Security Act of 1954.* June, 1954. Washington: 1954.
>
> _____. *The Southeast Asia Collective Defense Treaty.* November, 1954. Washington: 1954.

————. Committee on Armed Services and Committee on Foreign Relations, Joint Hearing. *The Southeast Asia Resolution.* August, 1964. Washington: 1966.

————. *Foreign Assistance, 1965.* March and April, 1965. Washington: 1965.

————. *Supplemental Foreign Assistance, Fiscal Year 1966—Vietnam.* [Known as the Vietnam hearings] January and February, 1966. Washington: 1966.

————. *U.S. Policy With Respect to Mainland China.* March, 1966.

————. *Foreign Assistance, 1966.* April and May, 1966. Washington: 1966.

————. *Foreign Assistance Act of 1968.* March, 1968. Washington: 1968.

————. *The Impact of the War in Southeast Asia on the United States Economy.* April-August, 1970. Washington: 1970.

————. *The Moral and Military Aspects of the War in Southeast Asia.* May, 1970. Washington: 1970.

————. *China and the United States: Today and Yesterday.* February, 1972. Washington 1972.

————. *The Causes, Origins, and Lessons of the Vietnam War.* May, 1972. Washington: 1972.

————. *The Future of United States-Soviet Relations.* November, 1983. Washington: 1983.

A useful collection of Fulbright's speeches and memoranda from 1940 to 1962 can be found in *Fulbright of Arkansas: The Public Positions of a Private Thinker* (Washington: Robert B. Luce, Inc., 1963) edited with an introduction by Karl E. Meyer, and with a foreword by Walter Lippmann. The *Congressional Record* is another source for some of Fulbright's comments. For Fulbright's most detailed expositions of his dissent from postwar American foreign policy, see the books written by the Senator, especially *The Arrogance of Power* (New York: Random House-Vintage Books, 1967), *The Pentagon Propaganda Machine* (New York: Random House-Vintage Books, 1971), and *The Crippled Giant: American Foreign Policy and its Domestic Consequences* (New York: Random House-Vintage Books, 1972). I have discussed *The Arrogance of Power* and *The Crippled Giant* in detail, of course. *The Pentagon Propaganda Machine* is an expansion of a series of Senate speeches Fulbright delivered in 1969 in an effort to make the Senate and the public aware of the quietly pervasive nature of the Defense Department's public relations activities. For the Senator's foreign policy positions in 1964, *Old Myths and New Realities* (New York: Random

House-Vintage Books, 1964), is a useful source. The earliest and probably the least important of Fulbright's books was *Prospects for the West* (Cambridge, Massachusetts: Harvard University Press, 1963). *The Role of Congress in Foreign Policy* (Washington: American Enterprise Institute for Public Policy Research, 1971) is a transcript of a debate between Fulbright and Senator John C. Stennis of Mississippi concerning the proper roles of Congress and the President in the formulation of foreign policy. Fulbright stressed his familiar theme of opposition to the excessive expansion of the executive's power, while Stennis, an opponent of both the Cooper-Church and McGovern-Hatfield amendments, did not express any particular concern over the Presidency's leadership in foreign policy decision-making in recent American history.

I consulted various State Department publications and the *Public Papers of the Presidents of the United States* for the administrations of Truman through Johnson. The memoirs of the Presidents and their principal aides are also interesting, such as Dean Acheson's *Present at the Creation: My Years in the State Department* (New York: Norton, 1969); Dwight D. Eisenhower's *Mandate for Change, 1953-1956* and *Waging Peace, 1956-1961* (Garden City, New York: Doubleday, 1963-1965); Lyndon Baines Johnson's *The Vantage Point: Perspectives of the Presidency, 1963-1969* (New York: Holt, Rinehart, Winston, 1971); Henry A. Kissinger's *White House Years* and *Years of Upheaval* (Boston: Little, Brown and Company, 1979 and 1982); and many other memoirs. For a collection of Adlai Stevenson's correspondence and other documents relating to his career, I used *The Papers of Adlai E. Stevenson*, edited by Walter Johnson, especially *Volume VIII, Ambassador to the United Nations, 1961-1965* (Boston: 1969).

For contemporary journalistic accounts and analyses of postwar American diplomacy, I studied past editions of the *New York Times, Washington Post, Arkansas Gazette, St. Louis Post-Dispatch, Time, Newsweek,* and *U.S. News and World Report,* and other journals. I read these newspapers and magazines basically to capture the mood of some of the public responses to events as they happened.

In a few passages I relied upon three letters (each of three or four single-spaced pages) Senator Fulbright had written me in which he commented upon the rough drafts of the book's chapters. I also interviewed Fulbright, John Sparkman, Claude Pepper, George McGovern, Bob Snider (a former aide to John McClellan), and a few others. The interviews were *not* one of the crucial sources, since problems of relying upon the participant's recollections as well as other difficulties weaken interviewing as a source.

245

The most notable secondary work which has been previously published concerning Fulbright's career is the biography by Haynes Johnson and Bernard Gwertzman, *Fulbright the Dissenter* (Garden City, New York: Doubleday, 1968). I have cited chapters from Johnson and Gwertzman in my treatment of Fulbright and U.S. foreign policy in the 1940s, the Bay of Pigs, and the Dominican controversy of 1965. Generally, *Fulbright the Dissenter* is a perceptive biography; as the title indicates, in most chapters it emphasizes Fulbright's activities as a critic of crusading anti-communism during much of his career. Johnson and Gwertzman's book was limited by the fact that it was published in early 1968, when many important events were still in the future, including the last five years of Fulbright's opposition to the Vietnam war. Their biography's treatment of the period from mid-1966 until early 1968 is very brief. However, *Fulbright the Dissenter* is an interesting account of the Senator's career up to early 1966.

There is at least one important inaccuracy in the Johnson and Gwertzman volume. They stated that Fulbright "always refused to try and repeal" the Gulf of Tonkin Resolution. In fact, Fulbright *did* vote to repeal the Tonkin Resolution on March 1, 1966 (as I explained in Chapter 8). Only four other Senators voted with Fulbright in favor of repealing the Resolution, and thus the March 1, 1966 vote was one of the memorable acts of political courage in the Arkansas Senator's career. It was true that after the debacle of the ninety-two to five vote defeating repeal, Fulbright did not advocate attempts to obtain repeal until the dissenters could expect to attract considerably more than five votes; in 1966 such attempts had no chance of gaining a majority, and the administration publicized such results as the March 1, 1966 vote as triumphant endorsements of the escalation policy. Johnson and Gwertzman mentioned the reasons for Fulbright's reluctance to support repeal in 1967-68 but they neglected to discuss the Senator's vote for repeal in 1966; apparently they did not know about it. The important fact was that Fulbright had been courageous enough to publicly repudiate the Tonkin Resolution at a relatively early date, in comparison to the vast majority of Senators. Many political analysts were surprised in 1966 that Fulbright would go so far in opposing the President as to vote for repeal. There were so many momentous events happening in 1966 that most foreign policy analysts and historians seem to have later forgotten the effort to repeal the Resolution.

Kurt Tweraser's *Changing Patterns of Political Beliefs: The Foreign Policy Operational Codes of J. William Fulbright, 1943-1967* (Beverly Hills, California: Sage Publications, 1974) is written in the jargon of political science, and hence, unfortunately, is relevant only for political scientists. A more useful source is Tweraser's 1971 Ph.D. dissertation at American University, "The Advice and Dissent of Senator Fulbright" (which has not been published, to my knowledge). This dissertation is based on extensive research and focuses on Fulbright's responses to the Cold War. Tweraser acknowledges that the Senator was a dissenter after 1965, but I would not agree with his depiction of Fulbright as a "Cold Warrior" during the period from 1946 to 1964. Fulbright made some anti-communist statements during those years, especially the late 1940s and early 1950s, but in my assessment, what deserves the greatest emphasis was Fulbright's opposition to the most destructive and extreme manifestation of anti-communism, such as McCarthyism, some of Dulles' more erratic actions in the late 1950s, the U-2 fiasco, the Bay of Pigs, and the Senator's frequent criticism of the radical right. My view is closer to that in Daniel Yergin's article, "Fulbright's Last Frustration," in *The New York Times Magazine*, November 24, 1974. Yergin argues that the Arkansan was quietly and carefully beginning to question the Cold War consensus at an early date: "While Henry Kissinger was just turning his Ph.D. thesis into a book and describing scenarios for limited nuclear warfare, Fulbright was pointing the direction toward what a decade and a half later became known as detente."

Tristram Coffin's *Senator Fulbright: Portrait of a Public Philosopher* (New York: E.P. Dutton, 1966) is an exercise in hero-worship and was not valuable for my research.

Twenty years ago Walter Johnson and Francis Colligan wrote *The Fulbright Program: A History* (Chicago: The University of Chicago Press, 1965), an account of the exchange program, with a foreword by J. William Fulbright.

There are vast numbers of articles on Senator Fulbright. The following is a short list of some of the most important articles: Charles B. Seib and Alan L. Otten, "Fulbright: Arkansas Paradox," in *Harper's*, June, 1956; Sidney Hyman, "Fulbright—The Wedding of Arkansas and the World," *The New Republic*, May 14, 1962; Brock Brower, "The Roots of the Arkansas Questioner," *Life*, May 13, 1966; Russell Warren Howe and Sarah Trott, "J. William Fulbright: Reflections on a Troubled World." *Saturday Review*, January 11, 1975; Gary Herlick, "J.W. Fulbright: Democratic Senator from Arkansas," in *Ralph Nader Congress Project: Citizens Look at Congress*, (Washington: Grossman, 1972), edited by Ralph Nader. Lloyd E. Ambrosius, "The Goldwater-Fulbright Controversy," *The Arkansas Historical Quarterly*, Autumn, 1970, deals with Fulbright's debate with Goldwater concerning Soviet-American relations in the early 1960s. In a series of articles written in 1967, I.F. Stone delivered a sympathetic yet searching criticism of Fulbright's evolution from pro-administration figure to dissenter: "Fulbright of Arkansas, Part 1," December 29, 1966; "Fulbright: From Hawk to Dove, Part 2," January 12, 1967; "Fulbright: The Timid Opposition, Part 3," January 26, 1967, in *The New York Review of Books*. One should also consult the many articles on recent U.S. foreign policy in *Foreign Affairs*.

The scholarly literature on the Cold War and the Vietnam war is voluminous. I might note a few of the works which were useful in my research. For McCarthyism, see Richard M. Fried, *Men Against McCarthy* (New York: Columbia University Press, 1976); Robert Griffith, *The Politics of Fear: Joseph R. McCarthy and the Senate* (Lexington, Kentucky: The University Press of Kentucky, 1970); and Richard Rovere, *Senator Joe McCarthy* (New York: Harper and Row, 1959). A few of the best volumes on Vietnam are Frances Fitzgerald, *Fire in the Lake: The Vietnamese and the Americans in Vietnam* (New York: Random House-Vintage Books, 1972); George C. Herring, *America's Longest War: The United States and Vietnam, 1950-1975* (New York: John Wiley and Sons, 1979); David Halberstam, *The Best and the Brightest* (Greenwich, Connecticut: Fawcett Crest, 1972); Halberstam, *The Powers That Be* (New York: Dell, 1979), for press coverage of the war; and Bernard B. Fall, *Last Reflections on a War* (New York: Schocken Books, 1967). The best book on Sino-American relations is John King Fairbank's *The United States and China*, Fourth edition (Cambridge, Massachusetts: 1979). I also profited from Fairbank's lecture, "The Chinese Revolution," at Newcomb Hall of the University of Virginia, April, 1983. For a journalist's observations on the China of 1973, see the collection of articles, *A Visit to the People's Republic of China* (Little Rock: 1973) written by my father, James Powell, when he led a group of journalists on a month-long visit through the mainland; this was one of the first groups to enter China after President Nixon's journey to Peking in 1972.

The following is a short list of works on the Kennedy, Johnson and Nixon years. Two of Arthur M. Schlesinger's books were particularly valuable: *A Thousand Days: John F. Kennedy in the White House* (Boston: Houghton Mifflin, 1965); and *Robert Kennedy and His Times* (New York: Ballantine, 1978). Also see John Kenneth Galbraith, *A Life in Our Times* (New York: Ballantine, 1981). Schlesinger's *The Imperial Presidency* (New York: Popular Library, 1974) includes several discussions of Fulbright's responses to the expanding power of the postwar Presidency. Doris Kearns' *Lyndon Johnson and the American Dream* (New York: Signet, 1976) is an interesting biography, although it does not provide a thorough analysis of the Fulbright-Johnson conflict over Vietnam. For Clark Clifford, Fulbright, and Johnson in 1968, I relied upon Herbert Y. Schandler, *Lyndon Johnson and Vietnam: The Unmaking of a President* (Princeton, New Jersey: Princeton University Press, 1977). Also see Harry S. Ashmore and William C. Baggs, *Mission to Hanoi: A Chronicle of Double-Dealing in High Places* (New York: G.P. Putnam's Sons, 1968); and Neil Sheehan, et al., editors, *The Pentagon Papers* (based on investigative reporting by Neil Sheehan, written by Neil Sheehan, Hedrick Smith, E.W. Kenworthy, and Fox Butterfield. New York: Bantam 1971). Three of the most engrossing volumes on the Nixon years are Jonathan Schell, *The Time of Illusion* (New York: Vintage, 1975); William Shawcross, *Sideshow: Kissinger, Nixon, and the Destruction of Cambodia* (New York: Washington Square Press, 1979); and William Safire, *Before the Fall* (New York: Ballantine, 1975).

Ronald Steel's biography, *Walter Lippmann and the American Century* (Boston: Little, Brown, and Company, 1980) was a significant source because of Fulbright's long and rewarding friendship with the famous columnist. Especially interesting are the chapters which describe Lippmann's initial euphoria for Johnson's leadership, followed by his gradual disillusionment with the President, and finally his outrage at the colossal blunders of the U.S. intervention in Vietnam.

C. Vann Woodward presented an incisive observation on Fulbright in a brief passage of *The Burden of Southern History* (Enlarged edition; Baton Rouge: Louisiana State University Press, 1968). Woodward noted that some opponents of the Vietnam war had admitted "that America has at last encountered problems that are difficult to reconcile with traditional myths of indomitable optimism—invincibility, success, innocence, and the rest." "Senator J. William Fulbright," he continued, "who harbors a keen awareness of the incongruity between national myth and national policies, has observed that 'a nation whose modern history has been an almost uninterrupted chronicle of success ... should be so sure of its own power as to be capable of magnanimity.'" In Woodward's opinion, Fulbright was "thoroughly American, but to the ears of anyone attuned to the traditional rhetoric of American myth," his words set up an immediate dissonance. "In the American past, and in the predominant mind of the present [1968] as well, all wars end in victory and all problems have solutions. Both victory and solution might require some patience—but not much. The idea of admitting defeat and the prospect of living patiently with an unsolved social problem are, to borrow Senator Fulbright's expression, 'unthinkable thoughts' for most Americans." The historian argued that Fulbright's ability to renounce the myths of innocence, victory, and virtue had led him to an unusually perceptive and realistic viewpoint on American foreign policy.

For the background of American diplomatic history, I have relied upon several of the works of George F. Kennan and Norman A. Graebner. Kennan's realistic analysis of U.S. foreign policy and of Soviet-American relations is presented in many of his writings, among them *Russia and the West Under Lenin and Stalin* (New York: Mentor, 1961); and *Memoirs, II: 1950-1963* (Boston: 1972). Norman A. Graebner's *The Age of Global Power: The United States Since 1939* (New York: John Wiley and Sons, 1979), is a general history of America from the late 1930s to the late 1970s. Graebner's *The New Isolationism* (New York: The Ronald Press Company, 1956) was one of the earliest critical evaluations of the Eisenhower-Dulles foreign policies; the historian stressed the administration's attempt to create the impression of more determined foreign policies than those of Truman, basically by employing Dulles' dramatic rhetoric. The Republican administration's rhetoric promised greater success at less risk and cost than the Truman administration accomplished; in reality, Dulles' dramatic phrases left American policy exactly where it had been in the late Truman era. For the Cold War, see Graebner's *Cold War Diplomacy, 1945-1975* (New York: D. Van Nostrand, 1977, Second edition).

Graebner's *Ideas and Diplomacy* (New York: Oxford University Press, 1964) is a massive collection of readings in the intellectual tradition of American foreign policy, edited with extended commentary by the author. This book analyzes the conflict between the realistic and ideological approaches to diplomacy from the eighteenth century to the post-World War II epoch. As Graebner demonstrates, during the early history of the republic, George Washington, Thomas Jefferson, John Quincy Adams, and other realists controlled the basic U.S. foreign policy decisions. These decisions (along with other historical factors) facilitated the effective and often brilliant U.S. diplomacy of early American history. In the twentieth century (for a variety of involved reasons) those who advocated the ideological approach came to dominate the formulation of U.S. foreign policy. Interestingly, *Ideas and Diplomacy* ends with a chapter including two of Fulbright's speeches: "Old Myths and New Realities" of 1964, and one of the addresses Fulbright delivered in his debate with Goldwater in the early 1960s. Graebner describes Fulbright's positions as following in the realist tradition; the Senator pleaded that the nation's commitments abroad should be limited by the interests, power, and capabilities of the United States. Fulbright's conservative approach to the use of power seems reminiscent of one of Jefferson's realistic statements, quoted near the beginning of *Ideas and Diplomacy:* "I hope our wisdom will grow with our power, and teach us, that the less we use our power, the greater it will be."

Index